NO BETTER PLACE

ARTHUR CONAN DOYLE, WINDLESHAM AND COMMUNICATION WITH THE OTHER SIDE (1907-1930)

ALISTAIR DUNCAN

First edition published in 2015

Paperback ISBN 978-1-78092-797-8
ePub ISBN 978-1-78092-798-5
PDF ISBN 978-1-78092-799-2

Published in the UK by MX Publishing
335 Princess Park Manor, Royal Drive, London, N11 3GX

This book is dedicated to my wife Kate whose support for all my endeavours, both sane and not so, is unwavering.

I also dedicate this book to Paddy, Archie and Bailey. Three faithful friends, sadly missed.

PRAISE FOR 'NO BETTER PLACE'

"Arthur Conan Doyle was an incredibly interesting and complex person and packed an awful lot into his time on Earth. In this book, as in others before it, Alistair Duncan has given us a careful, considerate and informative look at a distinct period in Doyle's life. This book is a good read and may inform you of a few things you didn't know about Doyle during his "Windlesham" years. Duncan writes well and has turned out, what could have been in the hands of another writer simply a dry recounting of Doyle's activities, a definitive and entertaining account of the last 23 years of Doyle's life."

Bill Barnes
President of The Sydney Passengers

"No Better Place" completes the cycle of Alistair Duncan's writings on the specifics of Arthur Conan Doyle's life. This book gives an overview of his last twenty-three years - the happy years at Windlesham with his second wife and family. These years were dominated by Conan Doyle's obsessive interest in spiritualism, and Alistair Duncan deals fairly and dispassionately with this, and also gives a balanced account of the unfortunate affair of the Cottingley fairies. This whole cycle of books is a triumph of research and is a worthy contribution to the biographical material on Conan Doyle's complex character.

Georgina Doyle
Author of Out of the Shadows

By The Same Author

Eliminate the Impossible

Close to Holmes

The Norwood Author

An Entirely New Country

ACKNOWLEDGEMENTS

Thanks are due to Mrs Georgina Doyle who was generous with her time and permitted me to reproduce extracts from the papers of Mary Conan Doyle as well as photographs from her private collection.

Further thanks are due to Brian Pugh of the Conan Doyle (Crowborough) Establishment for his unrivalled knowledge of Conan Doyle's life and access to his enviable collection of photographs. Thanks are also due to him for his excellent Conan Doyle Chronology without which this book would have been much harder to write.

Others meriting thanks include: Bill Barnes; David Stuart Davies; Roger Johnson; Oscar Ross; Tom Ruffles of the Society for Psychical Research; Dr. Richard Sveum; Jean Upton and Doug Wrigglesworth.

The photographs and other images used within this book have come from many collections, including that of the author. None are to be used without the permission of the owner of the relevant collection.

ABOUT THE AUTHOR

Alistair Duncan has been a Sherlock Holmes enthusiast since 1982 and has spoken on radio, television and at live events about both Sherlock Holmes and his creator Sir Arthur Conan Doyle.

He is a member of The Sherlock Holmes Society of London, The Conan Doyle (Crowborough) Establishment and The Sydney Passengers.

He lives with his wife in Surrey.

'...Saturday will bring us to Windlesham, where I shall live and die, I expect. No better place.'[1]

[1] Excerpt from a letter written by Arthur Conan Doyle to his mother in November 1907. Lellenberg, Jon et al. *Arthur Conan Doyle: A Life in Letters.* Harper Press. 2007.

CONTENTS

Foreword xvii

Introduction xxi

1907 25

Making Changes 27

1908 31

Sherlock Holmes Begins His Last Bow 33

Olympic "Games" 41

1909 51

A Sense of Mortality 53

The Curtain Rises 58

1910 75

The Curtain Falls and Rises 77

George Newnes Passes On 88

1911 101

Motoring and Home Rule 103

The End of the Beginning 110

1912 117

The Lost World and The Lost Ship 119

1913 129

Billiards, Tunnels and Suffrage 131

Sleuthing on the Silver Screen 138

1914 143

Into the Valley 145

The East Wind Arrives 154

1915 159

Writing, Lecturing, Volunteering and Loss 161

1916 169

Stepping Into The Light 171

1917 179

His Last Bow 181

1918 193

A Test of Faith 195

1919 203

Challenge and Counter Challenge 205

"I am so happy" 217

1920 221

Enter Houdini 223

The Coming of the Fairies 228

The 'Champion of Spiritualism' 234

Fifteen Days & Eight Lectures 253

The End of an Era 260

1921 261

Farewell Australia 263

Holmes on Screen, Stage and Page 272

1922 279

Back to America 281

The Public Rift Opens 296

1923 305

The New Paget? 307

A Man Deceived? 315

1924 319

Vampires, Clients and Garridebs 321

1925 327

Bookshop, Belfast and The Land of Mist	329
Paris and Bignell Wood	339
1926	347
Keeping a Low Profile?	349
The Case For and Against	353
1927	359
The Canon Complete	361
The Convict Released	365
1928	371
Flood Damage	373
Taking the Message to Africa	380
1929	387
'I am that Ghost'	389
1930	395
Breaking the Link	397
Doyle's Work is Done	401
Bibliography	411
Index	415

FOREWORD

To the man in the street, Arthur Conan Doyle is known as the creator of Sherlock Holmes – if he is known at all. But he is much more than that, as this volume clearly demonstrates. For many years Doyle was regarded as an unimportant author. When I was at university in the 1970s I wanted to write my final dissertation on Doyle. However, I was told that he was not significant enough to warrant such a study. For many years, the Sherlockian community referred to ACD, in rather dismissive terms, as 'the Literary Agent', denying him his role as the creator of the great Sherlock Holmes. Happily, things are very different today. There has been a seismic shift since the1980s and now Arthur Conan Doyle is appreciated as a fascinating and important character in his own right. As he should be. There is now a thirst for knowledge about the man, his writings and his life.

Those eager to learn more about the real Conan Doyle must have been very disappointed when they got their hands on his autobiography, *Memories and Adventures* published in 1924. It reveals little of his private life, granting the reader no real insight into what made the great man tick. And make no bones about it, Conan Doyle was a great man. It is not just the creation of one of literature's major characters or his other writings alone that make him deserving of this accolade. His brilliance shines through his involvement in many diverse public activities from campaigning to reform the divorce laws, fighting legal injustices, and sitting on the 1916 Olympic Games committee to supporting new inventions, to mention just a few of his passions. His vitality and persistence were remarkable. But there was also a dark side to him which he was at great pains to conceal in his autobiography, such as his rather shabby treatment of his daughter Mary. He was also economical with the truth concerning his relationship with Jean Leckie, who became his second wife. Although he had been having an unconsummated love affair with Jean for many years, while his invalid first wife was still alive, he does not mention this in his autobiography and passes off their union with one brief misleading, some might say down right deceptive, sentence: 'On September 18, 1907, I married Miss Jean Leckie, the younger daughter of a Blackheath family whom I had known for years, and who was a dear friend of my mother and sister.' Smoke and mirrors, Sir Arthur, smoke and mirrors!

In *No Better Place*, Alistair Duncan helps to open that secret door to Conan Doyle's personal life through his admirable and exhaustive research into both the author's public and private activities. We are given a detailed blow by blow, virtually day by day, account of the doings of Arthur.

Apart from his varied literary efforts, Doyle had his fingers in many pies, from large important ones such as the promotion of the building of a Channel tunnel, the Edalji affair, the Oscar Slater case and his support of the French Red Cross to minor personal ones involving his skills in playing cricket and billiards competitively. One cannot help but be amazed at Doyle's energy in involving himself in so many eclectic activities and causes, which are detailed in this book through the aid of various reports, letters, biographical writings and newspaper articles. However, it is Duncan's perceptive interpretations of the facts and incidents that enhance the newly revealed story of this complex man. At one point Duncan uses the phrase, 'it is tempting to consider' and indeed he does 'consider' the facts, helping, through his encyclopaedic knowledge of ACD's life, to interpret them with a keen insight.

As a result we get to see Doyle unmasked, warts and all. Placed under Duncan's magnifying glass, it is a revealing and many faceted portrait.

This volume allows us to become privy to all Doyle did for the last twenty-three years of his life, a time when he found himself newly married to the real love of his life and settled in the last home he would know. At this time he was a famous figure, beloved because of his creation of Sherlock Holmes, respected because of his public activities and yet still compelled to survive financially. As Duncan notes: '[Doyle was] a man whose decisions were often driven by his desire for fiscal security.' It was also a period of his life in which gradually he gave most of his energies to the promotion of Spiritualism, an activity which brought him a great deal of criticism and ridicule. His unquestioning acceptance of Spiritualism and the backlash he received as a result makes fascinating reading. The debate concerning whether spirits in the afterlife wear clothes, for example, is as intriguing as it is risible. However, we can see that despite the naiveté of Doyle's stance, he retained remarkable courage and steadfastness in sticking to his beliefs.

It is clear that in the final stage of the author's life, he had only one use for Sherlock Holmes: as a means to secure finances. It is revealing that in his last interview regarding the character he admitted to the journalist that, 'I was tired of Sherlock Holmes from the beginning… but it was an excellent way for a struggling young man to get a foothold and to get money.'

Although for the most part Jean Leckie emerges as a shadowy figure, we gradually become aware of her influence on Doyle and her subtle controlling nature – even to the extent of replacing all the female servants at Windlesham with men. Maybe this was, as Duncan suggests, in order to do away with any competition.

Despite Doyle's inconsistencies and character flaws, he nonetheless emerges as a man to be admired. There are few individuals who could cram so much activity and incident into their lives while at the same time bringing great pleasure to so many through his writings, especially those about Sherlock Holmes which still continue to thrill and entertain readers all around the world.

This engrossing volume is not only a very engaging read but also a wonderful research tool for anyone with an interest in Arthur Conan Doyle, his life and his work, and of course, the Great Detective. It is a life crowded with incident, passion and a restless energy. Take a deep breath and dive in.

David Stuart Davies, 2015

INTRODUCTION

The fact that you are reading these words is something of a surprise to me for the simple reason that I never expected to write them.

When I completed my book *An Entirely New Country*, which looked at Arthur Conan Doyle's Undershaw years, people asked me if I planned to go onto the next phase of his life. To them all I had answered in the negative. My reasons for this were twofold. Firstly it had taken me over a year to do justice (in my opinion) to Conan Doyle's ten years in Surrey; the prospect of tackling a twenty-three year period seemed decidedly daunting. Secondly, I knew I could not write about this period without touching on the thorny subject of Spiritualism.

So, straight away, I give advance warning that I do not subscribe to Spiritualism any more than I do any other religion or faith. Consequently, I find myself in a similar position to the Doylean and Sherlockian writer Trevor H. Hall who once wrote 'It has been urged upon me that out of the presumed conflict of my devotion to Doyle as a writer and a man on the one hand, and my critical view of spiritualism on the other, some kind of balanced opinion might conceivably emerge'[2]. I hope I manage to get close to such a balance.

---

[2] Hall, Trevor H. *Sherlock Holmes and his creator*. Duckworth Publishing 1978.

The years covered within these pages rather neatly begin with a beginning. The move to Crowborough in 1907 followed Conan Doyle's marriage to his second wife Jean (nee Leckie). Jean and Conan Doyle had first met ten years earlier and she had taken something of a gamble waiting for the day when Conan Doyle would be free to marry her. It was a gamble because, at the time of their meeting, Conan Doyle was still married to his first wife Louise. Louise had been diagnosed with incurable tuberculosis (or consumption) in 1893 but, four years later, against all expectations, she had already lived longer than the experts had predicted. Thanks very much to her husband's efforts she survived thirteen years beyond her initial diagnosis.

Divorce law reform was one of the many causes that Conan Doyle championed during his life but it was not for him personally. He very much considered that death was the only justified exit from his marriage and, although he clearly loved Jean from the first moments, he warned her that he would not leave his wife for her and she should consider, essentially, looking elsewhere.

Jean Leckie has come in for a lot of criticism and a fair amount of it has been justified. She was, from the ailing Louise's point of view, the spectre at the feast – a constant reminder that her husband, to an extent, had his future planned out beyond her death. However, although it may be tempting to some, Jean cannot be seen as any kind of gold-digger. Her love for Conan Doyle was genuine and she willingly took the risk of waiting without any guarantee of marrying the man she loved.

Conan Doyle's life in Crowborough covered many major events both personal and national. He fathered three children with Jean and lost his son by Louise in the chaos of the First World War. The War was something in which he took a more than conventional interest and, during it, he visited the front and authored an account of the conflict. In the realm of fiction, he created the character for whom, after Sherlock Holmes, he is most known – that of Professor Challenger.

He lived long enough to see his two most famous creations portrayed on the silver screen and his devotion to Spiritualism brought him international adventure, acclaim and derision. It also turned friends into foes; the most notable of these being escapologist and anti-Spiritualist Harry Houdini.

Alistair Duncan, Surrey, 2015

1907

MAKING CHANGES

In November 1907 Sir Arthur Conan Doyle and the new Lady Jean Conan Doyle were in France en route to England having almost concluded their honeymoon. Conan Doyle was clearly the happiest he had been for some time. It was only a year and a half previously that he had buried his first wife Louise and he had battled (and was still battling) in the cause of George Edalji.

One of their final stops had been Constantinople on November 2nd where they had come to the attention of the Sultan of Turkey. He had professed himself to be a fan of the Sherlock Holmes stories and had not only presented Conan Doyle with, according to the newspapers, the Order of the Medjidieh (second class), but had also asked to be supplied with copies of everything he had ever written and everything he would write in the future. In what must have been an act of courtesy more than recognition, the Sultan presented the new Lady Conan Doyle with the Order of Nichan-i-Chefakat (also second class)[3].

In a letter to his mother that same month, Conan Doyle announced that he expected to be back in England very soon and would be staying in the Hotel Metropole upon his arrival[4].

---

[3] *Daily Express* and *The Daily Mirror* of November 11th 1907.

[4] Lellenberg, Jon et al. *Arthur Conan Doyle: A Life in Letters.* Harper Press. 2007.

The Metropole was a natural choice as it had good associations. His wedding reception had taken place there only a few months earlier and he had probably booked rooms there before departing on honeymoon. Characteristically, Conan Doyle was not planning on taking it easy upon his return. He informed his mother that Jean would be spending the day following their return looking for domestic staff (presumably via agencies) while he would be visiting the Home Office in connection with George Edalji[5].

The fact that Jean needed to interview potential servants for their new home clearly indicated that Conan Doyle had parted company with his previous valet Cleave. Cleave and his wife Elizabeth had been the centre of Conan Doyle's domestic staff at his Surrey home, Undershaw. Towards the end of Conan Doyle's time in Surrey, Cleave and his wife had become parents and had needed to set up a home of their own. Cleave continued in domestic service, but presumably did not find the idea of following his employer to Sussex palatable as it would have meant moving a distance from both his immediate and extended family.

This arrangement almost certainly suited the new Lady Conan Doyle as she very likely wanted to commence her married life without too many reminders of her predecessor. The notion of starting in a new house with a new staff must have appealed greatly. It was probably also a relief when it was determined that the stained-glass windows at Undershaw, which incorporated many family crests, were impractical to move to the new house.[6]

The new house, named Windlesham, was, unlike Undershaw, not built to Conan Doyle's design. That house had been designed largely to cater to Louise Conan Doyle's fragility which had been caused by her incurable tuberculosis. With a younger wife in excellent health, that kind of design was not

---

[5] Covered in greater detail in my book *An Entirely New Country.*

[6] *Some Fragmentary Notes on Undershaw Today* By George Welch (*Sherlock Holmes Journal* Spring 1959 Centenary Edition).

necessary. It is also rather likely that embarking on the process of designing and building another house was unappealing to Conan Doyle.

There were, of course, aspects to Windlesham that both Conan Doyle and Jean wished to change. In December Conan Doyle once again wrote to his mother and informed her that he was taking advantage of a period when Jean was absent to make changes to the mantel in the dining room. There was also the addition of an extensive music room which ultimately ended up accommodating Conan Doyle's billiard table and acted as a general living area.

Away from the house, the *Daily Express* of December 14th noted that one Albert Gilmer, in partnership with theatre impresario Charles Frohman, was going to take over the Princess Theatre in Oxford Street and commence renovations to the tune of twenty-thousand pounds.

Albert Hatton Gilmer was a twenty-nine year old playwright who would become a professor of speech and drama[7]. It seems reasonable to suppose that Frohman was the main partner in much the same way that he was with William Gillette. It was the intention of the incoming management to have the theatre opened for the August Bank Holiday of 1908 with a melodrama by Conan Doyle. It was not clear whether they intended to open with an existing play or a brand new one, but it was destined never to happen. Problems with the lease hampered efforts to transform it and the cost of renovations presumably rose far above the budgeted twenty-thousand. The theatre never reopened and eventually became a warehouse[8].

---

[7] Website Findagrave.com (http://www.findagrave.com/cgi-bin/fg.cgi?page=gr&GRid=8218838).
[8] Arthur Lloyd Theatre website (http://www.arthurlloyd.co.uk/Princess.htm)

The Undershaw stained glass windows which did not make the move to Windlesham
(The Collection of Georgina Doyle)

1908

SHERLOCK HOLMES BEGINS HIS LAST BOW

The year 1908 opened with sad news. On January 28th Sidney Paget, who had illustrated the Sherlock Holmes stories from *A Scandal in Bohemia* onwards, died at the age of 48. He had single-handedly defined the image of Sherlock Holmes and it was his vision that subsequent illustrators were compelled to adhere to, as were the vast majority of film makers in later years.

It seems odd that Conan Doyle did not make some kind of comment on the death of the man whose contribution to Holmes's success had been significant. Yet, in his letters to family and to the press, Paget's name does not come up at this time[9].

February 21st saw the publication of the book *Wheels of Anarchy*. Written by Max Pemberton it was the result of a promise made by Pemberton to one Bertram Fletcher Robinson who had died on January 21st 1907[10]. The core idea for the story had been Robinson's and, in the knowledge that he would never get to write it, he had asked Pemberton to ensure that the idea was brought to life.

---

[9] Based on the contents of the books *Arthur Conan Doyle: A Life in Letters* and *Letters to the Press* of the *Unknown Conan Doyle* series.

[10] Pugh, Brian. *A Chronology of the Life of Sir Arthur Conan Doyle.* 3rd Edition. MX Publishing 2014.

The news of the story's publication appeared in the issue of the *Daily Express* for that day, which was hardly surprising since Robinson had worked for them for some years. They also drew a, perhaps tenuous, parallel between this new story and Conan Doyle's *The Hound of the Baskervilles* by pointing out that the core idea for both stories had come from Robinson.

Four days later the same newspaper carried an advert for *The Strand* in which it was announced that a short story by Conan Doyle entitled *The Pot of Caviare* would feature in its imminent March issue. The advert stated that the story was 'perhaps, the best short story he has ever written.' It is unlikely that this was genuinely felt to be the case, at least not in a commercial sense, as little that Conan Doyle wrote ever did as well as his Sherlock Holmes adventures.

Turning to Holmes, it is tempting to wonder whether or not history was repeating itself based on a letter written by Conan Doyle to Herbert Greenhough Smith on March 4th 1908[11].

A little over ten years earlier, Conan Doyle had made it quite clear that he was feeling the pinch financially as a result of all his travelling and the building of Undershaw. He had done this in a letter to Greenhough Smith in which he had sought payment in advance for a story he was about to deliver[12].

Clearly the subject of contributions to *The Strand* had arisen and, once again, the one thing that its long-serving editor dearly wanted to see was more Sherlock Holmes. The last such story to have appeared in his magazine was *The Second Stain* in December 1904 but it was possible that it still irked Greenhough Smith that Conan Doyle had been persuaded by Norman Hapgood of *Collier's Weekly* to write the last set of stories, collectively known as *The Return of Sherlock Holmes*.

Conan Doyle did not need a huge amount of persuasion on this occasion, although he refused to commit to a series. Instead, he told Greenhough Smith that he would, from time-to-

---

[11] Lellenberg, Jon et al. *Arthur Conan Doyle: A Life in Letters.* Harper Press. 2007.

[12] *The Tragedy of the Korosko.*

time, write a new story as a 'reminiscence' of 'James Watson' – not the first time he had got Watson's first name wrong.

In the end he offered *The Strand* two stories; one for midsummer and one for Christmas. On April 11th he reported, in a letter to his mother, that he had finished the first[13]. However, this may not be entirely accurate, or perhaps he redrafted some of it, as other sources stated that in fact he completed the story on April 17th.[14]

The new outing for the Great Detective was *The Adventure of Wisteria Lodge* which would later be published in the magazine in two parts; the first, entitled *The Singular Experience of Mr J. Scott Eccles*, in September 1908[15] and the second, *The Tiger of San Pedro*, in October. The story would later give Holmesian scholars some trouble as it was set in 1892 following Holmes's battle with Professor Moriarty – and their mutual deaths - and before 1894 when Holmes returned from the dead in *The Empty House*[16].

Mary Doyle was still somewhat uncertain about her son's decision to resurrect Holmes. She had first voiced such concerns in 1903 following her son's acceptance of the commission from Norman Hapgood for *Collier's Weekly*. She clearly voiced it again despite the success of the stories that Conan Doyle had written following that commission. Once more Conan Doyle was forced to reassure her of his confidence that the quality of the stories would not harm his reputation and that the financial rewards would certainly be useful.

---

[13] Lellenberg, Jon et al. *Arthur Conan Doyle: A Life in Letters.* Harper Press. 2007.

[14] Lycett, Andrew. *Conan Doyle: The Man who Created Sherlock Holmes.* Orion. 2007.

[15] One month earlier in *Collier's Weekly.*

[16] This refers to the date of the story rather than the date of publication.

An illustration by Arthur Twidle for The Adventure of Wisteria Lodge

The challenge faced by Greenhough Smith was who should illustrate the two-part story in the absence of the now deceased Sidney Paget. The illustrator Arthur Twidle (1865-1936) was ultimately chosen and, as with later illustrators, he stuck to the successful Paget formula. Unlike Paget, Twidle was not destined to become the permanent illustrator for the Holmes stories. He would produce illustrations for the next story but no further stories after that. The reasons for this are open to speculation. It is unlikely to be down to the quality of his work as he had been producing illustrations for *The Strand* since December 1905[17]. It could easily have been the case that he disliked being constrained by the parameters put in place by

[17] Twidle's last illustrations for *The Strand* appeared in its December 1909 issue.

Paget to which *The Strand* and its audience clearly wanted to see future illustrators adhere.

In the meantime there were other items to be published. In May *The Grey Dress* appeared in the magazine *The Flag*.

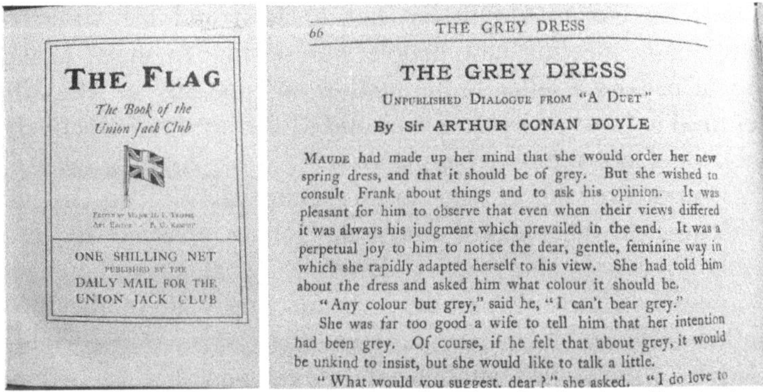

THE FLAG

The Book of the Union Jack Club

ONE SHILLING NET

PUBLISHED BY THE

DAILY MAIL FOR THE UNION JACK CLUB

66 THE GREY DRESS

THE GREY DRESS

UNPUBLISHED DIALOGUE FROM "A DUET"

By Sir ARTHUR CONAN DOYLE

MAUDE had made up her mind that she would order her new spring dress, and that it should be of grey. But she wished to consult Frank about things and to ask his opinion. It was pleasant for him to observe that even when their views differed it was always his judgment which prevailed in the end. It was a perpetual joy to him to notice the dear, gentle, feminine way in which she rapidly adapted herself to his view. She had told him about the dress and asked him what colour it should be.

"Any colour but grey," said he, "I can't bear grey."

She was far too good a wife to tell him that her intention had been grey. Of course, if he felt that about grey, it would be unkind to insist, but she would like to talk a little.

"What would you suggest, dear?" she asked. "I do love to

The Grey Dress as it appeared in The Flag (author's collection)

Billed as part of Conan Doyle's earlier work *A Duet* (which it was not – as yet) the piece was interesting in that it depicted a wife managing to convince her husband that it was his idea that she wear a dress to which he had initially objected[18]. Was it purely fiction or did it actually provide an insight in Conan Doyle's marriage to Jean?

June 16th saw Conan Doyle at the House of Commons. He was there to give evidence to a Parliamentary committee on the proposal to introduce daylight savings time to Britain. At the session the principal opponent was the Secretary of the London Stock Exchange. He pointed out that if Britain adopted a daylight savings policy and moved the clocks forward one hour it would mean that the stock exchange would be closed in Britain before its counterpart in New York opened and that this would affect trade. Conan Doyle, when called, did not tackle this point but simply observed that the introduction of such a

[18] *The Grey Dress* would be added to later editions of *A Duet.*

bill would contribute to general health and happiness – especially for children[19].

Events soon caught up with Conan Doyle and Jean. Ever since their return from honeymoon they had been busy and their home had been besieged with visitors. Many of these were known to Conan Doyle but not to Jean and the strain of continually meeting new people was starting to show. Conan Doyle penned a letter to his mother on June 30th in which he referred to how weary Jean was and of the need to, effectively, lock the doors and keep people away[20].

One of the visitors prior to this letter was William Gillette. Gillette, who had played Sherlock Holmes on stage to great acclaim, was in the country during May, along with theatre impresario Charles Frohman, in connection with another play called *Samson*, to which Frohman had secured the rights. Earlier, Gillette had announced to Frohman that he had no intention of acting in England again and, presumably, Frohman was working hard to persuade him otherwise[21].

It appears that Gillette visited Windlesham without Frohman because Conan Doyle later wrote to his mother to inform her of Gillette's visit without mentioning the impresario. Was this just a social call on Gillette's part or did the actor wish to seek Conan Doyle's opinion on whether or not he should reconsider his stance on acting in England?

In any event, the visit went well on a social level; Conan Doyle reported to his mother that Gillette and Jean had immediately got on well[22].

Conan Doyle had always been ready to support a cause he believed in, regardless of whether that support was physical or financial. However, it would appear that he could be taken in.

---

[19] *Daily Mirror* June 17th 1908.

[20] Lellenberg, Jon et al. *Arthur Conan Doyle: A Life in Letters.* Harper Press. 2007.

[21] Zecher, Henry. *William Gillette: America's Sherlock Holmes.* Xlibris 2011.

[22] Lellenberg, Op. cit.

On July 1st 1908 it was reported that he was amongst three people believed to have been defrauded by one Francis R. Crawford[23].

Lena Ashwell
(Author's collection)

Crawford had apparently written a number of letters to people involved in the theatre, including Conan Doyle, pretending to be an actress named Margaret who had fallen on hard times. He was clever enough to target the one group of people who were likely to have the most sympathy. The lady singled out as having been taken in the most was the actress and theatre manager Lena Ashwell, who by this time was running her own theatre named Kingsway which was located in Great Queen Street, London[24]. Ashwell had sent thirty shillings in

---

[23] *Daily Express* July 1st 1908

[24] As an aside it is interesting to note that James Boswell, the noted 18th century diarist, lived in this same street for a period of time. It

response to Crawford's initial approach and a further similar amount subsequently. After one letter too many, investigations were initiated and Crawford exposed. He was remanded at Bow Street on June 30th but it was not stated to what extent, if any, Conan Doyle had been conned.

---

was Sherlock Holmes who remarked to Dr. Watson that he would be lost without his 'Boswell'.

OLYMPIC "GAMES"

July was a hectic month for Conan Doyle. It commenced with a series of cricketing fixtures and social engagements. His daughter Mary arrived in England during the month and stayed at Windlesham, but it is not clear to what, if any, extent she was involved in her father's social diary.

Conan Doyle's business and writing commitments were also mounting up. In regards to business he was still involved with the firm Raphael Tuck & Sons Ltd. and attended their annual general meeting in Finsbury Circus.[25] On the writing front he was, as he later wrote to his mother, 'deep in a Sherlock'. This was *The Bruce-Partington Plans* which was due to be published at the end of the year.

However, the biggest event of the month was the Olympic Games which had commenced in April. The *Daily Mail* secured Conan Doyle's services as a correspondent and July 24th saw him present at the men's marathon.

This particular marathon was made famous by Dorando Pietri of Italy. He was so exhausted upon approaching the finishing line that he repeatedly collapsed and was helped to his feet by umpires. Some of the photographs taken on the day led to the idea that Conan Doyle himself was one of those who assisted the Italian. Although he did not physically assist Dorando, Conan Doyle could have been said to have assisted

[25] Pugh, Brian. *A Chronology of the Life of Sir Arthur Conan Doyle.* 3rd Edition. MX Publishing 2014.

him in his report. He described the moment the Italian entered the stadium:

> Out of the dark archway there staggered a little man, with red running-drawers, a tiny boy-like creature. He reeled as he entered and faced the roar of the applause. Then he feebly turned to the left and wearily trotted round the track. Friends and encouragers were pressing round him.

In his report Conan Doyle repeatedly remarked that Dorando fell to the ground with exhaustion but never mentioned that he was helped to his feet.

> He was within a few yards of my seat. Amid stooping figures and groping hands I caught a glimpse of the haggard, yellow face, the glazed and expressionless eyes, the lank dark hair streaked across the brow. Surely he is done now. He cannot rise again.
>
> Will he fall again? No, he sways, he balances, and then he is through the tape and into a score of friendly arms. He has gone to the extreme of human endurance. No Roman of the prime ever bore himself better than Dorando of the Olympics of 1908. The great breed is not yet extinct.

The American John Hayes crossed the line in second place and the American team lodged a complaint regarding the assistance Dorando had received. This was upheld and Dorando was disqualified. Although undoubtedly the correct course of action, there was much sympathy for the Italian amongst the British people. Queen Alexandra later presented him with a silver cup and Conan Doyle organised a fund through the *Daily Mail*. On July 31st Jean and Conan Doyle met Dorando at the newspaper's offices to present him with a gold cigarette case and a cheque for over three hundred pounds[26].

---

[26] Pugh, Brian. *A Chronology of the Life of Sir Arthur Conan Doyle*. 3rd Edition. MX Pub. 2014. Exact amount was £308 and 10 shillings.

Dorando Pietri is helped across the finish line in the 1908 Olympic Marathon

August gave Conan Doyle some respite from his hectic life and he was able, with his brother Innes, to play cricket for the MCC against East Grinstead (the match was a draw)[27].

The *Daily Express* of September 2nd observed that Conan Doyle and Jean had been recently staying in Worthing but were now headed for Scotland. It is not clear what the purpose (if any) of these trips was, but it is possible that golf played a part in the visit to Worthing. In his book *Adventures with Authors* Sydney Roberts recalled playing a game of golf with Conan Doyle at the Cissbury course near Worthing in 1911. In the absence of any firm information this seems a plausible explanation for his visit there.

The trips away may have been occasioned by the building work being undertaken at Windlesham. Conan Doyle remarked, in a letter to his mother, that the kitchen wing of the house was being extended. On the ground floor these changes were intended to provide a store room and book room. Above these were to be two further bedrooms for, as Conan Doyle said,

---

[27] Pugh, Brian. *A Chronology of the Life of Sir Arthur Conan Doyle.* 3rd Edition. MX Publishing 2014.

'When the crisis comes we shall want more rooms'[28]. The crisis in question was presumably the impending arrival of his new child.

Windlesham pre and post building work. The expansion is most obvious in the centre of the house
(The Collection of Georgina Doyle)

---

[28] Lellenberg, Jon et al. *Arthur Conan Doyle: A Life in Letters.* Harper Press. 2007.

On the subject of children, Mary and Kingsley were staying at Windlesham at this time and spending time travelling around the immediate area together. However, while Kingsley would be at the house for Christmas, Mary was to be back in Dresden where she was studying.

The Daily Mirror of October 2nd reported that Conan Doyle's book *The Great Boer War*, which had first been published in 1900, was to be published in a more accessible edition as part of publisher Nelson and Sons' 'shilling library' dedicated to making more accessible works relating to history and travel. It would be formally published five days later[29].

Four days later the *Daily Express* reported the return to the police courts of one Cecil de Smith. In 1904 the newspaper had reported on how he had been brought before the courts for impersonating a match-seller cum beggar in the city in order to secure money. The money was used by Smith to rent an expensive villa near Crystal Palace and entertain several ladies[30]. It was a scheme lifted directly from Conan Doyle's Sherlock Holmes story *The Man with the Twisted Lip*.

Smith was now back before the courts for not paying money due to his wife under the terms of an alimony order. In court it was explained that he had been preaching religion at Clapham Common and had cheated people 'right and left by posing as a philanthropist'. The judge threatened him with three months' imprisonment if the money was not paid.

[29] Reported in *The Daily Mirror* of October 7th.

[30] *An Entirely New Country* by your present author.

Kingsley and Mary in 1908
(The Collection of Georgina Doyle)

October 19th saw Conan Doyle in Cambridge. He attended a dinner in the city's Guildhall to bid farewell to cricketer Kumar Shri Ranjitsinhji, more usually known as Ranji[31]. Ranji, who was returning to his Indian principality, had been in England recovering from illness.

Ranji c1897

[31] *Daily Express* October 20th 1908.

Despite attracting controversy he was clearly held in high esteem – especially for his cricket (for England, Sussex, and Cambridge University) and it was this connection that took Conan Doyle to Ranji's farewell dinner. Newspaper coverage described Ranji as being honoured not only as the ruler of an Indian state but as a 'popular undergraduate'. At the dinner, also representing the nation's cricketers, was W.G. Grace who had both bowled out and been out bowled by Conan Doyle some years earlier.

The *Daily Express* of November 5th carried an interesting article about the Authors' Club. The club had been founded in 1891 by the writer Walter Besant and Conan Doyle had been an early member. The newspaper article referred to the 'reconstruction' of the club which had been accomplished 'with the cordial co-operation of the majority of the former members'. The article went on to list the names of those members who now made up the society's general council. Amongst them were Conan Doyle, Anthony Hope Hawkins and H. Rider Haggard[32].

November closed with an appearance at a bazaar in Tunbridge Wells in connection with Barnardo's. *The Daily Mirror* of November 20th reported that Conan Doyle had advocated the use of small holdings for the boys of Dr. Barnardo's homes. It was not spelt out in the article exactly what was meant by this but, presumably, it was the aim to show the boys something of animal management.

This was followed, on the 24th, by an appearance to support the 18th annual smoking concert organised by the students of Middlesex Hospital[33]. Conan Doyle then took the opportunity

[32] The latter two being the authors of *The Prisoner of Zenda* and *King Solomon's Mines* respectively.

[33] Pugh, Brian. *A Chronology of the Life of Sir Arthur Conan Doyle*. A smoking concert was a social event, attended by men only, at which they smoked and discussed the issues of the day while listening to live music.

to reward himself with a break and took Jean to the south of France for a short holiday[34].

December saw publication of *The Bruce-Partington Plans*. For the final time, this was illustrated by Arthur Twidle. The year closed with Christmas at Windlesham. Kingsley and Innes were present but Mary spent the holiday back in Dresden[35].

---

[34] Pugh, Brian. *A Chronology of the Life of Sir Arthur Conan Doyle*. 3rd Edition. MX Publishing 2014.
[35] Pugh, Op. cit.

1909

A SENSE OF MORTALITY

1909 opened with health issues. Conan Doyle was taken ill with an intestinal blockage[36]. It was serious enough to require an operation which was carried out at Windlesham. The situation did not put him in the best of moods and he took some of his frustration out on his daughter Mary.

Mary was shocked when her father accused her of not showing any interest in his state of health. This was both unfair and inaccurate. It was unfair as he had hardly been the best of fathers, leaving his daughter out of two successive Christmases since the death of his first wife (and Mary's mother) Louise.

It was also inaccurate as Mary had written no less than three letters from Dresden to offer sympathy and enquire as to his situation. In later letters to her brother Kingsley, to whom she was very close, she came across as, unsurprisingly, very hurt by her father's attitude. However it is likely that Conan Doyle was not quite as in the wrong as the situation suggested.

The plain and simple fact was that letters to Windlesham were only likely to pass through three pairs of hands. The first being Conan Doyle's, the second those of his secretary Alfred Wood and, finally, those of the new Lady Conan Doyle.

It was believed in certain parts of the family that a jealous Jean had taken advantage of an opportunity to intercept Mary's

---

[36] Pugh, Brian. *A Chronology of the Life of Sir Arthur Conan Doyle.* 3rd Edition. MX Publishing 2014.

letters in order to sow seeds of discord between father and daughter[37].

Conan Doyle's health became a subject of national interest and led to an amusing anecdote appearing in the pages of *The Daily Mirror* January 14th issue. The article remarked that Conan Doyle was one of the country's most popular literary men and one of the few with a genuine European reputation. The article went on to state that Conan Doyle must be unique in being an author of 'books for boys' whose books were also considered 'edifying reading for nuns'.

The explanation for this, which the paper stated was well known, concerned the mother superior of a convent who had bought Conan Doyle's book *Micah Clarke* believing it to be a work by the Roman Catholic priest Canon Doyle. Upon reading it aloud to the nuns it was discovered that the book was 'too good to be true or, rather, too interesting to be good'. The mother superior, upon realising her mistake, decided to continue on the grounds that, having paid for it, it 'would be wasteful were we not to read it to the end'.

Conan Doyle spent the latter half of January recovering and was clearly shaken by the nature of his illness. His first child with Jean was due in March and the operation had clearly made him think about what would happen to his family in the event of his death.

At the very beginning of February he wrote to his mother to inform her that he had updated his will[38]. He had written to his mother about a previous will just before he had headed to South Africa during the Boer War in 1900. His aim then had been to ensure that his family were catered for in the event of his death. This new health scare may have encouraged him to amend it to ensure that his new wife and imminent child were looked after. It is quite possible, given all that had gone on since his marriage to Jean in 1907, that he had not got round to updating his will to

---

[37] Doyle, Georgina. *Out of the Shadows*. Calabash Press. 2004.

[38] Lycett, Andrew. *Conan Doyle: The Man who Created Sherlock Holmes*. Orion. 2007.

take into account his new circumstances. Even if he had amended it to include Jean it is unlikely that such an amended will had accounted for any children they had together[39].

Around this same time modifications were made to parts of Windlesham in preparation for the new child. The principal losers through these changes were Mary and Kingsley, whose rooms in the house were appropriated for a nursery. In a letter Mary wrote to Kingsley her feelings were clearly muted. She was resigned, it appeared, to being, effectively, second-class and said that she had felt no personal claim over the lost room as she had spent virtually no time in it[40].

March 1st saw Conan Doyle preside over a meeting held at the Whitehall Rooms in the Hotel Metropole[41]. The purpose of the meeting, which had been organised by the Authors' Club and to which Conan Doyle was accompanied by his son Kingsley, was to honour Edgar Allen Poe who had been born one hundred years previously[42].

In his debut Holmes novel *A Study in Scarlet*, Conan Doyle had jokingly mocked Poe's creation, detective Auguste Dupin, having Holmes remark to Watson that '…in my opinion, Dupin was a very inferior fellow'. In reality Conan Doyle understood fully well the debt he owed to Poe and the *Daily Express* of the following day reported him as saying 'What writer of detective stories is not prepared to admit his indebtedness to Poe?'. *The New York Times* of the same date quoted Conan Doyle as also saying 'It is the irony of Fate that he, as he said, should have died in poverty, for if every man who wrote a story which was indirectly inspired by Poe were to pay a tithe toward a monument it would be as such as would dwarf the pyramids'.

---

[39] This was far from the last time his will would be updated. The last occasion was not long before his death (see 1930 section).

[40] Doyle, Georgina. *Out of the Shadows*. Calabash Press. 2004.

[41] Pugh, Brian. *A Chronology of the Life of Sir Arthur Conan Doyle*. 3rd Edition. MX Publishing 2014.

[42] It was not an exact anniversary as Poe was born on January 19th 1809.

Other speakers at the event, according to the same newspaper, were the U.S. Ambassador and Captain Poe – 'the oldest surviving member of the Poe family'.

All Saints Church, Crowborough (2011)

Fifteen days later, on March 17th Jean gave birth to their first son. The matter was deemed sufficiently significant that it featured in the March 20th issue of the *Daily Express* under its section *World News in Brief*. Just shy of a month later, on April 15th, he was baptised Denis Percy Stewart Conan Doyle at All Saints Church in Crowborough.

The impressive list of names was partly as a result of some extensive dispute. Conan Doyle's mother was determined that the name Percy be used but Conan Doyle was less keen, pointing out to his mother than his new son already had a cousin of that name. The ultimate compromise was to have the name featured but second to that of Denis.

Towards the end of May 1909 Conan Doyle found what he believed to be a dinosaur footprint in Crowborough. News of this find reached Arthur Smith Woodward who was Keeper of the Geology Department at the British Museum (Natural History)[43]. In turn, he communicated it to amateur archaeologist and geologist Charles Dawson.

Charles Dawson (1864-1916)

Dawson was intrigued and wrote back to Woodward, 'I am interested in what you say about Crowborough and the footprints. I shall be very pleased to make Sir A. Conan Doyle's acquaintance'[44].

---

[43] Since 1992 it has been formally known as the Natural History Museum – a title which had only been informal prior to that date.

[44] Spencer, Frank. *The Piltdown Papers*. Oxford University Press 1990.

THE CURTAIN RISES

On Friday June 11th 1909 Conan Doyle's play *Fires of Fate* opened at Liverpool's Shakespeare Theatre[45]. The play, which was based on his story *The Tragedy of the Korosko,* starred Lewis Waller who had also starred in Conan Doyle's dramatization of his Brigadier Gerard stories in 1906.

The previous day had seen him write to his mother from the Hotel Metropole in London[46]. His reason for being at the Metropole was not something that he went into in his letter but it is possible that his brief stay there was connected to events in the Congo. He did however inform his mother that he would soon be staying at the Adelphi Hotel in Liverpool while he oversaw his latest play's opening.

He claimed, in the same letter, to be unfamiliar with the Shakespeare Theatre. This demonstrates how divorced he was from his Sherlock Holmes play of 1901. That play, which had been redrafted, presumably to a significant extent, by William Gillette, had opened at the same theatre before its move to the Lyceum Theatre in London. Conan Doyle, like Gillette before him, clearly viewed the Liverpool Theatre as little more than a proving ground describing it to his mother as nothing more than 'dress rehearsals with audiences'.

---

[45] Pugh, Brian. *A Chronology of the Life of Sir Arthur Conan Doyle.* 3rd Edition. MX Publishing 2014.

[46] Lellenberg, Jon et al. *Arthur Conan Doyle: A Life in Letters.* Harper Press. 2007.

While there, both Conan Doyle and his leading man Waller were interviewed for *The New York Times* which published an article on June 13th. Entitled *Conan Doyle's Play Condemns Suicide*, the article began by detailing that negotiations were taking place with Waller with a view to him touring the United States in a number of productions.

On the subject of *Fires of Fate* Waller was naturally positive describing it as a 'very intense drama' that contained 'plenty of adventure'. He went on to state, incorrectly, that Conan Doyle had adapted the play from his story 'The Tragedy of the Nile'.

Waller went on to the sensitive subject of suicide, explaining that 'The piece is a powerfully developed lesson against self-murder. It shows mainly that whatever a man may be suffering or may have to suffer of shame or sorrow, it is the height of cowardice, and, indeed, of crime, for him to take his life, however tempted'.

Conan Doyle stated that the play was about faith, remarking that 'no skepticism [sic] can really shake - the faith in a primal cause, in something beyond chance in the universe, in a definite design which controls everything both material and spiritual.'

The following Tuesday (15th) the play opened at the Lyric Theatre in London where it gained positive reviews from the likes of the *Daily Express* and *Daily Mirror* in their issues of the following day[47]. Conan Doyle's brother Innes and sister Connie watched the opening performance in London and dined with him at the Metropole afterwards.

To what extent Conan Doyle's mind would have been on his play is debatable as it was not the only thing occupying his thoughts.

Quite possibly secondary to both his play and its critical reception were affairs in the Congo. It is feasible that before heading up to Liverpool, Conan Doyle had stopped in London to meet with Edmund Dene Morel. If he didn't on this occasion he certainly did so later.

---

[47] Pugh, Brian. *A Chronology of the Life of Sir Arthur Conan Doyle*. 3rd Edition. MX Publishing 2014.

The Congo Free State had been established in 1885 and had been ruled by Leopold II of Belgium. The word 'Free' was definitely out of place as Leopold had presided over the systematic enslavement of the local population and widespread human rights abuses were alleged.

Adelphi Hotel Liverpool c1909

This so enraged Conan Doyle that he penned *The Crime of the Congo* which would be published that October. This work aided the cause of the Congo Reform Association, one of the earliest human rights movements, whose leading figures included Morel and Roger Casement.

The Association's efforts ultimately resulted in international condemnation of Belgium which forced its parliament to wrest control from Leopold and create the now named Belgian

Congo. The agenda of the 1909 meeting between Morel and Conan Doyle is not known for certain, but it would seem likely that it was to discuss a series of appearances that both men were to make up and down the country on the subject.

Edmund Dene Morel – founder of The Congo Reform Association

Conan Doyle began these appearances close to home with a speech on 'Congo Atrocities' in Crowborough. With his book on the subject due to be published a little under two months later it was a good way of generating publicity for both book and cause.

Around this time, Conan Doyle's daughter Mary visited Windlesham and met her new half-brother for the first time. The baby left a very favourable impression on her and she and Denis were to remain on good terms for the whole of his life. On this visit Mary was able to personally see the changes to the house that her brother Kingsley had told her about. Despite the fact that the changes had impacted on her and her brother, Mary was impressed with how they had been carried out[48]. Perhaps

[48] Doyle, Georgina. *Out of the Shadows*. Calabash Press. 2004.

her less frustrated impression had been facilitated by her fondness for her new half-brother.

Roger Casement – Supporter of The Congo Reform Association

Mary's good mood appears to have been put under severe strain by her step-mother. Since her mother's death Mary had become accustomed to looking after herself and was very much an independent person. Jean felt that this was inappropriate. Mary later recorded in her diary how Jean had told her that the purpose of a married woman was to support her husband and, essentially, to forget all thought of personal goals. While Mary went out of her way to compliment Jean – observing that she ran Windlesham well and the positive effect she had on her father – she could not bring herself to accept Jean's view of a woman's role[49].

[49] Doyle, Georgina. *Out of the Shadows*. Calabash Press. 2004.

While Jean probably believed wholeheartedly in what she was saying, her motivation for saying this to Mary was highly dubious. Jean had voluntarily adapted to role of wife and mother thus putting paid to any possibility of a singing career. She was clearly insecure and wanted no female rivals for her husband's attention. Her lecture to Mary on how women should behave was, in all probability, the beginning of attempts to ensure that Mary never outshone her.

The *Daily Express* of July 21st reported that *Fires of Fate* was to change theatres to make way for a production by the Moody-Manners Company. The newspaper either did not know or did not report the exact schedule but the play transferred to the Haymarket Theatre and was there from August 12th to the end of the month. After a short pause it returned to the Lyric for performances between September 6th and October 9th.[50]

Conan Doyle was far from done with the theatre; around the same time he decided to try his hand at another play with the hope of performing even better. The topic to pursue may have occurred to him during September while on a cruise with Jean that saw them visit Portugal, Spain and Morocco[51]. He settled on the idea of dramatizing his 1896 novel *Rodney Stone*. The story largely revolved around bare-knuckle boxing in Regency England and was one of the books he had written during his time in Davos while caring for his ailing first wife Louise.

It was clear that his success in the theatre to date had been mixed. His one-act play *Waterloo* had become a major success

[50] *The London Stage 1900-1909: A Calendar of Productions, Performers, and Personnel* by J.P. Wearing. According to *Arthur Conan Doyle: A Life in Letters* by Jon Lellenberg et al. The final performance of the play was October 8th.

[51] Pugh, Brian. *A Chronology of the Life of Sir Arthur Conan Doyle*. 3rd Edition. MX Publishing 2014.

for Henry Irving and his Sherlock Holmes play, although essentially rewritten by William Gillette, had been, and was continuing to be, something of a crowd pleaser.

Conan Doyle, all too conscious of the work that Gillette had done, almost certainly did not count *Sherlock Holmes* as a personal success[52]. On the other hand, his 1906 dramatization of his Brigadier Gerard story, that had starred Lewis Waller, was a success that he could certainly claim for himself.

So while, from a public perspective, Conan Doyle had enjoyed some success, from his personal perspective, *Waterloo* remained *his* most successful work (in terms of longevity at least) and it was nearly twenty years old. This state of affairs was something he was clearly determined to change with his new boxing play.

The signs were bad from the start. Not a single theatre showed an interest in staging the play. Presumably this was because all the theatre managers and owners could see that the subject matter was of limited appeal. Bare-knuckle boxing was seen as barbaric, especially in light of the relatively new incarnation as structured by the Queensbury Rules, and really only of any interest to men.

Ultimately, such was his confidence, Conan Doyle leased London's Adelphi Theatre for six months. This was a significant gamble as, during this period, all the theatre's running costs fell to him. Later, he was able to report to his mother, in a letter dated November 11th 1909, that his 'Boxing Play' was in rehearsals.

In the midst of all this Conan Doyle was approached about refereeing an actual boxing match. On December 9th Irving Jefferson Lewis, the Managing Editor of the *New York Morning Telegraph*, wrote to him, following up on an earlier cable, and

---

[52] It seems reasonably clear that only three men at most knew how much of the play William Gillette had rewritten. Arthur Conan Doyle, William Gillette and Charles Frohman (who produced it). Conan Doyle's original stage play had burned in a fire along with Gillette's first rewrite and Gillette had rewritten it from memory.

asked Conan Doyle if he would be prepared to referee the forthcoming match between world heavyweight champion Jack Johnson and retired world heavyweight champion James Jeffries[53].

Illustration from Rodney Stone

[53] Doyle, Arthur Conan. *Memories and Adventures*. Wordsworth Editions Ltd. 2007.

The letter ran thus:

NEW YORK,
December 9, 1909.

MY DEAR SIR,—

I hope you will pardon the liberty I took as a stranger in cabling to you asking if you would act at the championship battle between Jeffries and Johnson. The fact is that when the articles were signed recently your name was suggested for referee, and Tex Rickard, promoter of the fight, was greatly interested, as were many others. I believe it will interest you to know that the opinion was unanimous that you would do admirably in the position. In a voting contest several persons sent in your name as their choice. Believe me among sporting men of the best class in America you have many strong admirers; your splendid stories of the ring, and your avowed admiration for the great sport of boxing have made you thousands of friends.

It was because of this extremely friendly feeling for you in America that I took the liberty of cabling to you. I thank you for your reply.

It would indeed rejoice the hearts of the men in this country if you were at the ring side when the great negro fighter meets the white man Jeffries for the world's championship.

I am, my dear Sir,
Yours sincerely,
IRVING JEFFERSON LEWIS,
Managing Editor New York Morning Telegraph.

Johnson had been world heavyweight champion since December 26th 1908 but, as an African American, his win had stirred up racial animosity amongst whites who had called out for a 'Great White Hope' to take the title back. Several such 'hopes' had stepped forward and all had been beaten.

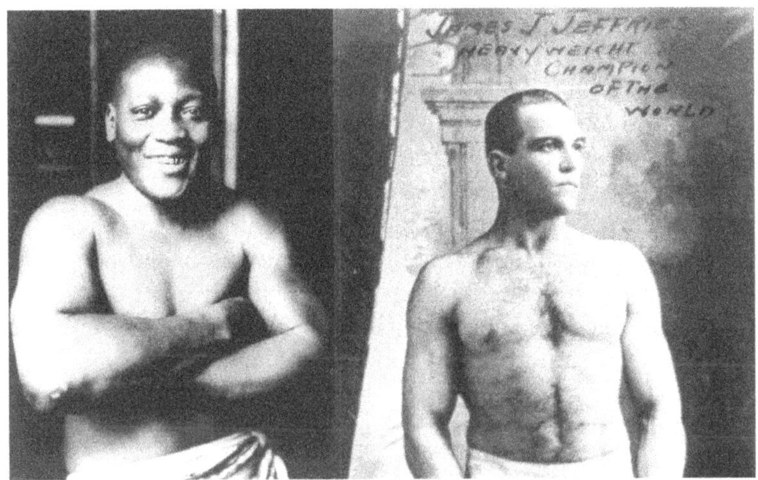

Boxers Jack Johnson and James Jeffries

People started to approach James Jeffries to come out of retirement and fight Johnson. Jeffries had retired undefeated some six years previously and had no interest in such a fight and was certainly not motivated by the racial prejudices of others. Ultimately, a substantial sum was dangled in front of him and he acquiesced.

The next problem was that of securing a referee acceptable to both sides. It was at this point that Conan Doyle's name had come up and the approach made. In his autobiography, after quoting the letter from Lewis, Conan Doyle stated:

> I was much inclined to accept this honourable invitation, though my friends pictured me as winding up with a revolver at one ear and a razor at the other. However, the distance and my engagements presented a final bar.

As a result of Conan Doyle's refusal the promoter Tex Rickard had to referee the match. When it took place in July 1910 the fight ultimately went to reigning champion Johnson.

Returning to October 1909 it was clear that Conan Doyle had enough on his plate. On Tuesday October 5th, only a few days before *Fires of Fate* was to close, a reporter from the *Daily Express* visited him at Windlesham. The purpose of the visit was to interview Conan Doyle about the situation in the Congo and the speeches he was due to give around the country. He was clearly pleased at the newspaper's interest and stated to the reporter 'I am glad the "Express" has taken up the matter with a view of putting the facts before the public. The Government cannot do anything effectual until the people of this country are enlightened as to the real horrors of the Congo Free State and are behind the Government as a driving force'.

He then showed the reporter a photograph of a mutilated child which the newspaper featured in its article of the following day and which also featured on Conan Doyle's pamphlet. In their later issue of October 7th the paper quoted part of Conan Doyle's book which detailed how a man was shot for daring to spend the day fishing rather than working for the rubber industry and how a young boy was ordered to cut off the man's hand while he was still alive.

Twelve days later, on the 19th, the *Daily Express* drew the attention of its readers to an attack on Conan Doyle by the Belgian journal *Petit Bleu*. It was clear that the journal, like Conan Doyle himself, was not going to pull any punches.

'The case of Conan Doyle,' it stated, 'seems to have a pathological character. Sherlock Holmes has evidently been bitten by the Hound of the Baskervilles and the action of the rabies virus is too strong for us to count on the efficiency of the serum. All the same, his spiteful utterances find a ready echo in certain quarters.' The journal went on to object to a power (i.e. Great Britain) claiming the right to impose '…reforms that she has not as yet applied to her own colonies. This takes away from her all moral right to raise her voice in protest'. The journal then went on to detail the reforms that were apparently taking place.

The mutilated child image that appeared on Conan Doyle's Congo Pamphlet. A fuller version with background appeared in the Daily Express (1909)

The activity created by Conan Doyle's position on the Congo was certainly not lost on his daughter. In a letter to her brother during the same month she remarked that her father was '…making a fine stir over this Congo business'. Then, revealing some of her hurt feelings regarding her treatment, she observed '…Daddy was born to be a Public Man and a husband, but not to be a father'[54].

Mary Conan Doyle was, at this time, once more in Dresden and a letter she had received from her father had clearly contributed significantly to her mood. One of her great

[54] Doyle, Georgina. *Out of the Shadows*. Calabash Press. 2004.

pleasures was singing and she now found herself in receipt of a letter in which her father cast doubt on her abilities and whether it was worth her time (or his money) to continue. She realised at once that her step-mother was behind the scenes. Under the guise of needing to conserve money (ostensibly caused by the costs occasioned by the arrival of her new half-brother Denis) Jean was aiming to prevent Mary reaching the stage where she could upstage her. Mary wrote to Kingsley 'I realise that in all future dealings it is Jean and not Daddy with whom I shall have to reckon with.'[55]

On October 31st, Conan Doyle appeared at the Whitefield's Tabernacle to discuss the situation in the Congo. The event was covered in the following day's *Daily Express*. The meeting was popular, attracting sixteen hundred people according to the paper. Conan Doyle's comments on the regime were described as 'scathing'. So robust and alarming were his words that some members of the audience were reported as shouting out 'murderer' whenever King Leopold's name was mentioned.

Conan Doyle drew his audience's attention to devastated villages and the fact that as many as ten million natives had allegedly died under Belgian rule. He was dismissive of reforms that Belgium claimed to be implementing and stated 'I believe in my heart that the administration of the Congo is not only a crime, but the very greatest crime ever committed in the history of the world'.

Less than a month later saw Conan Doyle and Edmund Morel give what was possibly their first joint speech on the Congo at Newcastle Town Hall. This was followed by a series of similar speeches which followed the most bizarre geographical route.

From Newcastle, the two men went to Plymouth where they spoke on November 18th. The following day Conan Doyle made a solo speech at the Albert Hall in London which Jean was able to attend. Four days after this he and Morel appeared at the

---

[55] Doyle, Georgina. *Out of the Shadows*. Calabash Press. 2004.

Artillery Hall in Hull before an appearance at Liverpool's Sun Hall on the 24th[56].

The 25th saw them in Edinburgh and the 26th in Manchester. Conan Doyle then gave another solo speech in Brighton on December 12th. All of this activity must have made it somewhat difficult for him to closely monitor his fledgling play.

On December 17th Mary arrived in London from Dresden. She had been almost absent from her father's life since his remarriage. Mary had spent the Christmases of 1907 and 1908 in Dresden and must have been hurt by it. Kingsley had missed out the same Christmases but, unlike his sister, he had visited his father and Jean at Windlesham in January 1908.

One of Mary's first journeys following her arrival was to visit her brother at Eton; but, by December 21st, she was finally in her father's company. They had lunch together before attending a rehearsal of the play. It is hard to imagine Mary enjoying the subject matter but her diary entry for that day suggested otherwise:

> Had lunch with Daddy. Thought he looked very well, though more absorbed in outside matters than ever. We went to a rehearsal of House of Temperley. Very interesting. Nice cheery lot actors – tirelessly energetic, and very nice to one another[57].

She was probably simply grateful for some time with her father even though he was effectively working. Conan Doyle's absence from theatre matters, due to his Congo speaking engagements, may well have meant there were a great many things about the play that needed changing and the opening night was six days away.

The press were clearly admitted during December as both the *Daily Express* and *The Daily Mirror* carried articles on how the rehearsals were proceeding. The *Daily Express* of the 22nd

---

[56] All Congo speech dates from *A Chronology of the Life of Sir Arthur Conan Doyle* by Brian Pugh.

[57] Doyle, Georgina. *Out of the Shadows*. Calabash Press. 2004.

reported that rehearsals for the play were 'in full swing' and also stated that Conan Doyle was 'superintending' events each day. In reality, given his Congo commitments he could only have been overseeing events since his last speech in Brighton. *The Times* reported that during at least some of this time he was staying at the Piccadilly Hotel in London which implies that there was enough to attend to that he felt the need to be on hand rather than lose time by travelling to and from Crowborough. *The Daily Mirror* of December 23rd featured a photograph of the rehearsal of a boxing match along with the inaccurate statement that the play was to be 'produced' on Boxing Day – no pun was apparently intended.

Mary and Kingsley were both at Windlesham for Christmas, the first Christmas that they had all been together since their mother's death[58]. It is hard not to imagine it has having been a tense time. Despite the joy of being together at Christmas and with their father they must have still felt a little like intruders into their father's new family. Conan Doyle must have also been distracted to a certain extent not only by that new family but also by his play's imminent debut.

December 27th 1909 saw said debut at the Adelphi and it went well. Conan Doyle's brother Innes noted that the producer, Mr Jarman, had been so pleased with its reception that he had kept them all up talking about it until 2.30am. Innes clearly liked the play also as he saw it again only a short while later[59]. It appeared that Conan Doyle might actually prove the naysayers wrong.

As the year came to a close Conan Doyle was also hoping for another success although this was not related to the stage. He wrote to his mother to inform her of his hopes for an invention known as the Auto-wheel. This device was designed to be attached to a conventional bicycle and render it motorised. Conan Doyle owned sixty out of ninety shares in the maker

---

[58] Pugh, Brian. *A Chronology of the Life of Sir Arthur Conan Doyle.* 3rd Edition. MX Publishing 2014.
[59] Doyle, Georgina. *Out of the Shadows*. Calabash Press. 2004.

Wall & Co (which he had purchased in November) and appeared confident of a healthy return[60].

Advertisement for the Autowheel

[60] Lellenberg, Jon et al. *Arthur Conan Doyle: A Life in Letters.* Harper Press. 2007.

1910

THE CURTAIN FALLS AND RISES

Just under two weeks after the debut of *The House of Temperley*, on Thursday January 6th 1910, the *Daily Express* carried a feature entitled *Melodrama of the Ring* which showed photographs from a performance of the play along with portraits and mini-biographies of the principal actors and actresses. Many of these same photos could also be seen in issue ninety of the magazine *The Play Pictorial* which devoted a whole issue to Conan Doyle's latest stage offering.

The *Express* gave an upbeat assessment of the play, in one issue even describing it as 'The most thrilling exhibition of the noble art of fisticuffs ever seen on the stage'. In truth, despite the positive opinions in the press and amongst the family, the play was in trouble.

Simply put, the concerns that had very likely deterred theatres from staging the play had turned out to be all too justified. People in general were not attracted to the subject matter and women in particular had little or no interest. Conan Doyle, a man whose decisions were often driven by his desire for fiscal security, had, simultaneously, leased a theatre at enormous expense and effectively excluded fifty per cent of his potential audience. Despite this, there was one man who thought the play could serve a useful purpose.

The Play Pictorial (issue 90) The House of Temperley Issue
(Author's collection)

His name was Reginald Brett – the second Viscount Esher. Lord Esher was chairman of the government's Defence Committee and had been involved in the set-up of Britain's Territorial Force[61]. The TF had been formally created on April 1st 1908 and the desired number of recruits had been decided on a per-county basis. Lord Esher was involved in the raising of the London quota and he knew that quota was going to be hard to achieve. He would later report (as recorded in *Hansard*) that London had only signed up around eighty-five per cent of the men it had set out to recruit.

Lord Esher

An important fact about the TF was that its members were not obliged to deploy overseas. This situation had its roots in the fact that it was made up of former units generally considered to be a home guard. Early in 1910 members of the TF had been asked to volunteer for 'Imperial Service' which meant that they could then be deployed anywhere within the Empire. Take up of this offer had been low, less than ten per cent, and Esher clearly felt that something had to be done.

[61] The forerunner of today's Territorial Army - a force of part-time soldiers designed to supplement the army in times of need.

Presumably at Lord Esher's suggestion or instigation, the London County Association, the official body responsible for raising London's TF quota, booked out the entire Adelphi Theatre on the night of February 11th 1910. The audience for that evening's showing consisted entirely of members of London's TF. The idea behind this was clear – to encourage the men to volunteer for overseas deployment. *The Daily Mirror* of that day reported that Captain Temperley's rousing speech in the play's second act was thought to be something that would inspire those attending.

The idea certainly found favour with Conan Doyle who wrote to his brother Innes that it was a great advertisement and that he expected audience numbers to swell off the back of it[62]. Above and beyond commercial considerations the idea must have appealed to Conan Doyle on a patriotic level. He was a frustrated soldier, former Boer War doctor and champion of the rifle club as a means of training the nation to defend itself. Anything that could inspire his countrymen to assist the Empire would have undoubtedly pleased him.

His struggling play was not the only theatrical issue on the agenda at this time. Not long before, on February 2nd, he had appeared, along with J.M. Barrie and E.W. Hornung before Mr. Justice Warrington in connection with a dispute concerning their mutual theatrical agent[63].

Conan Doyle and his fellow writers had allowed their affairs to be handled by one Addison Bright. Bright had run an agency in partnership with one A. F. Hardy but had suddenly died in 1906, three years into a ten year agreement. Subsequently it was discovered that he had retained approximately twenty-thousand pounds that should have been handed to authors he represented. Barrie, Hornung and Conan Doyle all recovered some money from Bright's estate with Conan Doyle recovering eight thousand out of nine thousand he was owed.

---

[62] Lycett, Andrew. *Conan Doyle: The Man who Created Sherlock Holmes.* Orion. 2007.

[63] *The Daily Mirror* of February 3rd 1910.

The executors of the estate were seeking further funds from the agency in order to settle other outstanding debts. Hardy, who was not accused of any personal wrongdoing, was fighting this and sought the annulment of the partnership with the aim of removing any personal liability for the debts owed by Bright.

The outcome was not ideal for Hardy. The judge refused the annulment of the partnership but did limit the amount of any further money that would be expected to be repaid to writers who were out of pocket. It is not clear whether Conan Doyle received the one thousand pounds that was outstanding.

So confident was Conan Doyle of a change in his theatrical fortunes that he turned his attention to other matters. The first of these being his interest in the idea of establishing a cyclists' cavalry service. He wrote to the *Daily Express* on the subject a few days before the TF performance of his play[64]. A response in the issue of the 11th from one W. Pollin offered support and went on to suggest that a volunteer brigade of motor-cyclists would be a good and popular idea. This letter was followed with a number of others also in favour.

The second matter also revolved around transport. It had come to Conan Doyle's attention that some former bus drivers had lost their pensions due to the winding up of the fund that underwrote them. Conan Doyle was later named, along with the Duke of Bedford, body-builder Eugen Sandow and the actor Henry Irving as being supporters of a fund, started by the *Daily Express*, designed to offer relief to these men in the absence of their pensions. The *Daily Express* of February 21st was able to report that the fund held over eight hundred pounds at the time of publication[65]. By Wednesday March 2nd the newspaper was able to report that the fund had reached over two thousand pounds[66].

These matters attended to, Conan Doyle and Jean took a holiday in Cornwall between March 7th and 21st during which

---

[64] His letter was published in the February 8th issue.

[65] Exact sum was £861 12s. 9d.

[66] Exact sum was £2,214 18s. 4d.

he would later confess that he got inspiration for the Sherlock Holmes story *The Devil's Foot*[67]. The area they chose, called Mullion, was a short distance from Poldhu Cove, Mount's Bay and Helston. All were areas that found their way into his 'Cornish horror' which would be published in December.

Back in Theatreland, despite Conan Doyle's confidence and the full-house of February 11th, *The House of Temperley* continued in its failure to attract audiences. By April 21st even Conan Doyle admitted it was going downhill[68] and, on May 6th, the play's demise was sealed with the death of King Edward VII. Despite only having reigned for just short of a decade Edward had been a popular King who was seen as having helped Europe stay at peace. It was feared in some circles that the loss of his calming influence would be felt and it is a fact that the First World War began only four years later. The country went into mourning and entertainment was the last thing on people's minds. An area where this was felt immediately was the West End of London where theatres closed. For Conan Doyle, whose play was teetering on the edge of financial disaster, this was the last straw.

King Edward's funeral was to take place on Friday May 20th. Even though he was under considerable financial pressure Conan Doyle elected to report on the King's funeral for the *Daily Mail*. The article was quoted liberally by *The New York Times* of the following day.

Conan Doyle used his article to pass comment on a number of issues. The first of these was England's negative attitude toward the German Kaiser. The Kaiser rode at the head of, what Conan Doyle described as, 'the troop of Kings who escorted their dead peer'. He added, 'England has lost something of her old kindliness if she does not take him back into her heart to-

---

[67] Lellenberg, Jon et al. *Arthur Conan Doyle: A Life in Letters.* Harper Press. 2007.

[68] Ibid. He would later admit, in August, that the collapse of the play had cost him £5000.

day'. Whether or not Conan Doyle remembered this four years later is open to speculation.

He went on to mention the Kings of Spain, Portugal and Belgium. The latter he briefly linked to the issue of the Congo before he let something of his immediate situation and frustration slip. 'The great dead has been honoured and the world is now for the living'. The living, in this instance, could certainly be said to include the theatre-going public of whom Conan Doyle was in desperate need. The question was what to give them. Ultimately, as he had done before in times of financial crisis, he turned to the one man he could rely on to bolster his bank balance – Sherlock Holmes.

Of the Sherlock Holmes stories Conan Doyle's favourite was *The Speckled Band*. This was not widely known at the time but would be revealed some years later. As recently as February he had begun work on an adaptation entitled *The Stonor Case* and by April he had reported to his mother that it was half done[69]. It is not clear when he had originally anticipated this work going into production but he recognised that he needed the play ready more swiftly than originally planned. According to one source[70], he began again from scratch for reasons unknown, although this is not universally agreed. In any event, a play, with the more familiar title *The Speckled Band* was ready and in rehearsals before the end of May.

For Holmes, Conan Doyle approached H.A. Saintsbury who had made a success as the great detective in a touring version of the William Gillette play. For the villain Rylott (renamed from the original Roylott) Conan Doyle cast Lyn Harding.

Harding's intended approach to the character of Rylott did not appeal to Conan Doyle. Depending on which source you read, Harding's portrayal was either too melodramatic for Conan Doyle or insufficiently melodramatic and mutual friend

---

[69] Lellenberg, Jon et al. *Arthur Conan Doyle: A Life in Letters.* Harper Press. 2007.
[70] Ibid.

J.M. Barrie was brought in to arbitrate. Barrie sided with Harding's depiction and Conan Doyle caved in[71].

Turning to the other principal parts - the role of Watson was taken by Claude King and that of the terrified Enid Stonor was played by Christine Silver.

The name changes for the characters were not the only departures from the original story. Curiously, and for the first time since his original preparatory notes for *A Study in Scarlet*, Conan Doyle moved Sherlock Holmes back to *Upper* Baker Street. Were these changes deliberate or, perhaps more likely, were they the result of an author in a hurry who was more concerned about reversing a financial crisis than being consistent with his characters and locations?

S. FISHER
has removed to more commodious premises
— 75 —
New Bond St., W.
COSTUMES from 7 Gns.
Season 1910.
NOW ON VIEW
The Latest Parisian Models.

KEITH, PROWSE & CO., LTD.
THE LARGEST THEATRE TICKET DEALERS in the World
Branches all over London.
162 NEW BOND STREET
YOU Want Best Seats. WE Have Them.

LONDON'S LATEST RESTAURANT
NEW GALLERY RESTAURANT and WIENER CAFE.
AFTERNOON TEAS.
HERR GOTTLIEB and his Celebrated Orchestra.
121 REGENT ST.

LIBERTY & CO'S
SILK SCARVES
12/6
15/6

ROYAL ADELPHI THEATRE.
Sole Lessee: Mr. GEORGE EDWARDES. STRAND, W.C.
Proprietors: Messrs. A. & S. GATTI
Manager: Mr. J. A. E. MALONE.

TO-NIGHT AT 8.30,
THE SPECKLED BAND:
An Adventure of Sherlock Holmes.
By ARTHUR CONAN DOYLE.

Dr. Grimesby Rylott	Mr. LYN HARDING
Enid Stonor (Dr. Rylott's Step-daughter)	Miss CHRISTINE SILVER
Mrs. Staunton	Miss AGNES THOMAS
Rodgers	Mr. A. S. HOMEWOOD
Ali, an Indian	Mr. WILTON ROSS
Mr. Scott Wilson (engaged to Enid's Sister)	Mr. ARTHUR BURNE
Mr. Armitage	Mr. SPENCER TREVOR
Mr. Longbrace (Coroner)	Mr. J. J. BARTLETT
Mr. Brewer (Foreman of the Jury)	Mr. FRANK RIDLEY
Inspector Downing	Mr. GEOFFREY HILL
Coroner's Officer	Mr. GEORGE LAUNDY
Mr. Holt Loamimg	Mr. A. G. CRAIG
Mrs. Soames	Miss GWENDOLEN FLOYD
Mr. James B. Montague	Mr. A. CORNEY GRAIN
Mr. Milverton	Mr. FRANK RIDLEY
Billy (Page to Mr. Sherlock Holmes)	Master CECIL F. LOWRIE
Dr. Watson	Mr. CLAUDE KING
Peters	Mr. C. LATER
Mr. Sherlock Holmes	Mr. H. A. SAINTSBURY

Jurors at the Inquest.

Act I.		The Hall of Stoke Place, Stoke Moran
Act II.	Scene 1	Dr. Rylott's Study, Stoke Place
	Scene 2	Mr. Sherlock Holmes' Rooms, Upper Baker Street, London
Act III.	Scene 1	The Hall of Stoke Place
	Scene 2	Enid's Bedroom, Stoke Place

PROGRAMME OF MUSIC

MATINEES WEDNESDAY & SATURDAY AT 2.30.

PRICES OF ADMISSION

BOX OFFICE (Mr. A. P. OXLEY) open 10 to 10.

Acting Manager — Mr. CHARLTON MANN
Stage Manager — Mr. W. W. KEENE
Assistant Stage Manager — Mr. A. BACHNER

THE CHARGE FOR THIS PROGRAMME IS 2d.

Odol The World's Dentifrice
When the teeth are cleansed with Odol the whole mouth is rejuvenated as the body is by a bath.

ON HIRE
AT LITTLE MORE THAN CAB FARES
Private Motor Carriages,
Landaulettes and Open Cars
Charge for Evening (DINNER, THEATRE) from 10/6. 15 miles
WEDDINGS A SPECIALITY.
MOTOR JOBMASTERS LIMITED
LONDON, S.W.

The theatre programme for The Speckled Band
(The collection of Roger Johnson)

71 When the play was filmed in 1931, Harding was the only cast member to reprise his role. He also went on to appear as Professor Moriarty on film opposite Arthur Wontner's Holmes.

Lyn Harding and H. A. Saintsbury

In the middle of all this activity Conan Doyle found time to meet with a former head of state. Theodore Roosevelt was in England and staying at the London home of Arthur Lee the M.P for Fareham[72]. The *Daily Express* of May 25th published a summarised itinerary of the former president in which it was stated that he had met (presumably the previous day) various literary men at Lee's house for lunch. Amongst these were Conan Doyle and Owen Seaman - the editor of *Punch*.

The first performance of *The Speckled Band* took place at 8.45pm on June 4th 1910[73]. Conan Doyle stayed overnight at the Hotel Metropole and wrote to his mother from there on the 5th to let her know that the play had gone down 'wonderfully well'[74]. This opinion of the play was shared by his son Kingsley in a letter to his uncle Innes Doyle. Innes also agreed that the play was a success and personally noted on June 12th that the

---

[72] Arthur Lee and his wife later bought the house known as Chequers which they left to the nation for use as the official country retreat of British Prime Ministers from 1921 onwards.

[73] Pugh, Brian. *A Chronology of the Life of Sir Arthur Conan Doyle.* 3rd Edition. MX Publishing 2014.

[74] Lellenberg, Jon et al. *Arthur Conan Doyle: A Life in Letters.* Harper Press. 2007.

first week's takings had been £1,301. The profit on this amount was £650 – nearly fifty per cent[75].

Almost a week before, on June 6th, *The Daily Mirror* had given a review in which it praised the play but credited its success to its snake:

> *The melodrama, which was very heartily received, owes little of its success to most of its actors and actresses. But the snake was magnificent. It would wriggle any drama into posterity.*

The *Daily Express* of the same day was inclined to overlook the snake and give credit to the actors. It remarked that the audience was so enthusiastic that they called for Conan Doyle for over twenty minutes following the play's conclusion (a point ignored by the *Mirror*). The, presumably relieved, author eventually appeared, bowed once and vanished resisting calls to give a speech. The newspaper could not pile enough praise upon leading-man Saintsbury saying 'H.A. Saintsbury does not merely act the part. He is the great Sherlock, as surely as though he had stepped out of the pages of Sir Arthur's book.'

Claude King, as Watson, was also praised. His portrayal was described as 'honest, simple, and even a trifle thick-witted, just as we all know him.' In its conclusion the paper stated:

> *Melodramatic, no doubt, the piece is; but it is the best melodrama. It holds the audience from first to last, and the heart of the most hardened playgoer knocks against his ribs when the victim and her rescuers wait breathlessly in her darkened room for the coming of the unknown horror against which locked doors and shuttered windows are of no avail.*

---

[75] Doyle, Georgina. *Out of the Shadows*. Calabash Press. 2004. The play would be consistent in its earnings. On July 12th Conan Doyle mentioned to Innes that the previous week's takings for the play were £1,660.

Claude King c1923

The Speckled Band, which had been a source of terror for the Stonors and a source of thrills for fans of Holmes was, for Conan Doyle, a saviour from financial embarrassment as he got back all the money he had lost on *The House of Temperley* and more besides[76].

King (Watson) and Saintsbury (Holmes) on stage

---

76 Lellenberg, Jon et al. *Arthur Conan Doyle: A Life in Letters.* Harper Press. 2007.

GEORGE NEWNES PASSES ON

Any joy Conan Doyle felt about the success of his play must have been tempered when he learned of the death of George Newnes which occurred on June 9th[77]. It was the faith that Newnes and Herbert Greenhough-Smith had shown in him that was responsible for giving him the platform to launch his Sherlock Holmes short stories, which even he had to admit had led to his present fame and fortune as an author.

The Daily Mirror stated 'Not merely London journalism, but the modern world lost a typical figure yesterday by the death of Sir George Newnes, which took place at Lynton.' It went on to give a sketch of Newnes' life, beginning with his first job in a 'fancy goods warehouse' eventually leading on to his founding of Tit-Bits magazine in Manchester. Naturally, the article mentioned the foundation of *The Strand Magazine* and how it had placed Conan Doyle 'in the first rank of living novelists and led to his later triumphs on the stage'.

A curious article appeared in the July 4th issue of the *Daily Express*. It referred to the now imminent Johnson-Jeffries boxing match that Conan Doyle had been asked to referee. It predictably mentioned the issue of black versus white and pointed out 'The contest is racial in its significance, and that is perhaps, in the circumstances, the worst aspect of the affair'. In another part of the article it remarked that the sport was not what it was but pointed to the support of men such as Conan

---

77 *The Daily Mirror* June 10th 1910.

Doyle as one of the reasons that the sport had 'never quite lost its glamour'. The most bizarre element was the assertion that the '...success of the prize-fighting play, "The House of Temperley," was but the last of the many evidences of its [boxing's] popularity'. It would appear that the paper's definition of success was somewhat at odds with that of Conan Doyle and the theatre-going public.

Sir George Newnes (1851-1910)

July saw Conan Doyle overtly involved in two acts of charity. The *Daily Express* of the 11th named him as one of the people involved in raising money for E. D. Morel, his colleague in the Congo struggle. The Earl of Cromer had used the newspaper to launch an appeal to raise funds for Morel who had been forced to devote his energies to the Congo at the expense of his 'private interests'[78] which presumably referred to his work as a journalist.

The *Daily Express* of July 29th carried an interesting advertisement for signed picture postcards. The proceeds were for charity in aid of the Fresh Air Fund. The fund had been established by the newspaper's founder Arthur Pearson as far back as 1892 with the aim of funding breaks to the countryside for children from city slums[79].

Over two hundred celebrities had been approached to sign picture postcards of themselves which the newspaper then sold on for one shilling each. The exceptions to this included Conan Doyle whose picture and signature were deemed to be worth five times that amount due, it was stated, to the limited supply.

August 4th saw Conan Doyle in Littlehampton staying at the Beach Hotel. Looking at a map today the distance between Littlehampton and Crowborough does not seem large enough to merit a stay at a hotel but Conan Doyle wrote to his mother on the same day and explained that he viewed it as a well-earned break following all the stress associated with *The House of Temperley* and *The Speckled Band*. He was also able to report that he had finished a new Sherlock Holmes story and that it had run to ten thousand words. This was *The Devil's Foot* - the story inspired by his visit to Mullion in Cornwall[80].

Also on the 4th he paid a visit to nearby Arundel Castle but his later movements are unclear[81]. Around the same time as his arrival he wrote to Roger Casement in connection with a book,

---

[78] In the October 21st issue of the *Daily Express* it was reported that the fund had reached £2,000.

[79] *Derby Telegraph* February 28 2011 (online edition).

[80] Lellenberg, Jon et al. *Arthur Conan Doyle: A Life in Letters.* Harper Press. 2007.

[81] Pugh, Brian. *A Chronology of the Life of Sir Arthur Conan Doyle.* 3rd Edition. MX Publishing 2014.

quite possibly ideas for *The Lost World*, which he would begin the following year.

On the 12th Conan Doyle turned out for the MCC in a cricket match against the local Littlehampton side[82]. It resulted in a win for the MCC following which he returned to Windlesham. The timing of the visit to Littlehampton was interesting as it meant he was absent for the transfer of *The Speckled Band* from the Adelphi theatre[83]. It might seem rather careless of Conan Doyle not to supervise the transfer of his play but, given that his break in Littlehampton was motivated, at least in part, by theatre related stress it is no great surprise that he maintained a distance. The play's destination was the Globe Theatre (presently known as the Gielgud) which had been renamed from its former name – The Hicks Theatre – by Charles Frohman in 1909 when he became its manager.

It was also in August that Mary Conan Doyle saw *The Speckled Band* for the first time. She considered it some of her father's best work '..because, female interest nil, love interest likewise nil'.[84]

Her cutting remarks were no doubt strongly influenced by the fact that her father had refused to fund any further education in Germany. To say that this must have been a frustrating time for her is clearly an understatement. She had been sent to Germany very much against her wishes. Her requests to come back, in the early days, had been rebuffed and now, as she was settling in and making progress, she was being forced to return.[85]

September 1st saw Conan Doyle return to the theatre. On this occasion it was not one of his own plays. The *Daily Express* of September 2nd reported that Conan Doyle and Jean had attended the first-night performance at His Majesty's Theatre of *Henry*

---

[82] Pugh, Brian. *A Chronology of the Life of Sir Arthur Conan Doyle*. 3rd Edition. MX Publishing 2014.
[83] This took place on August 8th – (Ibid).
[84] Doyle, Georgina. *Out of the Shadows*. Calabash Press. 2004.
[85] Ibid.

VIII which starred Sir Herbert Tree. Tree, many years earlier, had been offered Conan Doyle's Sherlock Holmes play but had lost it after demanding changes that Conan Doyle was not comfortable agreeing to. Conan Doyle and Jean were described as sharing the box with friends but further details were not revealed.

A little over two weeks later Conan Doyle accepted the presidency of the Divorce Law Reform Union[86]. He had long considered that divorce was not available to those who needed it. John Lamond, one of his earliest biographers, noted that Conan Doyle was especially concerned for women who were, as Lamond put it, 'chained for life to a husband who might be in a lunatic asylum, or to one who had become an habitual drunkard'[87].

This view almost certainly came from how Conan Doyle had viewed his parents' marriage with his father Charles spending a large amount of time drunk and then confined, with his mother only released, in 1893, by Charles' death. As a strong believer in marriage Conan Doyle was not attempting to make divorce an easy option (he said that 'laxity in the marriage tie is an evil'[88]) but he thought that where a marriage was beyond hope, for whatever reason, divorce needed to be easier to obtain. His support for marriage had long since been committed to public record with his book *A Duet* and, at around this time, his latest Brigadier Gerard story *The Marriage of the Brigadier* was published in *The Strand*.

The subject of divorce reared its head in his latest completed Sherlock Holmes story *The Devil's Foot*, which was to be published in December. The character of Dr. Leon Sterndale, who can be seen, quite reasonably, as a prototype for the character Conan Doyle was yet to invent – Professor

---

[86] Pugh, Brian. *A Chronology of the Life of Sir Arthur Conan Doyle.* 3rd Edition. MX Publishing 2014.

[87] Lamond, John. *Arthur Conan Doyle: A Memoir*. John Murray 1931.

[88] Doyle, Arthur Conan. *Memories and Adventures*. Wordsworth Editions Ltd. 2007.

Challenger, remarks to Sherlock Holmes about '...the deplorable laws of England...' that prevented him from divorcing a wife who had long since abandoned him. Conan Doyle would later echo this sentiment in his autobiography when he remarked that England lagged behind other countries and that this had led to the situation where marriages 'which are obviously disgusting and degrading are maintained in this country while they can be dissolved abroad'.

October was a busy month for Conan Doyle. The first significant event took place on the 3rd and was an address by him to medical students of St Mary's Hospital. The October 4th issues of the *Daily Express* and *The Daily Mirror* covered the event. The former with an article and the latter with a captioned photograph. The speech, entitled *The Romance of Medicine*, was part of the procedure of opening the 'Winter sessions'. For nearly an hour he spoke, covering the medical issues surrounding all manner of famous figures including Napoleon Bonaparte[89].

October 4th saw Kingsley depart the country for Lausanne in Switzerland. Conan Doyle distracted himself from this by taking Jean to a performance of *Elektra* at the Royal Opera House in Covent Garden[90].

The following day was apparently a quiet one beyond the fact that Conan Doyle's daughter Mary resumed her studies in the country. After this brief interlude the schedule resumed apace. October 6th saw Conan Doyle and Jean at the Whitehall Rooms, in the Hotel Metropole, for an event held by the Anti-Slavery and Aborigines Protection League and the 7th saw Conan Doyle at the Holborn Restaurant at a reception for the French actress Sarah Bernhardt[91].

---

[89] An abridged version of the speech later found its way into *The Lancet.*

[90] *Daily Express* October 5th 1910.

[91] Pugh, Brian. *A Chronology of the Life of Sir Arthur Conan Doyle.* 3rd Edition. MX Publishing 2014.

Globe Theatre, London (now Gielgud Theatre) c1910

During the same month, writing to his mother, Conan Doyle announced that he intended to go and see some of the Crippen case. This of course referred to Hawley Harvey Crippen (known as Dr. Crippen) who was on trial accused of the murder of his wife Cora. The other item of note that Conan Doyle reported was that Jean had recently changed nurses[92]. What brought this about was not clear but, so close to term with her second child, it must have been something significant.

Finally, during this month, Conan Doyle was made Captain of Crowborough Beacon Golf Club (for one year) and President of Crowborough Gymnasium Club[93]. It seems probable that Conan Doyle was made Captain of his Golf Club before October 11th. The reason for this being that *The Daily Mirror* of the 11th carried an article entitled *Bonus for Territorial Caddies* in which it was reported that Conan Doyle had convinced the members of the club to pay a bonus of ten shillings 'for each caddy over the age of eighteen who undergoes the annual training'. Although he could have said this before his appointment it seems likely that this suggestion was made either as part of an acceptance speech or after his appointment when his position would have given his idea more weight.

November brought, on the 19th, the birth at Windlesham of Conan Doyle and Jean's second son Adrian. He would be baptised at the same church as Denis in January of 1911. Two days later *The Speckled Band* opened in New York at the Garrick Theatre[94].

Rather surprisingly, the play, which had done well in Britain and had saved Conan Doyle's nerves and bank balance, did not match that success in the United States. In the end it ran for a mere thirty-two performances which Conan Doyle largely blamed on Charles Frohman's scheduling[95].

While there may have been an element of truth in this, the review that appeared in *The New York Times* of November 22nd gave a number of other reasons.

---

[92] Lellenberg, Jon et al. *Arthur Conan Doyle: A Life in Letters.* Harper Press. 2007.

[93] Pugh, Brian. *A Chronology of the Life of Sir Arthur Conan Doyle.* 3rd Edition. MX Publishing 2014.

[94] *The New York Times* of November 20th 1910 reported that the play was to open the following day.

[95] Lellenberg, Op. cit.

The reviewer first described the introduction of Sherlock Holmes into the play as a 'too labored effort' and then went on to describe the second act, which took place mostly in Holmes's rooms, as 'retarding the development of the main story'.

However, in the eyes of this particular reviewer, the most significant problem with the play was the absence of William Gillette. William Gillette was now so identified with the role that anyone else attempting to play Holmes was expected to give an impersonation of Gillette as Holmes rather than their own interpretation. Charles Millward, who played Holmes, was praised as a 'good actor' but 'there can be no doubt that in this instance a far more effective performance for the purpose would have resulted if he had succeeded in imitating the mannerisms and slow, drawling method of Mr. Gillette'.

Edwin Stevens, playing Rylott was praised as the most convincing and Irene Fenwick, as Enid Stonor, was criticised for struggling with anything requiring 'depth or passion'.

The December issue of *The Strand* saw the publication of *The Devil's Foot.* For this story the illustrating duties were picked up by one Gilbert Holiday (sometimes recorded as Halliday)[96]. Holiday (1879-1937) was an artist who specialised in sporting scenes and scenes involving horses[97]. His talent for depicting horses would later lead to commissions featuring horses in military service during the First World War.

Holiday had illustrated for *The Graphic* and *The Illustrated London News* but had only been producing illustrations for *The Strand* since May of 1910. You could be forgiven for thinking that he regretted accepting *The Strand*'s commission to

[96] Whitt, J.F. *The Strand Magazine 1891-1950 A Selective Checklist.* 1979.

[97] *The Horse and Hound in Art.* http://www.horseandhoundart.com/Gilbert_Holiday.htm

illustrate the *The Devil's Foot*. This interpretation is not unreasonable when you consider that he not only illustrated only one story but also that none of the illustrations he produced appear to bear his mark. His initials or full signature were frequently to be seen on other works he produced. Following his work on the latest Sherlock Holmes story he left *The Strand*, returning briefly to produce illustrations for its January 1913 issue.

For the family, the year concluded with the happy news that Conan Doyle's brother Innes was engaged to a young Danish woman by the name of Clara Schwensen[98].

[98] Pugh, Brian. *A Chronology of the Life of Sir Arthur Conan Doyle*. 3rd Edition. MX Publishing 2014.

Holmes and Watson are visited in their Cornish retreat in The Devil's Foot (by Gilbert Holiday)

The engagement photograph of Innes Doyle
(The Collection of Georgina Doyle)

The engagement photograph of Clara Schwensen
(The Collection of Georgina Doyle)

1911

MOTORING AND HOME RULE

1911 opened with Jean following on the heels of her husband by being appointed the Ladies' Captain at the Crowborough Beacon Golf Club. Early February saw *The Speckled Band* begin performances at the Strand Theatre which was operating under that name for the second time[99].

March brought the publication, in *The Strand*, of the latest Sherlock Holmes story *The Adventure of the Red Circle.* This was published over two successive issues of the magazine. For the first and only time the illustrating duties were picked up by two new artists – Henry Matthew Brock and Joseph Simpson[100].

Brock (1875-1960) had been a contributor to *Punch* and had produced artwork for posters and advertisements for the D'Oyly Carte Opera Company. Simpson (1879-1939) had also done some advertising work but would later go on to produce portraits and sporting subjects. It is possible that it was through their advertising work that they came to the attention of Greenhough-Smith at *The Strand.* Brock produced his first illustrations for the magazine in April 1910 and Simpson had done so a month earlier. Their careers at the magazine ran in parallel to a certain extent. Brock ultimately produced his last

---

[99] It is today known as the Novello Theatre.

[100] Whitt, J.F. *The Strand Magazine 1891-1950 A Selective Checklist.* 1979.

illustrations for *The Strand* in December 1912 and Simpson in May of the same year.

Henry Matthew Brock and Joseph Simpson (self-portrait)

April brought a nice review of Conan Doyle's book *The Last Galley*. The *Daily Express* of April 25th reported that the book was to be published that day, although later sources disagreed, saying that it was actually published on the 26th[101]. Aside from any issues of accuracy, the newspaper's reviewer was happy with the book, describing it as 'decidedly good reading'.

During April, Conan Doyle took Jean, their two sons, a maid and a nurse to the Royal Bath Hotel in Bournemouth. From there he wrote an undated letter to his mother in which he remarked upon the poor weather[102]. His decision to go to

---

[101] Lycett, Andrew. *Conan Doyle: The Man who Created Sherlock Holmes.* Orion. 2007 - is one of the sources that gives the 26th.

[102] Lellenberg, Jon et al. *Arthur Conan Doyle: A Life in Letters.* Harper Press. 2007.

Bournemouth rather than anywhere else is not something that he elaborated on in his letter or indeed anywhere else.[103]

Clearly it was a family holiday, but was it also a research trip? The idea for what would later become *The Lost World* was in his mind by this time and fossilised leaves had been discovered in Bournemouth.[104]

On May 5th, in another letter to his mother, Conan Doyle reported that he was to take part in The Prince Henry of Prussia Cup which was an idea of said Prince Henry – the brother of the Kaiser. The event, which would see Germany and Britain compete in a motor trial through the two countries, had been proposed by way of celebration of the impending coronation of King George V. The plans of Germany aside, Britain naturally had plans to mark the crowning of its new King.

The *Daily Express* of May 13th reported that, on the previous day, Conan Doyle was at the Crystal Palace to witness the opening of the Festival of Empire. The festival was a long series of events designed to celebrate the coronation that was to take place on June 22nd.

The King was described as nervous, this made all the more obvious by his twitching hand. He was described as 'face to face with his people for the first time'. The grounds of the Crystal Palace were filled with examples of replicas of buildings and products from all the countries of the Empire. The festival would, over the course of its duration, feature music and various sporting events.

Two days after the coronation, on June 24th, *The Daily Mirror* offered a series of brief book reviews under the heading *Coronation Books and Others*. In it, amongst various works, Conan Doyle's *The Last Galley* was mentioned. It was described as 'As fine a collection of stories as anyone could wish to read'. Despite this endorsement the entry *"De*

---

103 None of the sources consulted by your present author contained any ideas.

104 Letters from Charles Darwin to J.D Hooker in 1866 confirm this and are held at the University of Cambridge.

Profundis", a story appearing in the book's second part, was described as best avoided by 'all with weak nerves' as it 'passes the limits of what is advisable in the way of horrors'.

On July 4th the Prince Henry of Prussia Cup commenced in the German town of Homburg. The first stage took the competitors to Cologne on the 5th, Münster on the 6th and Bremerhaven on the 7th where the cars were loaded on board ship for the crossing to Southampton[105].

Each car in the competition was allowed one driver and one passenger. In addition, each car had an observer from the opposite country in order to ensure fair play. Conan Doyle took Jean as his passenger and their German observer was one Count Carmer. Once on British soil the cars headed out from Southampton (on July 9th) to Leamington (10th), Harrogate (11th), Newcastle (12th), Edinburgh (13th) where they rested before heading to Windermere on the 15th. The final stops were Cheltenham (16th) and London on July 18th.

Britain was declared the victor in the competition and a celebratory banquet was held on July 19th. At the time, Conan Doyle was very positive about the contest, but he noted the pessimism amongst some British army officers who were taking part. They were convinced that the competition was simply a ruse for German officers to get valuable intelligence on Britain before the outbreak of any war between the two countries. Much later, Conan Doyle saw the wisdom of this, describing the event as a ploy by Germany to 'create a false entente by means of sport'.

Conan Doyle's observer Count Carmer was initially considered, by him, to be rather cold and aloof. By the end of the competition he had 'thawed' considerably and visited Conan Doyle at Windlesham[106]. However, in 1920, a Count von Carmer was named by *The New York Times* as a 'War Culprit'. In its issue of February 5th 1920, Major Count von Carmer,

---

105 Lellenberg, Jon et al. *Arthur Conan Doyle: A Life in Letters.* Harper Press. 2007.
106 Ibid.

described as 'garrison commandant' was wanted for 'arbitrary requisitions, bad treatment of civilians and systematic pillage'.

Conan Doyle did not remain in the country for long following Britain's motoring victory. On August 2nd he fulfilled the duties of best man at the wedding of his brother Innes to Clara Schwensen in Copenhagen. He was then back in the country before the end of the month in order to take part in an Authors versus Publishers cricket match at Lords. The match ended in a draw[107].

Around the same time, Kingsley enrolled as a medical student at St Mary's Hospital in Paddington. While Conan Doyle was undoubtedly proud, his mind at this time was occupied by a great many things, the most notable of which came to the attention of the public at the end of September.

The event in question was Conan Doyle publicly abandoning his long held opposition to Irish Home Rule. This change in attitude had been brought about by a number of things, but the most notable influence was almost certainly Roger Casement. Conan Doyle chose to announce his new position on the 22nd through the pages of the *Belfast Evening Telegraph* and *The Times*[108].

In his letter Conan Doyle acknowledged that he had twice stood for Parliament as a Unionist but pointed out that even in those days he had acknowledged that Home Rule '…could only come with time, that it would only be safe with an altered economic condition and a gentler temper among the people…'.

He now considered that these conditions had been met and pointed to what he saw as the successes of Home Rule in South Africa and Canada. These 'two successes' clearly indicated, to his mind, that the Empire need not fear a failure with Ireland. To underscore his sincerity he made it plain that if the

---

[107] Pugh, Brian. *A Chronology of the Life of Sir Arthur Conan Doyle*. 3rd Edition. MX Publishing 2014.

[108] Gibson, John Michael and Green, Richard Lancelyn. *Letters to the Press*. Martin Secker & Warburg Ltd. 1975.

newspaper did not publish his letter he would do so himself in order to ensure that the wider public were aware of '…how I stand in the matter'.

The Festival of Empire in the grounds of the Crystal Palace (1911)

THE END OF THE BEGINNING

October 4th brought the sad news of the death of Dr. Joseph Bell at his home in Midlothian. Conan Doyle had been clear from the moment that Sherlock Holmes became popular that Bell had been the inspiration for the character or, more specifically, his powers of deduction. It was therefore no surprise when he was approached by the press for his reaction to the news.

In its article entitled *Detective of the Surgery,* the *Daily Express* quoted a letter written by Conan Doyle about his late mentor. 'Personally, I can say very little of Dr. Joseph Bell, for I have never met him in his own house, and really only knew him as my professor. As such I shall always see him very clearly; his stiff, bristling, iron-grey hair, his clear, half-humorous, half-critical eyes, his eager face and swarthy skin.'

Conan Doyle went on to remark on Bell's dry humour and his energy but the letter seemed lacking in sadness. Bell had, in many respects, been the inspiring father figure that Conan Doyle's own father had been unable to be. Bell had taken Conan Doyle under his wing by appointing him as his clerk and it was the close proximity that Conan Doyle had to Bell that enabled him to study Bell's diagnostic method which in turn led to the eventual creation of Sherlock Holmes.

Perhaps it was Conan Doyle's dislike of being known for Holmes that caused him to be somewhat cool in his initial reaction[109].

Dr. Joseph Bell JP, DL, FRCS (1837-1911)

---

109 *The Daily Mirror* produced a similar article in its October 5th issue. It did not take the trouble to contact Conan Doyle for comment and simply reprinted quotes that Conan Doyle had made about Bell when he was still alive.

It would later emerge that Bell had been decidedly unhappy about his association with Sherlock Holmes. Despite making appreciative noises in public, presumably through a desire to avoid hurting his former pupil's feelings, Bell was more candid in private.

For a good part of his life, Bell was close friends with one Jessie Saxby who, for a time, was President of the Edinburgh, Orkney and Shetland Literary and Scientific Association. Saxby's husband, also a lifelong friend, was, like Bell, a physician. Saxby published over thirty volumes of stories, poems and other items in her lifetime and her last known work was a short and posthumous biography of Bell entitled *Joseph Bell, M.D., F.R.C.S., J.P., D.L., etc. An Appreciation by an Old Friend*. It was published in 1913 and came in at just under one hundred pages including some illustrations.

In this short work, Saxby quoted a letter on the subject of Holmes and his association with Bell that Bell had written to her (the exact date of the letter is not clear).

> 'Why bother yourself about the cataract of drivel for which Conan Doyle is responsible? I am sure he never imagined that such a heap of rubbish would fall on my devoted head in consequence of his stories'.[110]

Given that this was Bell writing, in confidence, to a lifelong friend we can be fairly certain that Conan Doyle was not aware of his position. It is tempting to wonder, however, whether Conan Doyle ever saw (or owned) a copy of Saxby's work and thus learned of Bell's feelings about the attention the Holmes association had brought him. Even though Conan Doyle's own attitude toward Holmes was ambivalent at best, he would surely have been slightly wounded to hear that Bell's private position was so at odds with his public utterances of support and admiration.

---

[110] All information about Saxby's work was obtained from *Sherlock Holmes and his creator* by Trevor H. Hall. Saxby died in 1914.

The Last Galley received comment in the October 8th issue of the *New York Times*. The story itself was well received, but far more interesting was the comment made by the article's author in relation to Sherlock Holmes. He observed, because Conan Doyle was so identified with Holmes, that 'readers in general will be disappointed-for a time, at least-with everything he does which leaves that popular favourite out of account…'.

This was hardly a revelation but what was interesting was the suggestion that '…now that Mr. G.K. Chesterton has found time…to invent a rival to Mr. Sherlock Holmes in the person of the ingenious cleric Father Brown, it may not be unwise for Sir Arthur to imitate the historic example of Sir Walter Scott when Byron took to writing poetry- and seek another métier'.

It demonstrated that, in the eyes of this particular reviewer, Sherlock Holmes's place at the top of the pile was no longer secure.

This probably mattered little to Conan Doyle who was now hard at work on *The Lost World*. It was now that, it could be said, he paid his respects to the late Dr. Bell. His new hero, Professor Challenger, was described as being educated at Edinburgh University but this could equally be said to be based on Conan Doyle himself rather than his late mentor.

Dinosaurs reared their heads again in November. On the 19th Conan Doyle was convinced that a fossilised Iguanodon footprint had been found in the grounds of Windlesham[111].

This news, presumably, went, once again, to Arthur Woodward who passed it on to Charles Dawson. Dawson took the opportunity to combine business with pleasure and took both himself and his wife down to Windlesham where they met Conan Doyle and Jean. In a letter dated November 30th,

---

111 Pugh, Brian. *A Chronology of the Life of Sir Arthur Conan Doyle*. 3rd Edition. MX Publishing 2014.

Dawson wrote to Woodward that he had explained to Conan Doyle that what he had was in fact a 'concretion of oxide of iron and sand'[112]. He went on to write 'I was so sorry at his disappointment – he is such a good fellow'.

Any disappointment that Conan Doyle had felt due to Dawson's opinion must have been fleeting as he wrote to his mother on December 3rd to report that his book was complete and that he was 'very busy superintending the making of some pictures which will purport to be photos of the Lost World…'[113]

December 8th saw Conan Doyle and Jean at the Criterion restaurant in Piccadilly at an Incorporated Society of Authors event to honour the establishment of The Imperial Copyright Act which was due to receive Royal Assent on the 16th. This act consolidated and replaced all the various copyright laws that had existed up until that point and applied them across the Empire[114].

The act brought in a number of new elements that must have been popular with all authors. The need to register copyright was removed and copyright was deemed to exist from the moment a work was created rather than when it was published. The length of the copyright term was increased to life plus fifty years. It also extended copyright protection to the creators of sound recordings. There were other changes connected to the newly emerging medium of film.

December also saw the publication of *The Disappearance of Lady Frances Carfax*. This would feature the talents of artist Alec Ball[115]. Ball had produced his first illustrations for *The Strand* in December of the previous year. The illustrators of the previous story, Brock and Simpson, were still working for the

---

[112] Spencer, Frank. *The Piltdown Papers*. Oxford University Press 1990.

[113] Lellenberg, Jon et al. *Arthur Conan Doyle: A Life in Letters*. Harper Press. 2007.

[114] It was applied in phases over the years that followed.

[115] Whitt, J.F. *The Strand Magazine 1891-1950 A Selective Checklist*. 1979.

magazine at this point and it is fair to say that they, along with Ball, were the main artists for *The Strand* in 1911. Simpson illustrated another story in the same issue of the magazine which explains why he was not called upon for the latest Holmes adventure. Brock's lack of involvement is less easy to account for. His last work for the magazine had been to illustrate a P.G. Wodehouse story in the September issue and he had certainly produced less work that year than Ball who, in 1911, had illustrated five stories prior to the latest Holmes adventure.

None of these artists would have the opportunity to illustrate a Sherlock Holmes story again as all three were destined to leave *The Strand* before the next adventure saw the light of day.

1912

THE LOST WORLD AND THE LOST SHIP

An interesting article appeared in the February 14th issue of the *Daily Express*. It was entitled *Boxing Popular in France* and, as its title made plain, talked about the popularity of the sport amongst the French.

The article did not limit itself to the actual sport however; it also talked about the depiction of boxing in the arts and in particular the stage. No less than three stage productions were referred to; the last of which was *Maison Temperley*, the French version of Conan Doyle's unfortunate boxing play.

What was curious was the statement that the play was to be staged at the Théâtre Sarah Bernhardt. It was only in October of 1910 that Conan Doyle had attended a reception in Bernhardt's honour in London's Holborn restaurant. She had been running the theatre that had previously been the Théâtre des Nations since 1899, so it seems fairly possible that Conan Doyle's presence at the reception in 1910 was as much business as it was pleasure.

Conan Doyle was not only battling for his own play but also for the plays of others at this time. The *Daily Express* of February 15th reported that he was uniting with other dramatists in defiance of the Lord Chamberlain. The play concerned was *The Secret Woman* by Eden Phillpotts.

Eden Phillpotts (1862-1960)

Conan Doyle and his fellow dramatists (who included J.M. Barrie, Anthony Hope, George Bernard Shaw and Jerome K. Jerome) were angered at the decision of the Lord Chamberlain's office to ban the play which meant that it could not be staged for money. The advice given to the Lord Chamberlain that had resulted in the ban had apparently come from the Examiner of Plays. The new holder of the position at the time being the actor Charles Brookfield.

Charles Brookfield (1860-1913)

Conan Doyle would probably have protested against the censorship of Phillpott's play in any case, but he would have been encouraged by any chance to cross swords with Brookfield. Brookfield had starred as Sherlock Holmes in a parody play entitled *Under the Clock* in 1893 and he had also, allegedly, given information to help the Marquess of Queensbury in his court battle with Oscar Wilde, which had resulted in Wilde being convicted and jailed on a charge of gross indecency.

Brookfield's appointment as Examiner of Plays had angered supporters of Wilde and, five days after the *Express's* article they converged on the Prince of Wales's Theatre to protest at the revival of Brookfield's own play *Dear Old Charlie*[116]. It was felt that Phillpott's play was being unfairly discriminated against and that the best way of demonstrating this was to stage Phillpott's play for free, in parallel, thus circumventing the ban, at the Kingsway Theatre. The first of these showings was on February 22nd just after Brookfield's play had reopened.

In total, Conan Doyle and his fellow dramatists were underwriting three thousand six hundred theatre seats. It demonstrated that Conan Doyle's recent theatre experience had not discouraged him from taking financial risks – especially in the cause of defending a fellow dramatist.

This was not their only act of defiance. They also wrote a letter to *The Times* in which they said, of the Lord Chamberlain, '…he knows no better. We do not doubt the kindliness of his intention when he offers to show us how to alter our work to his satisfaction; and we are sure he does not understand that these offers to save us from ourselves and hush the matter up are to authors the greatest insult of all.'

There was also, of course, an element of self-interest being shown on the part of all Phillpott's supporters. They understood and acknowledged that it could one day be any of them on the receiving end of the same treatment.

In March *The Lost World* began serialisation in *Associated Sunday Magazine*[117]. *The Strand* began serialisation the

[116] http://www.mr-oscar-wilde.de/ See the page specifically on Brookfield.
[117] Pugh, Brian. *A Chronology of the Life of Sir Arthur Conan Doyle.* 3rd Edition. MX Publishing 2014.

following month[118]. Its editor, Greenhough-Smith, told Conan Doyle that it was the best serial he had produced other than Holmes, and Conan Doyle reported this in a letter to his mother[119]. A few weeks earlier, on February 14th, Charles Dawson, who had dismissed Conan Doyle's fossilised Iguanodon footprint, wrote to Arthur Smith Woodward confirming that Conan Doyle was writing 'a sort of Jules Verne book on some wonderful plateau in S. America…I hope someone has sorted out his fossils for him!'.[120]

Meanwhile, *The Strand*'s advertising reflected its editor's glowing opinion. An advert appeared in *The Daily Mirror* of March 26th in which it was stated that Professor Challenger '…is a Great New Personality and will Create as Profound a Sensation as CONAN DOYLE'S other Immortal Characters'.

The advert went on to state that Conan Doyle had never written 'more brilliantly, more effectively'. Readers were assured that they would be gripped by the latest product of Conan Doyle's imagination. However, the imagination of the population was soon to be gripped by something much more potent.

In the early hours of April 15th RMS Titanic sank in the North Atlantic Ocean. Given the massive loss of life and the ship's supposedly unsinkable status, the story naturally dominated the news across the world. Conan Doyle was as shocked and captivated as everyone else and was, unsurprisingly, moved by the stories of heroism that began circulating in the aftermath. In London it was decided to stage a benefit matinee at the Hippodrome. Conan Doyle contributed a poem entitled *Ragtime* which was to be performed and appear in the souvenir brochure.

---

118 Lellenberg, Jon et al. *Arthur Conan Doyle: A Life in Letters.* Harper Press. 2007.
119 Ibid.
120 Spencer, Frank. *The Piltdown Papers.* Oxford University Press 1990.

The *Daily Express* of April 27th pointed out that anyone who was not able to attend the matinee could apply for copies of the brochure (at 2s 6d) and thus assist the fundraising effort. Conan Doyle and fellow author Max Pemberton were amongst the many contributors to the content of the brochure mentioned by the newspaper.

Absent from this list was George Bernard Shaw. Shaw had elected to question the tales of heroism through the press and this angered Conan Doyle who had been brought up from the cradle on tales of such heroism. He also took to the letters pages of the press to take Shaw to task and he was backed up by *The Daily Mirror*.

In its issue of May 23rd the newspaper drew a comparison between Shaw and a character called Joey the clown '...who consistently turned up, at awkward moments, with a shout of "Only me!"'. The newspaper's ire was not, however, reserved purely for Shaw. The article went on to observe '...the constant cropping up and intervention of our celebrities, in any event of an importance worth their attention.' The article continued with 'The celebrities were growing restive under the diversion of many eyes from *them* to *this.*' This was a clear reference to the fact that the disaster had drawn people's attention away from the work of famous authors and playwrights.

In the newspaper's opinion it was this lack of the spotlight that had motivated Shaw's negative viewpoint. '...he makes it appear that all but himself are lying in their accounts of what happened and have been lying consistently from the first'. Then, referring to Conan Doyle's rebuke to Shaw, the article went on to say '...we regret that Bernard Shaw cannot take his rebuke quietly and leave it alone, but has to come capering up again and trying to be funny in order to cover his rather ugly fall...'.

By this time Conan Doyle had a new distraction and it was another battle against injustice. He had become aware of the case of one Oscar Slater. Slater had been jailed in 1909 for the murder, in Glasgow, of one Marion Gilchrist. The police were able to determine that, despite the chaos and mess, the only item missing was a diamond brooch. The murder was immediately viewed as a burglary that had gone wrong. In the absence of evidence, and on some very shaky witness testimony, Slater was identified as a person of interest and, when it was determined he was in America, his extradition was sought.

Slater voluntarily returned to Scotland and was put on trial. Despite the lack of evidence he was convicted of the murder by a majority verdict and sentenced to death. The sentence was later commuted to life imprisonment. Conan Doyle read of the case and, seeing a case which had been as badly handled as that of George Edalji, decided to campaign for Slater's release. He also began work on a book called *The Case of Oscar Slater*.

Conan Doyle's mother, when she learned of this, was not impressed and expressed her doubts about Slater to her son. Conan Doyle was unmoved by her opinions and firmly requested that she trust his judgement in the matter[121].

In the meantime *The Lost World* was clearly doing good business for *The Strand*. The magazine sold out of its June and July issues in a mere fourteen days. They did not claim that this was down to the presence of Conan Doyle's serial but, in their advertisement for the August issue, they went out of their way to mention it[122].

The summer of 1912 was a very social one for Conan Doyle. In June he was at the Savoy to mark the tenth anniversary of the founding of the Pilgrims Club. There was also a family holiday to Eastbourne, a cricket match for the MCC and visits to Windlesham by Anthony Hope and J.M. Barrie. Aside from these social engagements Conan Doyle found the time to be on the organising committee for the 1916 Olympic Games and

---

[121] Lellenberg, Jon et al. *Arthur Conan Doyle: A Life in Letters.* Harper Press. 2007.
[122] *Daily Express* August 3rd 1912.

work on his book regarding Oscar Slater which was published in August[123].

Around this same time Conan Doyle began work on a follow-up to *The Lost World*. It would ultimately be entitled *The Poison Belt*.

October 15th saw the publication of *The Lost World* in book form by Hodder and Stoughton[124]. *The Daily Mirror* of that date was very much in favour of the story, using such words as 'exciting' and 'fantastic'. The newspaper clearly considered the story a success.

Two days earlier *The New York Times* had reported on the American publication of the book by George H. Doran. Conan Doyle was compared with H. Rider Haggard and his 'passion for detail' and 'exact scientific knowledge' were noted. The newspaper concluded with the hope that '...we have not heard the last of Lord John, that, indeed, he may succeed Sherlock Holmes in Conan Doyle's affections'. Given our knowledge of Conan Doyle's feelings toward Holmes at the time, this was not an unrealistic hope.

On the 17th, the *Daily Express* had offered its opinion. Despite hailing the story as a 'capital yarn' it went on to say that it was the kind of story that H.G. Wells would have written 'a dozen years ago' and observed that, had Wells done so, it would have been 'more scientific and less heroic'. Not done with the comparisons, they went on to observe that it could also have been written by Jules Verne but, in that eventuality, it would 'not have been so dramatic'.

The only person overtly unhappy at this time was Conan Doyle's mother. She chose this moment to remind her son that

---

123 Pugh, Brian. *A Chronology of the Life of Sir Arthur Conan Doyle*. 3rd Edition. MX Publishing 2014.

124 *The Daily Mirror* of October 15th 1912.

it was almost exactly ten years since he had been knighted and asked why he would not mention his title on his books. She deployed the argument, not for the first time, that his actions were an insult to the late King Edward who had conferred it upon him[125]. This argument had ultimately persuaded the reluctant Conan Doyle to accept the honour in 1902; on this occasion it failed and, on his literary output, he remained Arthur (or A.) Conan Doyle.

November 6th saw *Le Maison Temperley* staged at Théâtre Sarah Bernhardt[126]. On two occasions during the month Conan Doyle wrote to his mother to inform her that the play was doing well. In the second of these letters Conan Doyle also informed his mother that he had written twenty-thousand words of *The Poison Belt*. Curiously, he also made mention of a 'one-act Sherlock play'. This, as has been suggested elsewhere, could have been a reference to *The Crown Diamond* which Conan Doyle would eventually rework into the Sherlock Holmes story *The Mazarin Stone*[127].

Away from his literary efforts two other events occurred during November that were of note. The first affected Kingsley. He had volunteered for the Army Medical Corps and Conan Doyle learned that his son had been made an ambulance driver. Secondly were two reports delivered by the Divorce Commission. This body had been set up to look into many of the reforms of the law put forward by Conan Doyle and like-minded people. It had produced a 'majority report' which favoured many reforms and a 'minority report' which opposed reform in favour of the status quo.

The *Daily Express* of November 13th reported that a wide 'extension of the existing laws of separation and divorce is

---

125 Lellenberg, Jon et al. *Arthur Conan Doyle: A Life in Letters.* Harper Press. 2007.

126 Bibliothèque nationale de France (web site http://data.bnf.fr/39460131/la_maison_de_temperley_spectacle_1912/)

127 Lellenberg, Op cit.

recommended by a majority of the Commissioners'. The newspaper had taken the step of communicating, by telegram, with prominent people both for and against reform. Naturally, Conan Doyle was amongst these and stated 'I am overjoyed with the majority report. It is a triumph of common sense, and will bring hope to many people who have long lost it'.

Predictably, it was George Bernard Shaw who managed to have the controversial viewpoint stating 'The majority is not quite so idiotic as the minority, but the moral of both reports is: "Don't get married"'.

On December 21st Conan Doyle's daughter was born[128]. Once again, there was discussion between Conan Doyle and his mother on the subject of names. He suggested that the new arrival be called Lena Jean Noel Conan Doyle[129]. The mam's response to this is not known but presumably she either objected or Conan Doyle changed his mind. The names ultimately chosen were Lena Jean Annette but, during childhood, she would be known as Billy. Conan Doyle did not have too long to enjoy the happy event before life intruded.

The *Daily Express* of December 31st reported that he was the foreman of the jury at a coroner's court in Crowborough. The court had convened concerning the sudden death of one Captain Gordon Campbell Blair. Captain Blair had been taken to various parts of the country for rest following an episode, allegedly motivated by an unhappy love affair, in which he had '...run through Piccadilly in his pyjamas'. Christmas Day, which fell during his time in Crowborough, had seen him become 'excited and violent' to the extent where people present had deemed it necessary to tie him to his bed. He had died the following morning due, the newspaper reported, to 'cerebral excitement'. Conan Doyle returned the jury's verdict of death by natural causes on December 30th.

---

[128]Lellenberg, Jon et al. *Arthur Conan Doyle: A Life in Letters.* Harper Press. 2007.
[129] Ibid.

1913

BILLIARDS, TUNNELS AND SUFFRAGE

February 1913 saw the Amateur Billiard Championship take place in London and Conan Doyle took part. He stayed at the Hotel Metropole with Jean and his early heats went well, taking him to the competition's third round. When he found that there were a few days between his second round victory and the date of his third round heat, he decided that the family should have a day in Brighton. While everyone else went by car, Conan Doyle chose to make the trip utilising the auto-wheel. En route he had an accident but this did not prevent him joining the rest of his family[130].

In a letter to his mother on February 13th he discussed both the billiards championship and the auto-wheel. Regarding the former he was pessimistic and stated that he was convinced that he would lose[131]. In this he was proved correct two days later when the championship resumed[132].

When it came to the auto-wheel he was a good deal more confident. Despite having acquired his shares in the manufacturer towards the end of 1909 the device had yet to take off. He told his mother that he was still optimistic for its future

---

[130] Pugh, Brian. *A Chronology of the Life of Sir Arthur Conan Doyle.* 3rd Edition. MX Publishing 2014.

[131] Lellenberg, Jon et al. *Arthur Conan Doyle: A Life in Letters.* Harper Press. 2007.

[132] Pugh, Op cit.

and, in March, he wrote another letter on the subject informing her that he would make ten shillings and sixpence for every auto-wheel sold. However, by August he was still waiting for it to turn a profit.

Conan Doyle at the Amateur Billiard Championship 1913
(The collection of Brian Pugh)

Despite his busy personal schedule March saw Conan Doyle volunteer his services to the Olympic movement. The *Daily Express* of March 13th announced that Conan Doyle had been heavily involved in the formation of a committee to take control of the financing required for Britain's participation in the 1916 games in Berlin. It was also announced that he would remain active within the committee for at least one further year.

Also during March Conan Doyle lent his voice to the large group of businessmen and others in favour of the building of a Channel Tunnel. The discussions continued into April with a significant discussion being held in the City of London on April 16th. The following day it was reported that the idea made sense for England. In the opinion of the secretary of the French Chamber of Commerce, England had nothing to lose and there was 'a very great deal to be gained'.[133]

Conan Doyle, when approached for his opinion, stated that it was 'a matter of such urgent national interest that it should be pressed forward at once to completion'. He added, 'But it should be a Government undertaking, for it is far too important to be in private hands'. He went on to state that, if carried out, the building of such a tunnel would rival the Suez Canal as a wise investment.

In truth, Conan Doyle's interest in the idea of a Channel Tunnel was not exactly driven by ideas of commerce. Rather it was driven by a desire to ensure the country's safety. In 1911 General Friedrich von Bernhardi of the German Army had published a book entitled *Germany and the Next War* in which he had set forth such arguments as the 'Right to Make War'. He was not an official army or government spokesman but his views were shared in some quarters. Conan Doyle had not initially believed that Germany was in the mood for war but had started to be convinced otherwise following the Prince Henry motoring competition of 1911. He decided to respond to Bernhardi's argument and *The New York Times* published his thoughts on March 23rd.

In his article he made it clear that naval warfare was his biggest concern and it was the rise of submarines that caused him to support the idea of a Channel Tunnel. Without such a tunnel, he argued, Britain was at the mercy of a submarine based blockade that could starve the country. 'But these dangers' he stated, '..can all be absolutely provided against in a manner which is not only effective, but which will be of equal value in peace and war. The Channel tunnel is essential to Great Britain's safety'.

He concluded his piece with a remark about Bernhardi, '…a man whose opinion is of weight and a member of the ruling class in Germany, tells us frankly that Germany will attack us

---

133 *Daily Express* April 17th 1913

the moment she sees a favourable opportunity…we should be mad if we did not take very serious notice of the warning'.

On the domestic front, April 22nd found Conan Doyle in court defending his pet dog Roy. *The Daily Mirror* of April 23rd reported that Conan Doyle had appeared at Mark Cross Police Court in Tunbridge Wells the previous day. Mr Arthur Hale, a local farmer, had alleged that Conan Doyle's collie had killed and 'worried sheep' on his farm. The story was considered so newsworthy that it also found its way into the American press[134].

Conan Doyle had elected to cross-examine Hale personally and asked the farmer if he was aware of a fold of sheep that were approximately 200 yards from his house. The farmer replied that he was to which Conan Doyle responded:

> 'Does it not strike you as being strange that my dog should pass this fold of sheep and go to a farm another mile on to worry sheep?'

A farm boy by the name of John Hornby had claimed that he had got close to the dog while it was amongst the sheep and that he was sure it was Conan Doyle's from the marks on its face. Conan Doyle swept this aside. He asked Hornby how close he had got to the dog. The boy replied that it was about ten yards. Conan Doyle then asked if the dog he had seen was running away when he approached it. Hornby replied that it had been. To this Conan Doyle said:

> 'The point is that it is very difficult to see a patch on a dog's nose if it is running away from you. You have seen my dog since and know that it has a white spot on its nose.'

When the young man confessed that he had not seen all the other collie dogs in the village and Conan Doyle pointed out

---

[134] An article entitled *Sherlock Holmes Wins* appeared in the May 4th issue of *The New York Times*.

that Roy was physically incapable of killing a sheep due to an issue with his jaw, the case was dismissed.

Six days following his court appearance, on April 28th, Conan Doyle gave a speech in Tunbridge Wells at a meeting of the National League for Opposing Woman Suffrage[135]. A little over two weeks earlier the pavilion of the Nevill cricket ground had been burnt down and 'militant suffragists' were suspected. As his daughter Jean would later recount, the violent actions of these groups shocked Conan Doyle who felt such actions were not becoming in women[136]. When he spoke on this matter he was opposing the violence more than the aim. Nonetheless his stance made him an enemy in the eyes of the suffragists.

It appeared that the cumulative pressure of all these events had taken their toll on Conan Doyle's health. On May 19th the *Daily Express* reported that Conan Doyle had been ordered by his doctor to take a holiday. The paper suggested that the destination, the Mediterranean, had been specified by the doctor. Conan Doyle and Jean soon acted on this advice. While they were out of the country the pillar-box outside Windlesham had a black fluid (or vitriol) poured into it[137]. It was suspected, but not proved, that members of the suffragist movement were behind this act of vandalism - perhaps encouraged by the news that Conan Doyle was abroad.

June 24th saw the birth of John Doyle, the son of Conan Doyle's brother Innes and his wife Clara[138]. One month later he was baptised with Conan Doyle as his godfather. It was a nice end to a very busy month which had not only seen him work on

---

135 Pugh, Brian. *A Chronology of the Life of Sir Arthur Conan Doyle.* 3rd Edition. MX Publishing 2014.

136 *In Conversation with Dame Jean Conan Doyle* by Christopher Roden - http://www.ash-tree.bc.ca/acdsjcd.htm

137 Pugh, Op cit.

138 Doyle, Georgina. *Out of the Shadows*. Calabash Press. 2004.

a Sherlock Holmes story, but also act as host to over one hundred members of the BMA Congress at Windlesham[139].

The *Daily Express* of August 6th carried an interesting article on the lot of the author. Entitled *Ten Pounds An Hour* it covered a variety of areas but its main aim was to manage the expectations of would-be writers with regards to income.

Unsurprisingly, fiction was deemed to be the form of writing that would bring the best financial rewards. Poetry fared worse, being described as having 'practically no monetary value'. Conan Doyle was named as one of only ten writers (presumably in Great Britain) who were earning around five thousand pounds from fiction (per year, one assumes).

On the subject of fiction *The Poison Belt* was published on August 13th[140]. The *Daily Express* of the following day provided a review which managed to, essentially, give away what the eponymous belt was, how the main characters avoided its effects and what ultimately happened to those who did not. The author of the review was clearly not overly excited by the story which perhaps explained why he was so cavalier with the plot details.

'Sir Arthur tells his story with all his characteristic skill and with several split infinitives...' was the summing up of the prose. As for the characters and plot, '...although its protagonists are the same as in "The Lost World", it has few of the thrills of that ingenious story'.

The less than satisfying conclusion was '"The Poison Belt" will make a railway journey enjoyable, provided that journey be no more than a hundred miles'.

---

[139] Lycett, Andrew. *Conan Doyle: The Man who Created Sherlock Holmes.* Orion. 2007 – BMA stands for British Medical Association. The story was *The Adventure of the Dying Detective.*

[140] *Daily Express* August 14th 1913.

Conan Doyle and his dog Roy
(The collection of Brian Pugh)

SLEUTHING ON THE SILVER SCREEN

The *Daily Express* of August 27th carried an article entitled *Sherlock Holmes on the Films*. The article referred to a series of nine Sherlock Holmes films, made the previous year, that had been secured for British release by the Fenning Company.

The nine films had, according to the article, all been filmed in Bexhill-On-Sea. The company behind the films was a French one – The Eclair Film Company. Conan Doyle had been heavily involved, right down to supervising the films on a scene by scene basis, and two men shared the directing duties. Roughly half of the films were directed by one Adrien Caillard. The remainder were directed by Georges Tréville. Both men were actors as well as directors but only Tréville starred in any of the films, taking on the role of none other than Sherlock Holmes.

The series began with *The Speckled Band* which was to be screened on October 27th. Then, at the rate of one per month, the others in the series. They were listed in the newspaper in the following order: *The Stolen Papers*, *The Silver Blaze*, *Mystery of Boscombe Vale*, *The Sign of Four*, *The Beryl Coronet*, *Adventure of Copper Beeches*, *The Reigate Squires* and *The Musgrave Ritual*. It was not clear whether this was the actual order of intended release.

The newspaper claimed that leading West End actors had been engaged to play the parts but no names were given.

Georges Tréville as Holmes with, presumably, Violet Hunter in Adventure of Copper Beeches (1912)

September 19th 1913 saw a private screening of *The House of Temperley* at the West End Cinema, Coventry Street, London. The film went on general release at the same cinema on November 3rd.[141] It was produced by London's Jury Company and directed by Harold M. Shaw. The film starred Charles Maude as Captain Temperley and ran for fifty minutes.

Novel efforts were made to advertise the film. *The Daily Mirror* reported, in its December 11th issue, that two young ladies had been spotted walking the streets of Richmond wearing clothes from the 1830s. Described as carrying sunshades of 'antique pattern' and wearing 'wide skirts, flounced up to the waist' the article revealed that, on close inspection, it had been determined that the ladies, taking part in what the paper described as an 'incursion into antiquity', were

[141] Pugh, Brian. *A Chronology of the Life of Sir Arthur Conan Doyle.* 3rd Edition. MX Publishing 2014.

'merely a scheme designed to advertise *"The House of Temperley"* a film drama founded on Sir Arthur Conan Doyle's novel'.

What remained unclear was whether the choice of ladies to advertise the film was done with the aim of stirring up female interest or to seize the attention of men.

October was a quiet month for Conan Doyle apart from one matter to which he chose to lend his support. In March 1911 a young boy called Andrew Yushinsky had left home, in Russia, to go to school. The alarm was raised when he did not arrive and his body was located several days later. The boy had been stabbed forty-seven times and his body had been drained of blood. Authorities concluded that it was a ritual killing and a local Jew named Mendel Beiliss was arrested[142].

Despite a distinct lack of hard evidence, the case was still proceeding nearly two years later and it was seen as being used as an excuse for Christians in Russia to stigmatise all Jews. Protest meetings took place in London at which prominent people spoke or had their messages of support read out. On October 28th one such meeting took place at the Memorial Hall, Farringdon Street[143]. Amongst the letters of protest from bishops and dukes were letters from Conan Doyle and Harry Gordon Selfridge, the founder of Selfridge's department store.

The December issue of *The Strand* saw the publication of *The Adventure of the Dying Detective*[144]. The artists previously employed by the magazine – Twidle, Holiday, Brock, Simpson and Ball – were unavailable. Yet, despite the fact that they had other artists on their books, the management of the magazine turned to Walter Paget[145]. Walter Paget was the younger brother

---

142 *Nelson Evening Mail* October 23rd 1913.

143 *Daily Express* October 29th 1913.

144 Published in *Collier's* the previous month. Pugh, Brian. *A Chronology of the Life of Sir Arthur Conan Doyle*. 3rd Edition. MX Publishing 2014.

145 Whitt, J.F. *The Strand Magazine 1891-1950 A Selective Checklist*. 1979.

of Sidney Paget and had been the man who Greenhough-Smith and George Newnes originally wanted to illustrate the Holmes stories when they first appeared in their magazine in 1891. The commission had, supposedly, fallen into Sidney's hands by accident as it had been addressed simply to 'Mr Paget'.

Despite being their first choice, Walter Paget had not done any drawings for *The Strand* following the mistake with the original commission. It seems likely, given their initial interest in him, that this was entirely down to Walter Paget himself – perhaps it was a sore subject.

Regardless of the reason, one can only wonder how he reacted when approached and what persuaded him to take on the commission for the latest Holmes adventure (which Conan Doyle had completed back in July[146]). It certainly did not herald the start of a long association as, following the commission, Walter Paget illustrated nothing else for *The Strand*.

[146] Lycett, Andrew. *Conan Doyle: The Man who Created Sherlock Holmes*. Orion. 2007.

Illustration by Walter Paget from The Dying Detective (The Strand December 1913)

1914

INTO THE VALLEY

Conan Doyle began work on his fourth and final Sherlock Holmes novel in 1914. Almost a year previously, in April of 1913, he had been visited at Windlesham by William Burns of the U.S. based Burns Detective Agency[147]. The two men discussed the work of the agency which was hardly surprising, given Conan Doyle's interest in crime true as well as fictional.

Their discussions about such subjects as the Molly Maguires – a nineteenth century secret society – inspired Conan Doyle, who decided to pit Sherlock Holmes against a similar organisation. Once again the question of illustrator arose. On this occasion the duties fell to one Francis Edmund Wiles who was more generally known as Frank Wiles.

Wiles had illustrated for *The Strand* as early as 1912 but it is not clear how he came to be considered for the latest Sherlock Holmes adventure. It is possible that his name came to the fore through the influence of his future father-in-law Walter Troughton who was connected to *The Studio* arts magazine[148].

Wiles would ultimately produce one of the most iconic images of Holmes and his efforts allegedly attracted the

---

147 Nollen, Scott Allen. *Sir Arthur Conan Doyle at the Cinema.* McFarland & Co Inc. 2004.

148 Theory put forward by the descendants of Wiles. Wiles married Mabel Troughton in June 1914.

admiration of Conan Doyle who supposedly stated 'This comes nearest to my conception of what he really looks like'[149].

William J. Burns (1861-1932)
(U.S. Library of Congress)

[149] http://www.classiccrimefiction.com/conandoylebiog.htm written by R.D. Collins.

The September 1914 Strand Magazine featuring the famous Frank Wiles illustration of Sherlock Holmes

A curious article appeared in the *Daily Express* of March 12th. The article was essentially one long advertisement for a book called *The Book of Public Speaking*. As the title implied, it was a guide to giving speeches and Conan Doyle was mentioned as one of the world's greatest orators, some of whose speeches would appear in the book. He was in good company, alongside such names as Winston Churchill and George Bernard Shaw.

Conan Doyle was busy at this time with two significant tasks. The first of these was the *The Valley of Fear*, which was nearing completion, and the second was the on-going quest for justice in relation to Oscar Slater. A representative of the *Daily Express* spoke with Conan Doyle on the latter subject on March 23rd and the resultant article appeared in the newspaper of the following day.

Conan Doyle referred to the original conviction of Slater as '…nothing short of a scandal…' and went on to praise Mr McKinnon Wood – the secretary for Scotland – for ordering the reinvestigation of the case. He demolished various aspects of the original case before concluding with 'Five out of fifteen jurymen voted for "Not Proven" and another for "Not guilty" a division of opinion which, under English law, would have resulted in a new trial'.

April 3rd found Conan Doyle defending himself from a charge of plagiarism. The French writer Joseph Henri Honoré Boex, known as J.H. Rosny, had suggested, it was alleged, that Conan Doyle's book *The Poison Belt* had been assisted by his work *La Force Mystérieuse*.

One of the first newspapers to pick this up was *The Daily Mirror* who took the step of telephoning Conan Doyle to inform him. Conan Doyle was not concerned, according to the newspaper's report in its issue of April 4th (which appeared in its section *This Morning's Gossip*). He said to the reporter that plagiarism was always being alleged against somebody and it was not usually worthwhile to deny it. He also told the reporter that, prior to the telephone call, he had not even been aware of Rosny's book.

The story was later picked up by *The Times* at which point Conan Doyle changed his stance and decided to respond. He wrote to his French translator, M. Labat, enclosing evidence from his agent A.P Watt, which proved that Conan Doyle's manuscript had been delivered to his publisher before Rosny's story had appeared, thus proving the accusations false. Labat saw to it that this was published in the French periodical *Le Temps*[150].

Whether Rosny had intended to accuse Conan Doyle of plagiarism or not, in the face of the evidence, he was quick to put out a statement and this was reported in the *Daily Express* of May 4th. Denying that he had been attacking Conan Doyle he stated that his actual intention had been to bring attention to the similarities of the two works in order to defend himself from charges of plagiarism in the reverse direction.

Towards the end of the month Conan Doyle and family headed to the United States. *The New York Times* of May 21st carried an article entitled *Conan Doyle Coming Here* in which it noted that Conan Doyle and Jean had embarked aboard the *Olympic* the previous day. According to the article, Conan Doyle and family were to spend a week in New York before heading to Canada.

For Conan Doyle the trip was a mix of business and pleasure. He was quoted as saying 'The principal reason that I am going now is that Lady Doyle has not seen the United States, and I have not seen Canada. I am looking forward to the camping trip. I am an outdoor man, you know'.

They arrived in New York on May 27th according to the same newspaper[151]. It observed, displaying a distinct lack of tact, that Conan Doyle was 'somewhat heavier than when he was here twenty years ago, and his hair is a little gray'.

Conan Doyle, for his part, was decidedly unimpressed with the American newspapers, observing 'I am in a wretched humour, all of it due to American journalism'. This bad temper stemmed partly from the fact that he had been giving individual interviews to members of the press and, at the time of his

---

[150] The website of the Sherlock Holmes Society of France.
[151] *The New York Times* of May 31st 1914.

interview with *The New York Times*, he had seen 'at least forty…since 9 o'clock this morning'.

His mood was also influenced by how the American press were reporting, according to him, his attitude towards 'the militants'. The 'militants' in this instance referred to those campaigning for women's suffrage.

He claimed to have good friends amongst 'the militants and those who favour the militant movement' but went on to say 'The militants have already gone too far, and I am afraid that the reaction is coming very soon, and that it is going to be disastrous'.

From there the interview went on to cover other topics including the Oscar Slater case and Irish Home Rule before moving onto Conan Doyle's schedule. The newspaper observed that Conan Doyle's Canadian schedule would take in the Selkirk Range of the Canadian Rockies and that he had camped in the area as part of his lecture tour twenty years previously. This was at odds with his statement to the newspaper's reporter on May 20th when he stated that he had 'not seen Canada'.

Conan Doyle's remarks on the suffragette movement did not pass without comment. One Marguerite Remington Charter was clearly incensed and wrote to *The New York Times* to protest.

She referred to Conan Doyle's talk of lynching as 'foolish' and stated that 'evidently the attention of the ships' reporters turned this man's head and encouraged him to talk great nonsense. By this time he is doubtless heartily ashamed of himself, and if he isn't, then he ought to be'. She also effectively accused Conan Doyle of cowardice by suggesting that he would not say in England 'the sentiments he thought profound enough for the American papers'.

Charter's ire was directed equally at Jean, who had made some remarks along similar lines to her husband. 'I'd like to assure Lady Doyle that there is plenty of militancy here, and that a lot of women will resent her light-hearted, perhaps I ought to say light-headed, remarks about her own countrywomen'. The newspaper did not publish the letter until

June 1st and it is possible that Conan Doyle and Jean remained ignorant of it.

On May 30th, Conan Doyle visited Sing Sing Prison with William J. Burns of the eponymous detective agency and was locked in a cell for five minutes[152]. He observed that it was the most restful time he had had since arriving in New York because '…it was the only chance I had to get away from the reporters'.

That compliment aside, Conan Doyle could find nothing good to say about the prison stating that it '…ought to be burned down'. It was a 'disgrace' for New York to have a prison that was '…a hundred years behind the times'. He was however impressed with the prison's Warden Clancy. 'I'd rather have a bad machine with Clancy at the head of it than a good one under an unsympathetic disciplinarian. His one idea is not to punish men, but to improve them'.

May 31st saw Conan Doyle and Jean visit Coney Island where, according to *The New York Times* of June 1st 'Sir Arthur saw everything that was to be seen and did many of the things for which Coney is famous'. Apparently both Conan Doyle and Jean enjoyed themselves, with the newspaper often describing them as laughing.

At six-thirty in the evening Conan Doyle's party (which included Burns and his family) dined at the Hotel Shelburne where Conan Doyle was apparently very impressed at some of the events that had been especially laid on. These included two seven-year-old children who performed modern dances.

Conan Doyle and Jean did not depart until after midnight, having seen pretty much all there was to see. When asked for an opinion Conan Doyle remarked 'Coney Island doesn't give one time to think. I'm trying to get myself together. I must do that before I can think. But I certainly had a good time'. His opinion was reportedly very much shared by Jean.

---

[152] *The New York Times* of May 31st 1914. This article was partly a summary of opinions made by Conan Doyle since the 27th.

After taking in a few other sights, Conan Doyle and Jean made their way into Canada, arriving in early June. It was a busy month with events every day. Conan Doyle gave lectures on Canadian literature, travelled on the Great Lakes, played some baseball, camped, and concluded the month with a visit on the 30th to Niagara Falls[153].

During his absence Conan Doyle had a book dedicated to him. German writer Walter Brugge-Vallon had penned a story called *That Strange Affair* and he had decided to dedicate it to Conan Doyle. The *Daily Express* of June 25th gave it a one paragraph review in which they observed that the German was 'almost as distinguished in Germany as a writer of detective stories as Sir Arthur Conan Doyle is in England'.

By the middle of July, Conan Doyle was back in England and in time to comment on the latest development in the case of Oscar Slater. An inquiry before a local Sheriff had taken place which had not gone well for Slater. On the 25th *The Spectator* published a letter from Conan Doyle detailing his reaction to the results[154].

'The result of this inquiry,' he wrote, 'was a decision that nothing should be done and the evidence given at it is now published in a Parliamentary White Paper. I think that no one who had mastered the facts can read this paper without amazement, for it appears to completely cut away point after point which told against Slater at the trial'.

He went on to predict that the case would become an 'immortal' example of 'official incompetence and obstinacy' and concluded by saying that only a fresh trial where all witnesses were under oath would be sufficient.

Apart from the developments regarding Slater and the annual meeting of Raphael Tuck & Sons Ltd. in London, Conan Doyle appears to have done little else. It was a good time to

---

[153] Pugh, Brian. *A Chronology of the Life of Sir Arthur Conan Doyle*. 3rd Edition. MX Publishing 2014.

[154] *The Spectator* article was quoted by *The New York Times* of August 9th.

take a rest as August was going to present him and the rest of the country with a good many challenges.

THE EAST WIND ARRIVES

Britain declared war on Germany on August 4th 1914. That same day a leaflet was circulated in Crowborough[155]. It ran thus:

IMPORTANT
A meeting
will be held
To-night, August 4
in the
Oddfellows' Hall
To discuss the feasibility of forming a Local Company or Companies for purposes of Drill and Efficiency, that we may be of service to our Country in this crisis.
Sir A. Conan Doyle, D.L.
will take the Chair at 8.30

Conan Doyle was, in a way, attempting to emulate his Rifle Club idea which he had conceived following his medical service in the Boer War. With his encouragement rifle clubs had sprung up across the country. The August 13th edition of the *Daily Express* carried a letter from him in which he described the structure of his volunteer force and added that he had already received two hundred and fifty requests for details

---

155 Lamond, John. *Arthur Conan Doyle: A Memoir*. John Murray 1931.

on his 'method or organisation' from people wishing to set up similar groups.

Unsurprisingly, the Government and Army were not enthused by the idea of series of autonomous units springing up. Not long afterwards a formal system was set up very much along the lines that Conan Doyle had envisaged. Conan Doyle signed up (having been refused permission to sign up for the regular army) and became Private Conan Doyle of the Crowborough Company of the 6th Royal Sussex Volunteer Regiment.

On August 26th the *Daily Express* carried an advertisement for *The Strand Magazine* in which it was announced that its September issue was 'now on sale at all Newsagents, Booksellers and Bookstalls', adding, '...admirers of Sherlock Holmes are recommended to obtain their copies AT ONCE'.

The serialisation of *The Valley of Fear* had commenced but it did not meet with universal approval. The son of Allan Pinkerton, founder of the famous detective agency, was annoyed at the parallels to his father's agency and considered that Conan Doyle's story was a breach of confidence in that it was based on private conversations between Conan Doyle and William Burns. Burns, it is said, was also unhappy and his friendship with Conan Doyle supposedly came to an end as a result[156]. However, it appears that time healed this wound, to some extent at least, as Conan Doyle and Burns would meet again in America in 1922[157].

The Valley of Fear was materially affected by the outbreak of war. Conan Doyle had originally written it in the third-person before altering it to a first-person narrative. Now it was altered further. Alongside a series of minor changes the Shafter

---

[156] Nollen, Scott Allen. *Sir Arthur Conan Doyle at the Cinema.* McFarland & Co Inc. 2004.

[157] Lycett, Andrew. *Conan Doyle: The Man who Created Sherlock Holmes.* Orion. 2007.

family of the story were changed from a German family to a Swedish one[158].

❧

It is only natural, if not necessarily justified, in time of war, for the press to attack the enemy. The *Daily Express* certainly subscribed to this attitude and did not pull its punches when it came to Britons who, in their view, aided the enemy.

In its issue of October 23rd it reported, with some apparent delight, on the successful rounding up of over a thousand Germans and Austrians in London the previous day. It did so under the title *1,200 Aliens Arrested.* The article drew its readership's attention to the fact that one such alien by the all too predictable name of "Fritz" (newspaper's quotation marks) had been serving as a barber in Aldershot for twenty years and had therefore, not surprisingly, had a lot of contact with British army officers.

Not far from this article was another entitled *No Quarter for the British* in which it was stated that various German officers had given orders demanding, with respect to the British soldiers, that 'all must be shot'.

Having presumably stirred its readers into an anti-German frenzy the newspaper elected to report on the activities of the Emergency Committee for the Assistance of Germans, Austrians and Hungarians in Distress. This organisation endeavoured to find safe houses in Britain for, what the newspaper described as, 'the country's enemies'.

A Saffron Walden Councillor by the name of Midgley had had his windows smashed by local townspeople when it emerged that he was 'harbouring' two Germans. In an attempt to explain himself he told the newspaper of his connection to

---

158 Gibson, John Michael and Green, Richard Lancelyn. *A Bibliography of A. Conan Doyle*. Hudson House, New York. 2000.

the Emergency Committee and how they had allocated him an elderly German couple.

Midgley also provided the newspaper with a booklet about the organisation which included a list, the newspaper reported, of people who had donated money for 'the comforting of the nation's enemies'. Amongst the many names was that of Conan Doyle who had pledged £2 2s.

Conan Doyle's position was entirely consistent with that he had adopted during the Boer War. He was ready to defend his country but he was never in the mood to attack people who did not merit it. On this basis he had defended the actions of many Boers during that conflict and he now sought to defend Germans whom he felt warranted it. Being the man he was he did not confine his support to the writing of a cheque. He had been attacked in September via the pages of *The Daily Mail* for defending some naturalised waiters who had been ruined by the war. This presumably meaning that they had lost their jobs due to having been born German[159].

November 25th saw Conan Doyle at the Guildhall in London for a meeting of the representatives of various volunteer training corps convened by the Central Association of Volunteer Training Corps.

The event was presided over by the Lord Mayor who began by addressing the notion that the volunteer forces were being touted as an alternative to conventional recruiting. He stated that if he had believed it to have had such an aim he would not have involved himself with it. Conan Doyle, in a move guaranteed not to improve his relationship with the suffragette movement, observed that a volunteer force without military training would be of no more use than women or professional footballers[160].

December 7th saw Conan Doyle speak at a recruiting meeting in Tunbridge Wells. In his speech he demonstrated that

---

[159] Lellenberg, Jon et al. *Arthur Conan Doyle: A Life in Letters*. Harper Press. 2007.
[160] *Daily Express* of November 26th 1914.

he shared the common belief that the war would be over quickly. 'If we meet in this room in a year's time it will be in a different world. We shall find ourselves in a world from which the curse of militarism has passed away'. He went on to say, 'The country is doing well. When we send forth our great armies in the spring it will not be long before the foe is on the run. Victory is certain'[161].

161 The *Daily Express* of December 8th 1914.

1915

WRITING, LECTURING, VOLUNTEERING AND LOSS

1915 opened with a flurry of war-based writing. Conan Doyle began his account of the campaign in France and, at the same time, became a contributor to *The War Illustrated*, a weekly magazine that had begun publication soon after the commencement of hostilities. It was designed to show the progress of the conflict through both articles and illustrations.

The Daily Mirror, in its issue of January 14th, carried a full page advertisement for the magazine in which it gave brief details of four contributors. F.A. McKenzie, a *Daily Mail* War Correspondent, was tasked with producing articles on the progress of the army; Commander Carlyon Bellairs of the Royal Navy was to chronicle the war at sea and, finally, C.G. Grey, a popular aviation writer, was to cover the war in the air.

With the main branches of the military covered, Conan Doyle's brief was more historical. For the latest issue he was listed as providing an article on how the Boer War had prepared the country for the current conflict. For this he had no doubt drawn on his earlier work *The Great Boer War*.

Much of February to June was spent travelling and lecturing on the war. Edinburgh, Sunderland, Bradford and Cheltenham were but a small number of the places visited. The pace was relentless and Conan Doyle only allowed himself a small break with Jean in Torbay during March[162].

Returning to the beginning of February, Conan Doyle found time to take on the American journalist James O'Donnell Bennett. Bennett had written what Conan Doyle described as a 'very courteous and moderate letter', questioning the accuracy of an article entitled *A Policy of Murder* which Conan Doyle had contributed to *The Daily Chronicle* towards the end of 1914.

Bennett's open letter had taken issue with the article, describing it as 'a very terrifying document - terrible in its wrath, in its passionate sincerity and in its massing of statements; terrifying in its effect upon the minds of neutral peoples if its statements are accepted'[163].

Bennett had then launched into a defence of Germany against many of the charges laid at its feet by Conan Doyle and had concluded by stating that, despite this defence of Germany, he was an American that loved England.

In his response, which appeared in *The New York Times* of February 6th, Conan Doyle was clearly frustrated, bordering on angry. He referred to the Germans laying mines in open water and how this could have brought about the sinking of the liner *Olympic*. He also referred to air attacks by Germany on unfortified towns where large numbers of civilians had died.

He concluded by quoting extracts from the diaries of German soldiers which described the burning of houses in Belgium and France, the hanging of women and the bayoneting of a girl of eighteen.

'Now, Mr Bennett,' wrote Conan Doyle, 'are these things really "lies, lies, lies?" Or am I justified in saying there has been a policy of murder all along the line…?'. He concluded by

---

162 Pugh, Brian. *A Chronology of the Life of Sir Arthur Conan Doyle*. 3rd Edition. MX Publishing 2014.

163 *An Open Letter to Sir Arthur Conan Doyle from James O'Donnell Bennett*. December 1914.

advising Bennett to read the evidence of the French and Belgian Commissions.

A typical illustration from The War Illustrated from 1915 featuring Private John Lynn VC DCM

Conan Doyle was back in Crowborough in mid-April and was photographed by *The Daily Mirror* carrying turf while working with the Crowborough Volunteer Training Corps. The newspaper described him as 'an enthusiastic volunteer,' who had, 'entered into the spirit of camp life with great earnestness'[164].

Following this the lecturing continued through to the end of May. At the very end of that month an article appeared in *The*

[164] *The Daily Mirror* of April 28th 1915.

New York Times which shed further light on the origins of *The Valley of Fear* and suggested the information that may have been conveyed to Conan Doyle by William Burns[165].

The author, who went by the name of W.M. Ossining, observed that the plot of the story was '…a very accurate account of the Molly Maguire difficulties in Pennsylvania in the early seventies'.

Ossining then proceeded to reveal some information that probably explained the anger felt by Burns and Pinkerton.

> 'The story of the Pinkerton detective, James McParlan, who was sent to investigate the Molly Maguires in 1873, is almost identical with that of John McMurdo in the "Valley of Fear," and many of his experiences are reproduced in Conan Doyle's book.'

Ossining continued:

> 'Various characters and situations are similar, and often names are only slightly changed'.

Ossining also stated that the passwords given in the story were among the published passwords of the Molly Maguires.

The anger felt by Burns and Pinkerton over what was seen as a breach of confidence by Conan Doyle begins to become understandable. James McParlan, also known as James McParland, was still alive (he would die in 1919) and could have been placed at risk. Having said that, one wonders if the link was already widely known if Ossining was so ready to reveal it in his article.

---

165 Issue of May 30th 1915.

James McParland (1843-1919)

At the beginning of June *The Valley of Fear* was published in book form. June also saw the formation of an organisation called France's-day. This organisation was, it appears, designed to raise funds for the French Red Cross. Arthur Conan Doyle was listed as one the many patrons and the date of July 7th was set as the date upon which events and fundraising would take place[166]. If Conan Doyle had hoped to be an active patron he was destined to be distracted by events.

In July the conflict came all too close to home. The 6th brought the first death from the younger generation. Oscar Hornung, the son of E.W. Hornung and Conan Doyle's sister Connie, was killed in action at Ypres[167]. Oscar had written to Conan Doyle previously to seek his help to get accepted for active service[168]. If Conan Doyle had done anything to aid his nephew it is tempting to wonder if he felt in any way responsible for the young man's fate. The 28th saw Conan Doyle's brother-in-law Leslie Oldham added to the list of personal losses.

Conan Doyle attempted to achieve something useful from these tragedies and wrote to *The Times* to advocate the notion that troops should be issued with both body and mobile armour. Curiously, to illustrate his argument he referred to events that had taken place on May 9th. It is therefore difficult to tell whether his letter was motivated by recent family losses or whether he would have written it in any case. It is tempting to suspect an element of both. Conan Doyle probably avoided mention of his family not only to avoid upsetting his sister and brother-in-law, but also to avoid his request being dismissed by the unsympathetic as the action of someone motivated purely by personal loss.

In any event, his thoughts made it into other newspapers such as *The New York Times* which published them on July 27th. Two days later the *Daily Express* revealed that the conflict had impacted on Conan Doyle's commercial interests as well as

---

[166] The *Daily Express* of June 29th.

[167] Pugh, Brian. *A Chronology of the Life of Sir Arthur Conan Doyle.* 3rd Edition. MX Publishing 2014.

[168] Lellenberg, Jon et al. *Arthur Conan Doyle: A Life in Letters.* Harper Press. 2007.

his personal ones. It was reported that the German assets of the printing firm Raphael Tuck & Sons, of which Conan Doyle was a board member, had been sequestrated by the German Government. Commenting on the fact that the British Government had not done the same with German property in Britain, Conan Doyle said 'It will show to the world that England is a safe field for investment. I do not think that Germany will gain any benefit from her action'.

It emerged during August that all was not well amongst the volunteer forces in Britain of which Conan Doyle had been such an active and public part. Some volunteers had complained that they had all the disadvantages of being full-time soldiers without any positives. Conan Doyle had taken the side of the War Office against the volunteers but the press was more than willing to state that the volunteers had a point.

In an article entitled *The Better Way*, the *Daily Express* of August 18th highlighted that the War Office had refused to recognise the volunteers and, as a result, they were not subject to military law. It was pointed out that ordering volunteers to leave 'places of public entertainment' such as public houses was not lawful as it would be, during certain hours, for a serving soldier.

It was also pointed out that volunteers supplied their own uniforms and had marched, drilled and dug trenches thus saving the country money. Yet, it was observed, their '...enthusiasm and hard work are, however, unregarded and apparently unappreciated, and they are severely snubbed for wearing the uniforms which are, as a matter of fact, the outward and visible sign of their patriotic eagerness to be of use'.

For Conan Doyle the rest of 1915 passed by largely uneventfully. Various small pieces, many concerning the war, appeared between October and December. He rounded the year off with a piece in *The Daily Chronicle* in which he praised the efforts of Field Marshal Sir John French, the outgoing leader of the British Expeditionary Force, who was to be replaced by General Sir Douglas Haig[169].

169 Pugh, Brian. *A Chronology of the Life of Sir Arthur Conan Doyle.* 3rd Edition. MX Publishing 2014.

1916

STEPPING INTO THE LIGHT

Conan Doyle would, during 1916, declare his belief in Spiritualism[170]. To what extent this public admission was motivated by the War is open to debate. Conan Doyle had expressed an interest in what lay beyond earthly life from the late 1800s – particularly January 1893 when he had joined the Society for Psychical Research.

However, despite this, his initial concerns of the year were very much in the earthly realm. January and February both saw deaths. In January it was Jean's close friend Lily Loder-Symonds who had been bridesmaid at their wedding[171]; in February it was another blow for the Hornung family when Willie Hornung's nephew was killed in action.

Conan Doyle's brother Innes, who held the rank of temporary Lt. Col, was awarded the Distinguished Service Order. The award was to be presented to him by the King in April[172]. Conan Doyle himself continued his military lectures with events in London and Brighton.

The first four months of the year saw considerable literary output from Conan Doyle. This was largely conflict related but

---

170 Pugh, Brian. *A Chronology of the Life of Sir Arthur Conan Doyle.* 3rd Edition. MX Publishing 2014.
171 Lycett, Andrew. *Conan Doyle: The Man who Created Sherlock Holmes.* Orion. 2007.
172 Pugh, Op. cit.

also saw the commencement of regular contributions on Spiritualism in the magazine *Light*[173].

At the same time as Innes Doyle was receiving his DSO from the King, Kingsley Conan Doyle left England for France to join the British Expeditionary Force. However, his uncle Innes was not far behind him as Conan Doyle later met both of them, during May, in France at the Western Front.

So what took Conan Doyle to the theatre of war? In his autobiography, *Memories and Adventures*, he stated that he was approached by Lord Newton who was, at that time, Paymaster-General in the Conservative Government.

Newton explained to Conan Doyle that the Italian army wanted some limelight, presumably because they felt their efforts were underrepresented in the press. The British Government's answer to this was to offer to send people out to see them in action and write up accounts for publication. Conan Doyle wrote that he initially rejected the notion. When Newton asked why, Conan Doyle explained that he needed to first visit the British Front in order that he would have a basis for comparison. Newton agreed and Conan Doyle got to see the British and French lines.

From there he went to Italy to examine its military position and came close to being killed. As he would later report, in *The Daily Mirror* of June 27th, he asked that he be shown the town of Monfalcone where a dockyard had been recently captured from the Austrians. His Italian military escorts elected to take him in an open topped vehicle and, as they approached Ronchi, they came within range of the Austrian guns. Shells were fired and exploded, according to Conan Doyle's escorts, a mere ten metres above their heads. The soldiers were apparently mortified that they had placed Conan Doyle in such danger. He was more pragmatic and declared that it was he that owed them an apology, stating in his article, 'they had enough risks in the

---

173 Pugh, Brian. *A Chronology of the Life of Sir Arthur Conan Doyle.* 3rd Edition. MX Publishing 2014.

way of business without taking others in order to gratify the whim of a joy-rider'[174].

It was around this time that Conan Doyle encountered the French General Georges Humbert. During the course of their conversation Humbert asked Conan Doyle what Sherlock Holmes was doing for the war effort[175]. In reply, Conan Doyle stated that Holmes was now too old for such service. Despite this, the idea of Holmes serving his country was now firmly planted in Conan Doyle's mind.

General Georges Humbert (1862-1921)

---

[174] Conan Doyle would also include this event in his autobiography.

[175] Lycett, Andrew. *Conan Doyle: The Man who Created Sherlock Holmes.* Orion. 2007.

One of Conan Doyle's last acts was to visit the ruins at Soissons in northern France. A photograph taken by representatives of the French War Office was printed by *The Daily Mirror* of July 1st. Presumably he headed towards the coast from that point as he was back in England about a week later.

For one of Conan Doyle's acquaintances the war was not going so well. Sir Roger Casement, who had been an ally of Conan Doyle in his fight for justice in the Belgian Congo, and the man behind Conan Doyle's conversion to the idea of Irish Home Rule, had been tried for treason at the Old Bailey in London. He had turned against Britain and its empire, no doubt motivated to an extent by his experiences of colonial powers in the Congo, and had taken part in the Easter Uprising in Ireland. His involvement had been only a little short of farce and his trial had commenced around the same time as Conan Doyle had arrived at the British Front.

By the end of June he had been found guilty and sentenced to death[176]. Conan Doyle did not approve of Casement's actions but had no desire to see him die. Consequently he attempted to push the idea that Casement was mentally ill in an attempt to save his life. The authorities, however, were determined to hang him and when Casement's personal diaries revealed him to be homosexual it was all too easy, in a time when homosexuality was illegal, to use them to influence public opinion and undermine any support for clemency. Casement was duly hanged in August[177].

---

[176] Pugh, Brian. *A Chronology of the Life of Sir Arthur Conan Doyle.* 3rd Edition. MX Publishing 2014.
[177] Ibid.

Kingsley Conan Doyle in uniform in 1916
(The Collection of Georgina Doyle)

Conan Doyle had additional concerns at this time. Kingsley had been wounded at the Somme in July and invalided out of the army. As soon as he was sufficiently fit he returned to active service and he later fought in the battle of Arras. Conan Doyle, for his part, resumed his demands for body armour for the troops. This would, no doubt, have intensified when Jean's nephew was killed in action.

The remainder of the year held little cause for joy. The magazine *Light* ensured that no one was in any doubt of Conan Doyle's views on spiritualism by carrying his personal announcement of his conversion in its October issue. This news was conveyed to the readers of the United States by *The New York Times* in late November.

In its issue of the 26th it carried an article entitled *Conan Doyle Thinks We Can Talk with the Dead.* Following a short introduction it was simply a reprint of the article from *Light.*

Conan Doyle was conscious of how sudden his conversion seemed and began his article by stating that he had first subscribed to *Light* in 1887 and pointed out that after thirty years of thought 'I cannot be accused of having sprung hastily to my conclusions'. He went on to remark that his conclusions could be summed up in one sentence; that sentence being 'In spite of occasional fraud and wild imaginings, there remains a solid core in this whole spiritual movement which is infinitely nearer to positive proof than any other religious development with which I am acquainted'.

He stated that, in his opinion, further proof was 'superfluous' and that the emphasis was now on doubters to disprove rather than believers to prove. To Conan Doyle's mind the evidence to date clearly demonstrated the existence of life after death, the existence of higher beings and heaven. For him it was nothing less than a 'revolution in religious thought, a revolution which gives us as by-products an utter fearlessness of death and an immense consolation when those who are dear to us pass behind the veil'.

There was no going back; Conan Doyle had nailed his colours to the mast and he would become, as he must have known that he would, a focus of attack and ridicule by those who doubted his position.

Despite his new-found, and declared, direction in life, Conan Doyle still had plenty of business on this side of the veil. On December 20th he reported to his mother of another attempt to encourage him into politics. At the time some Universities were parliamentary constituencies in their own right. Edinburgh University had approached Conan Doyle about standing for election in the Edinburgh and St. Andrews seat.

He did not refuse them and, it appears, allowed his name to go forward, but he admitted to his mother that he did not really care if it came to nothing. When circumstances provided him with the opportunity to withdraw his interest he lost no time in doing so[178]. He now had much bigger battles on which to focus his considerable energy.

178 Lellenberg, Jon et al. *Arthur Conan Doyle: A Life in Letters.* Harper Press. 2007.

1917

HIS LAST BOW

The year 1917 saw the return of Kingsley Conan Doyle to the front at the end of January. Despite his newly declared calling, Conan Doyle was not done with matters military and, in February, he was invited to lunch with Prime Minister David Lloyd George and Major Albert Stern[179]. Stern was in charge of the Tank Supply Committee and the meeting could well have been an opportunity for Conan Doyle to understand what was happening in this area and how it could address, to some extent, his appeals for armour. He was invited to breakfast with the Prime Minister again in either March or April.

In late May Conan Doyle and Jean took a holiday in Harrogate[180]. However it seems highly likely that the holiday contained an element of business. Lord Furness, a shipping magnate, had established a hospital for officers in Harrogate. *The Daily Mirror* of June 20th, in its regular column *To-day's Gossip*, stated that it was hearing excellent reports about the hospital and noted that Conan Doyle had recently paid 'a flying visit'. In all likelihood this would have been during the aforementioned holiday.

It seems quite likely that the Sherlock Holmes story *His Last Bow* was complete or near completion before the trip to

---

179 Lycett, Andrew. *Conan Doyle: The Man who Created Sherlock Holmes*. Orion. 2007.
180 Ibid.

Harrogate as Conan Doyle wrote to Greenhough Smith on May 31st to discuss the issue of illustrations.

Major (later Colonel) Albert Stern

He seemed particularly concerned that the pictures should not give away the plot. In one paragraph he stated 'A picture of the American throttling the German would be ruinous' thus illustrating that the story was at least as advanced as the point where Sherlock Holmes reveals himself [181]. Why he went to the trouble of pressing the point on this occasion is not clear. As an experienced editor it is quite possible that Greenhough Smith would have been a little put out.

Perhaps, with the story being seen as Sherlock Holmes's war service, Conan Doyle thought it a little more important than he had rated Holmes's adventures to date. It is also possible that he was aware that he was, once again, placing his story in the hands of a new artist.

Frank Wiles, who had illustrated *The Valley of Fear*, had entered the army not long after the outbreak of war. This was clear as he would eventually receive the 1914-15 Star medal[182]. He was therefore not available to illustrate the latest adventure.

On this occasion the task fell to one A. Gilbert. Gilbert was not new to *The Strand*, he had been illustrating it since at least 1916, but he had not worked on any of Conan Doyle's material[183]. Was this the reason for Conan Doyle's concerns?

June saw Conan Doyle's mother give up her long residence in North Yorkshire. She had lived on the estate of her former lodger Bryan Charles Waller since the 1880s and her family had regularly visited her there. Now she was heading for West Grinstead in Sussex. This may seem surprising, given the strong affection she had for her son and the support she had received from him, but it seems likely that she moved to Sussex, in part, to be close to her daughter Connie and son-in-law Willie Hornung, to be a support following their son's death.

---

[181] Lellenberg, Jon et al. *Arthur Conan Doyle: A Life in Letters.* Harper Press. 2007.

[182] According to the website www.greatwar.co.uk, the 1914-15 Star (known informally as 'Pip') was established in December 1918 and awarded to all who served in the theatre of war between August 5th 1914 and December 31st 1915. Recipients also had to have the British War Medal and the Victory Medal as prerequisites to getting the Star.

[183] Whitt, J.F. *The Strand Magazine 1891-1950 A Selective Checklist.* 1979.

Kingsley Conan Doyle (fifth from left) with his comrades in 1917 (The Collection of Georgina Doyle)

July saw a considerable amount and variety of activity. On the spiritualist front Conan Doyle published an article in *The Strand* entitled *Is Sir Oliver Lodge Right? – "Yes"* in which he defended Lodge's position on spiritualism. The second volume of his account of the British campaign in France and Flanders was published and Kingsley was appointed Acting Captain. Finally, towards the end of the month, Conan Doyle attended a further meeting on the subject of Divorce Law Reform[184].

August, in stark contrast, appears to have seen Conan Doyle mostly at home with little about him appearing in the press. He did however dutifully continue his service for the National Volunteers and was spoken to, while in his private's uniform, by a reporter from *The Daily Mirror*. The resultant report was trivial, simply observing that Private Conan Doyle had been camping with his battalion in the heart of Sussex[185].

September finally saw Sherlock Holmes enter the War in *His Last Bow*. The title, period and conversations between Holmes and Watson were strong indicators that, once again, Conan Doyle intended to draw a line under Holmes's adventures. With his new found zeal for the spiritualist crusade Conan Doyle had no more time for the scientific detective.

Manchester played host to Conan Doyle at the beginning of October. He made an appearance in the city's Free Trade Hall on the 8th ostensibly to discuss Divorce Law Reform. The event was reported on by the *Daily Express* in its issue of the following day.

One of Conan Doyle's first demands, according to the report, was for 'immediate legislation' that would see separations of three years converted into divorces. This stated, he then went on to the somewhat tangential subject of population. In a statement which the newspaper understatedly called 'remarkable' he said that 'Germany is going to

---

184 Pugh, Brian. *A Chronology of the Life of Sir Arthur Conan Doyle*. 3rd Edition. MX Publishing 2014.

185 *The Daily Mirror* September 1st 1917.

monstrous lengths to strengthen her future position, and that the child born to the order of the State – where the parents are little more than strangers to each other – will be an element in this development'. Expressing the desire that Britain did not follow suit he concluded by saying that 'The official stud farm will find no place in this country, but is this a time to allow a considerable section of our population to be sterilised?'.

The rest of the month consisted of two talks on Spiritualism in Bradford and London the latter with Sir Oliver Lodge presiding[186]. Between these two events, on October 22nd, *His Last Bow*, the collection as opposed to the single story, was published by John Murray. The following day saw a robust attack on Sherlock Holmes in the pages of the *Daily Express*.

The article was entitled *The Derivative Detective – Sir Conan Doyle's Aged Marionette* and was written by one L. J. McQuilland. McQuilland clearly thought that Holmes had no business coming out of retirement and expressed this by saying 'It was rather unkind of his creator, Sir Arthur Conan Doyle, to take the aged marionette out of his retirement again, putting the string for his working into the hands of the stupidest interlocutor in all fiction, the egregious Dr. Watson. Holmes has worn very thin, but Watson has become an utter imbecile'.

McQuilland was just getting started and revealed his true agenda which was to praise Poe's character Dupin who was described as 'a really great creation' and presented as a 'great oil-painting' to Sherlock Holmes's 'clever oleograph'[187]. The criticisms continued, 'Sherlock Holmes repeats all his old performances, jumping in and out of shrubberies, dodging about railway stations, throwing himself flat on his stomach on lawns, chuckling, babbling and boasting'.

After further jibes at both Holmes and Watson, McQuilland concluded by stating himself to be alarmed at the return of

---

[186] Pugh, Brian. *A Chronology of the Life of Sir Arthur Conan Doyle.* 3rd Edition. MX Publishing 2014.

[187] A term used in relation to commercial prints.

Mycroft Holmes. For McQuilland, Mycroft was '…even more tiresome than Sherlock'.

The opinion expressed in *The New York Times* could not have been more different. The reviewer in its October 28th issue was evidently overjoyed with what he had read, declaring the stories to be written with '…as much vigor and spontaneity as if they had been composed in the first flush of the author's delight in his creation of that notable character….the stream flows as abundantly as when first tapped, and with the same apparent ease'.

October 27th saw a decidedly anti-spiritualist article appear in the pages of the *Daily Express*. It appeared in the wake of Conan Doyle's talk on the subject from two days previously. Entitled *Gulled by "Mediums"* it did not pull any punches and ascribed the 'boom' in spiritualism to the large volume of deaths brought about by the war.

'London has never been so full of "mediums" as it is at the present time, and these harpies, who live on the gullibility of the public, have never reaped such a harvest as they are now raking in week by week'. The article singled out widows and mothers as the most common victims, saying that they were the most 'anxious to clutch at any straw which promises to bridge the chasm of death'.

The newspaper was clearly not happy about Conan Doyle's support of the movement, declaring 'It is a red-letter day in the annals of spookery when a man with a name comes out as a champion of "spiritualism" and vouches for the genuineness of the dark-room brotherhood'.

The Strand Magazine (cover), vol. 54, no. 321, September 1917 (Special Collections Toronto Public Library)

Conan Doyle saw the article and wrote a response which the newspaper published in its issue of October 30th.

'Sir,- In your issue of Saturday last you state that I "vouch for the genuineness of the dark-room brotherhood."

As a matter of fact I advised my audience to trust to the literature of the subject rather than to personal experiment in coming to their conclusions, explained that the frequenting of séances led to mere sensation hunting, and warned them of the existence of fraudulent imposters'.

He went on to declare that he had no doubt of the existence of genuine mediums. The *Express* was clearly not moved and challenged him to provide a list of mediums whose powers had been proved so that the newspaper could subject them to testing. To this, they said, 'Sir Arthur Conan Doyle could not possibly object'.

The subject continued in the next day's issue with a Mr Duke writing to question elements of Conan Doyle's speech. In the speech, Conan Doyle had stated that hospitals for weak souls existed in the afterlife and that spirits wore clothes. Duke was prepared to let the former idea pass but not the latter.

'Why should spirits wear clothes? What is the necessity? We are told they do not feel pain, so there is no need for protection, and other reasons that apply on this physical sphere cannot apply there'. He went on to ask whether fashions were a part of the spirit world and if garments existed were there other articles such as motor cars and aeroplanes. He concluded by observing 'The more we are told of this spiritual life the less spiritual it appears and the more perplexing. Nevertheless, it is vastly entertaining'.

November 1st brought Conan Doyle's response to the *Express'* challenge. He declined, stating that no committee of people that the newspaper could assemble would be any more appropriate than a group known as the Dialectical Society, who had held forty meetings 'under test conditions, with the result that the sub-committee upon the phenomenon reported unanimously upon the truth of the claims made by the Spiritualists'.

Conan Doyle went on to comment on many sceptics in the 'Psychical Research Society' who had been converted and various other 'investigations'. He concluded by observing that people '...seem to be continually demanding new evidence when they have never taken the trouble to master the evidence which already exists'. He also took issue with the newspaper's use of the term 'spooks' saying that any investigation willing to use such terms was not one he wished to be associated with.

The newspaper offered no direct reaction to Conan Doyle's refusal. Instead they printed a letter in which the author reminded its readers that Spiritualism had 'originated with an American girl, totally fraudulent, and was consolidated mainly by the Davenport Brothers, also proved absolutely fraudulent...How can any credit be given to a system founded and built up on fraud, even if there should be, as there usually are, some grains of truth mixed up with the mass of deceit?'

The onslaught against Conan Doyle did not end there. The next salvo coming with the *Express'* issue of November 3rd. The relevant article was entitled *Spooks, Modesty and Clothes* and was written by several people each of whom posed different questions. One of these declared that he was prepared to believe that spirits did wear clothes as '...when I have grasped materialised "spirit forms" appearing at séances they have invariably been attired in the garments of the character which they represented'. The extent to which this writer's tongue was in his cheek is a matter of opinion.

Another said that it was asking too much for him to accept that he would still have to pay his tailor's bills after he had 'passed into the beyond'.

The newspaper ran similar articles up to the middle of the month. In one a man asked how his trousers would stay up if he had no physical body to support his braces[188]. After this it

---

[188] *Daily Express* November 5th 1917.

seems that the newspaper finally tired of mocking Conan Doyle or that the fight was not worth having if Conan Doyle would not participate.

He was robust enough not to be worried by the attacks in the press. He had been attacked in the press before and it seems clear that he considered such episodes as the price he had to pay if he was going to get his message out. The *Express*, despite its clear opinion on Conan Doyle's new-found direction, was still happy to support him in other areas. In its issue of December 27th it quoted parts of a letter that he had written to *The Times* in which he had suggested that officers ill-treated by the Germans should sign a statement to that effect, which could be circulated with the aim of not only informing the general public of Germany's actions, but also the cause of justice once the war was over.

1918

A TEST OF FAITH

The year 1918 was destined to be a year of highs and lows. Yet it began calmly enough. Kingsley enrolled at St Mary's Hospital Medical School and Conan Doyle's brother Innes was awarded the CMG by King George V at Buckingham Palace.

But January was very much Kingsley's month. In addition to resuming his medical studies, he became godfather to his uncle's new-born son and resigned his army commission[189].

All these family events occupied Conan Doyle's mind and this showed itself in his activities. On March 20th he lectured in London on marriage and parenthood and this was reported on by the *Daily Express* of the following day. During the conference at the Caxton Hall in London, Conan Doyle commented on how backward England was compared to other Protestant countries. 'Women are the greatest sufferers from the bondage and torture of unhappy marriages. When they turn to the Church for comfort and help they are merely told to bear their misfortune patiently…and are waiting for a reform of the laws to release them from degrading slavery'.

Also on matters domestic, his book *Three of Them*, which looked at the lives of his three children with Jean, began appearing in *The Strand*. Following this he resumed the activities with which he had been more recently associated.

---

[189] Pugh, Brian. *A Chronology of the Life of Sir Arthur Conan Doyle*. 3rd Edition. MX Publishing 2014.

April saw a lecture on Divorce Law Reform at the Lyceum Club in London and the Summer gave way to a major tour on Spiritualism during which Conan Doyle did find the time to tell the members of Our Society of his experiences at the various fronts he had visited[190].

The New York Times of June 9th decided to run an article on three prominent people whom it identified as being supporters of Spiritualism. These were Professor W.J. Crawford of Queen's University in Belfast, psychology Professor Emile Boirac (who had died the previous year) and Conan Doyle, although it was clear that the article focused primarily on Conan Doyle. The article went to some lengths to emphasise the conventional scientific background of all three men as if this background gave greater weight to their conclusions regarding Spiritualism. It was almost as if they were saying that three such scientific minds could not possibly be wrong. The article was clearly, like its subjects, pro-spiritualist.

Yet their subjects were badly chosen. This was especially the case with Crawford who had been investigating the so-called 'Goligher Circle' and Kathleen Goligher in particular (whose picture appeared in Crawford's stead in the article). Crawford had devoted some time to proving the authenticity of Goligher but, following his death two years later, his conclusions were found not be supported by the evidence and pictures he had taken were demonstrated to be fake, although it was made clear that Crawford had been deceived.

Returning to Conan Doyle, his tour schedule saw him visit places including Sheffield, Portsmouth and Bournemouth before he was once again called upon, in September, to involve himself in the war effort.

On this occasion it was the Australian High Command that sought his services and, at the end of September, he visited the Australian positions at the front and addressed the troops. This

---

190 Pugh, Brian. *A Chronology of the Life of Sir Arthur Conan Doyle*. 3rd Edition. MX Publishing 2014. The event took place in May.

done, he returned to Britain and resumed his lectures on Spiritualism.

Émile Boirac, taken from his book Our hidden forces ("La psychologie inconnue")

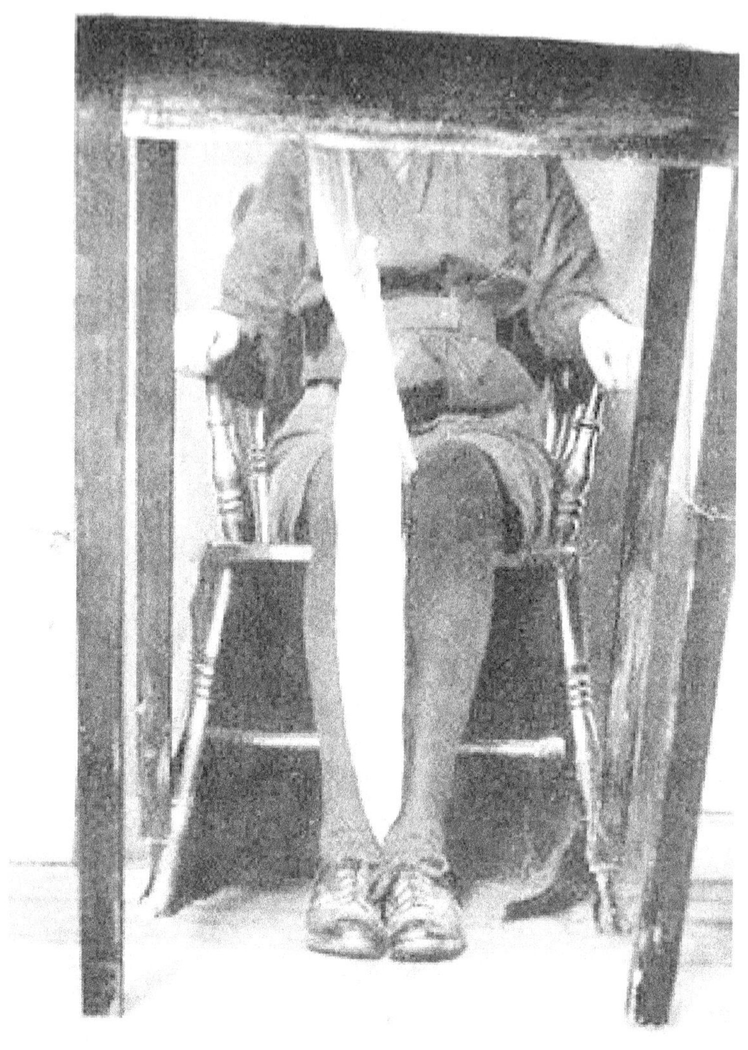

Kathleen Goligher's fake ectoplasm by William Jackson Crawford - The Psychic Structures at the Goligher Circle. (1921). New York: E. P. Dutton & Company.

Influenza was sweeping across Europe at this time and had reached epidemic proportions. *The Daily Mirror* of October 29th carried an article on the rate of infection in Britain and steps people could take to deal with the symptoms. A very concise part of the article, little more than a footnote, carried the following news 'Mr Arthur Conan Doyle, eldest son of Sir Arthur Conan Doyle, died of influenza at St Thomas' Hospital.'

Despite being known as Kingsley throughout his life, Conan Doyle's first son had been named after his father with Kingsley as his third name. He had died the previous day. In an act easily perceived as heartlessness, Conan Doyle did not immediately return to Windlesham or London, but delivered a scheduled talk on spiritualism in Nottingham on the same day as the *Mirror* informed the nation of his son's death.

He later wrote he would have been unable to speak had he not been a Spiritualist. It was the sure knowledge that his son had survived the grave and that they would be able to speak again that had enabled him to take to the stage as planned[191]. He later saw his son's body in the mortuary.

Kingsley was buried next to his mother in Grayshott on November 1st[192]. It is presumably no coincidence that a letter by Conan Doyle entitled *Life After Death* appeared in the *Daily Chronicle* a mere four days later[193].

Despite his recently declared faith it is reasonably clear that Kingsley's death had an effect on Conan Doyle, even if it was a rather delayed one. He did little for the rest of the year and the available evidence suggests that a planned lecture tour in Scotland and a further lecture in Nottingham both failed to happen[194]. Whether this was directly linked to Kingsley's death or not is a matter of speculation. It could equally have been the

---

191 Lellenberg, Jon et al. *Arthur Conan Doyle: A Life in Letters.* Harper Press. 2007.

192 Ibid.

193 Pugh, Brian. *A Chronology of the Life of Sir Arthur Conan Doyle.* 3rd Edition. MX Publishing 2014.

194 Ibid.

end of the War on November 11th that caused the cancellations in Conan Doyle's schedule. Free from the shadow of war the population was probably more concerned with celebrating the end of the conflict and the return, for some, of living relatives from the front as opposed to deceased ones from beyond the grave.

The pace of life did not resume in December. Aside from the publication of the latest instalment of *Three of Them* in *The Strand* and the book *Danger! And Other Stories* very little happened of note. Innes and Clara Doyle spent Christmas at Windlesham, presumably with their children.

The grave of Kingsley Conan Doyle in St. Luke's Churchyard, Grayshott
(Author's collection)

1919

CHALLENGE AND COUNTER CHALLENGE

For Conan Doyle, the year 1919 began in much the same way as the year 1918 had ended, with War and Spiritualism the dominant factors.

The War itself may have been over but the analysis and accusations were only just beginning. Conan Doyle initially confined himself to his lectures on Spiritualism with events in Hastings, Birmingham and Walsall. All of these took place in January but, before the month was out, Conan Doyle had returned to the subject of the recent conflict.

On January 27th he gave a speech entitled *Exploits of the Anzacs* at the Australian and New Zealand Luncheon Club in London[195]. The event was reported on the following day by *The Daily Mirror*. Conan Doyle was clearly irritated by what he described as the 'petty squabbling' of the allies in dividing the spoils of war. His particular concern on the occasion of his speech was the fleet of the German Navy. 'The first thing I would do with the German fleet,' he said, 'would be to take it out to sea, open the valves and sink the whole lot. That would save the petty squabbling among the Allies as to who was to have this and that'.

Around the same time Conan Doyle had his attention drawn to the activities of a Welsh medium named Tom Thomas and

---

[195] Pugh, Brian. *A Chronology of the Life of Sir Arthur Conan Doyle*. 3rd Edition. MX Publishing 2014.

decided to attend one of his séances. On February 13th Conan Doyle gave a lecture on *Death and the Hereafter* in Cheltenham's Town Hall[196]. Given Cheltenham's proximity to Cardiff it seems likely that the lecture was timed in order that the stay in Cheltenham could also serve as a rest stop en route to see Thomas.

On the 15th Conan Doyle and Jean, along with the local Chief and Deputy Chief Constables, attended a séance held by Thomas at the home of one Walter Wall in Cardiff. Wall was later interviewed by the *Cardiff Evening Express*[197]. 'They came to my house with a curtain, a tambourine, a few rattles and other toys'. Wall admitted to not having had much interest in the subject prior to the events in question. It may have been hoped, by some of those involved, that the use of Wall's house would be interpreted as a laudable attempt to allay any suspicion of fraud on the basis that it was neutral ground owned by a disinterested third-party.

Wall went on to describe how the curtain had been fixed across one corner of the room, furthest from the door and that the medium had been tied to a chair some twenty feet away by the Chief Constable. The items which had been placed behind the curtain started to 'fly about the room' a short while later.

During the course of the séance the Chief Constable reported being touched by some unknown hand when all the people in the room were holding hands and accounted for.

Conan Doyle was presumably impressed by the results as he wrote them up afterwards for publication. The next day he gave the Cheltenham lecture to an audience in Merthyr Tydfil. He also, according to his 1921 book *The Wanderings of a*

---

[196] Pugh, Brian. *A Chronology of the Life of Sir Arthur Conan Doyle.* 3rd Edition. MX Publishing 2014.

[197] The article was quoted in the May 30th edition of the Australian newspaper *Leader.* Twenty people were present in total at the séance.

Spiritualist, attended a further séance after which he said to Jean 'My God, if they only knew – if they could only know!'.[198]

The spiritualist cause was interrupted on February 19th by the death, in Halle, Belgium, of Conan Doyle's brother Innes from pneumonia. Conan Doyle soon had his brother's widow and son under his roof at Windlesham but does not appear to have made it to his brother's funeral in Belgium.

Sir David Ferrier FRS (1843-1928)

[198] Straughan, Roger. *Conan Doyle: "The St. Paul of Spiritualism"* taken from *The Arthur Conan Doyle Newsletter and Birthday File XXI* edited by Brian Pugh.

The *Daily Express*, which had delighted in attacking Conan Doyle's position on Spiritualism, returned to the fray in March. They opened the latest round with an article in their March 6th issue by Sir David Ferrier who was a leading neurologist. In his article he said that while he quite understood the desire of the bereaved to make contact with their loved ones, in his opinion, 'The alleged phenomena which Sir Arthur Conan Doyle appears to regard as a new discovery are not only an old story, but one which has never been capable of support when subjected to honest and impartial investigation'.

Two days later, another opponent named Stuart Cumberland, joined the debate. He told readers that Conan Doyle had not supplied '...proof of the unquestionable genuineness of the manifestations to which he apparently pins his faith'. Cumberland went on to describe the phenomena seen at séances as 'piffle...obviously of purely human imagination and of human delivery'. Once again Conan Doyle was challenged to provide proof. As an addendum to the article the *Express* noted that the famous magician Nevil Maskelyne had offered to reproduce the Cardiff séance, which Conan Doyle had attended, on Monday the 10th and that an invitation to attend had been extended.

The *Cardiff Evening Express* reported that the *Daily Mail* had also spoken to Maskelyne and quoted him as saying, in a 'tired voice', 'I've heard of it so many times. Nothing very fresh ever happens at these affairs...I have no doubt that with practice I could produce the same manifestations as those produced at Cardiff'[199].

Maskelyne's invitation was declined and Conan Doyle responded to both it and the comments of Cumberland in a letter published in the *Express's* edition of March 11th.

Bizarrely, Conan Doyle claimed that the 'dud miracles' and 'piffle' referred to by Cumberland had been 'endorsed by many

---

[199] All sources were quoted in the May 30th edition of the Australian newspaper *Leader.*

of the first scientific minds in Europe and America' and that he therefore did not take Cumberland's 'noisy dissent' seriously.

He went on to say that he would never take part in 'challenges which begin by violating the very foundation of all psychic investigation – namely harmonious conditions'. His detractors would have probably interpreted harmonious as meaning free of the checks that they would have insisted upon to ensure no trickery.

Nevil Maskelyne (1863-1924)
(State Library of Victoria)

He claimed that he could offer proof in the form of letters from ladies who had been to mediums that he had recommended and that these letters contained reports of what they had experienced. In a swipe at Maskelyne he said that an independent examination of the letters would be 'surely a more convincing test than a conjurer with his stage and his trapdoors'.

One is forced to wonder if Conan Doyle really believed that a simple set of letters would convince the sceptics of the truth of spiritualism. He would have understood from the newspaper reports that the doubters wanted first-hand physical evidence of contact with the other side and not reports from third-parties.

The problem was that, in reality, Conan Doyle was not really interested in converting the doubters unless they were prepared to be converted on his terms rather than their own. He had already declared his position on the whole matter very concisely in his book *The New Revelation* when he had stated:

> 'When the War came…the objective side of it ceased to interest, for having made up one's mind that it was true, there was an end of the matter. The religious side of it was clearly of infinitely greater importance.'[200]

Later in the year he would write to Sir Oliver Lodge and state 'I see it all from the religious angle, and so may drift away from the scientific'.[201] The onus was on the disbelievers to prove trickery rather than on him to prove authenticity.

But what of Maskelyne's reproduction? It does not appear to have taken place (as there was no further mention of it) and this may have been down to Conan Doyle's refusal to attend. However the *Express* had other ideas to fill its newspaper. Tom Thomas and his brother Will, also a medium, travelled from Wales to London as guests of the *Sunday Express* (presumably

---

[200] Hall, Trevor H. *Sherlock Holmes and his creator*. Duckworth Publishing 1978.
[201] Ibid.

beginning their stay on Sunday March 9th) and stayed in London up to Thursday March 13th.

They held a séance for the newspaper at its offices. Will Thomas described himself as 'perfectly happy with the results' and his brother Tom agreed. However, they clearly realised that their efforts had not been all that convincing as they went on to say '…we leave London still determined to provide complete proof of the genuineness of afterlife. You will see!'.

The brothers spent the rest of their London stay being entertained by the newspaper. They stayed at 'famous' hotels, went to the theatre and dined at the 'best' restaurants.

The *Daily Express* carried a report of all the events in its issue of March 14th and printed a letter from the brothers in which they declared that they were happy that the conditions of the séance were fair but they would 'have liked to know that the little phenomena produced was above suspicion, but the fault lies with the searching committee and not with us'.

It is clear that following the séance, and before commencing their week-long tour of theatres and restaurants, the Thomas brothers had given a report of the séance to Conan Doyle. The report was clearly not satisfactory to Conan Doyle and he took swift action which looked, on the face of it, to be an exercise in damage limitation. The Thomas brothers may have been upbeat about their performance and treatment but Conan Doyle appears to have viewed the whole exercise as damaging to the cause. The Thomas brothers were clearly a little naive and probably did not see that the *Express* had an anti-spiritualist agenda. Conan Doyle, following the regular criticisms and attacks he had received, knew otherwise.

It would appear that a representative of the newspaper was invited to Windlesham between the date of the séance and the 13th so that Conan Doyle could put forward a proposal.

'I should like to lift this controversy to a higher plane as these physical phenomena are, as I have always insisted, rather crude and material manifestations of outside power'.

The implication here is that, based on the report of the Thomas brothers, Conan Doyle knew full well what the *Express's* attitude was likely to be.

'I have a test ready to hand which would deal with the real question at issue – the survival of our loved ones, and the possibility of our communicating with them'.

Conan Doyle went on to suggest that representatives of various papers, six in all, should form a committee and then visit him at Windlesham where they could see and study reports from people who had attended séances (the same reports to which he had referred on the 11th). He went on to say that the committee would be welcome to take the reports away to authenticate them with their authors before reporting their conclusions. He felt that any report produced under these conditions would be able to get 'to the very roots of the matter'.

Conan Doyle then turned his attention to the Thomas brothers. He agreed that the séance had been held under fair conditions and that its results 'were not definite' but that it was 'not uncommon to have sittings which are absolutely blank'.

He concluded by remarking, in relation to the newspaper's séance, that 'it seems hardly fair first to search a man, and afterwards to declare that a bangle or others things which may appear were concealed upon his person'.

Did Conan Doyle expect his suggestion to be acted upon? It seems unlikely, at least in the short-term, as he embarked upon a brief lecture tour in Wales[202]. The *Express*, however, did run with the idea although not quite on the lines Conan Doyle had suggested.

Its sister paper the *Sunday Express* advertised a reward of five hundred pounds to the medium who could produce 'a bona-fide materialisation of the spirit of any person who has died within living memory'. It seems clear that this was done soon after the unsatisfying séance with the Thomas brothers (and hence just before Conan Doyle's suggestion was made).

---

[202] Pugh, Brian. *A Chronology of the Life of Sir Arthur Conan Doyle.* 3rd Edition. MX Publishing 2014.

The one and only respondent to this challenge was an unnamed and heavily veiled woman whom the newspaper took to calling the 'medium in the mask'.

The newspaper announced that the medium would appear at a séance on March 27th and they were inundated with requests from people who desired to be present. On the day the séance was due to take place they carried another article in which they stated that only a special committee would be permitted to be present. Interestingly the paper revealed that the woman had decided to withdraw from the chance of winning the award in order to make her success less open to suspicion. The paper also revealed that the séance was only going ahead because a test séance had taken place a week previously to see whether the main event was worth holding. The paper's 'special representative' declared that the results had 'fully justified the medium's claims to be seriously tested by the special committee'. Apparently the medium had succeeded in producing a cloud 'which grew in size and contour till it resembled an aged woman in a shawl'.

The committee destined to attend the séance on this occasion was interesting. Not all the members were listed but those that were included Conan Doyle, his detractor Stuart Cumberland and David Gow – the editor of *Light* in which Conan Doyle had publicly declared his conversion.

The séance duly took place at an unnamed flat in West London. It began with a test in which the medium was called upon to determine the nature of some personal effects of those present which were sealed in a box. She managed to describe some but not all. She also quoted words from a pre-sealed letter. These tests completed (if not necessarily passed) she produced a ghost. Predictably, the believers considered it the promised manifestation and the sceptics were, to use the words of the paper, 'not convinced upon the point'.

Curiously, Conan Doyle was not convinced by the performance of the medium and, in his mind, it probably vindicated his previous disinclination to take part in events organised by the press[203].

March also saw the *Express* pass comment on Conan Doyle's other major endeavour – his book *The British Campaign in France and Flanders 1917*. Three days prior to the séance they had reviewed the book and had clearly not been impressed. The reviewer was convinced that no serious account of the conflict was possible until a good period of time had passed during which all the facts could be collated and examined. The review concluded by stating that, while Conan Doyle would enjoy respect for his Sherlock Holmes adventures, his attempt in the realm of fact was 'not fortunate' and that a real history of the war would not be possible, in their opinion, for many years to come.

April saw Conan Doyle resume delivery of his lecture *Death and the Hereafter* in Scotland, play in a golf tournament in Crowborough and speak at the National Memorial Service for the Fallen at the Royal Albert Hall. This event was organised by the Spiritualists' National Union and, according to the *Daily Express* of April 26th (the day before the event took place), attendees who had actually communicated with lost relatives were requested 'to wear a white flower or ribbon'.

The paper that appeared on the 28th was able to report that many of those who attended had worn a white flower and that Conan Doyle had stated to those assembled that the army was 'largely impregnated with our doctrine'.

---

203 *The Daily Mirror* of March 16th 1920 carried a report where the medium's theatrical agent Percy Thomas Selbit had sued two theatrical producers for breach of contract. The 'Medium in the Mask' was reported as being a 'Legitimate Spoof' and Conan Doyle was reported to have regarded the séance he had attended as 'very clever'.

May began with some time at Windlesham before Conan Doyle resumed his lecture tour. Towns and cities including Doncaster, Manchester, Leicester and Portsmouth all received visits. In June, Conan Doyle did not tour. Instead he appears to have remained at Windlesham, leaving to deliver three lectures at The Queen's Hall in London, each talk being seven days apart. Both the *Express* and the *Mirror* covered the second of these lectures and produced articles in their respective editions of June 23rd. In the opinion of the *Mirror* the most significant thing Conan Doyle suggested during the talk was that Jesus was a psychic, had been an 'automatic writing medium' and had chosen his disciples for their psychic powers. Two days later an anonymous Christian had a letter published in the *Mirror* protesting at Conan Doyle's 'utterances', saying that to believe them would be to 'shatter the whole foundation of the Christian belief'.

July was similarly quiet with a few lectures in Sussex and August appears to have been largely devoid of travel. Aside from simply needing a rest from travelling, it is possible that Conan Doyle was using some of the time at home to work on his second spiritualist book *The Vital Message*. He also penned a poem entitled *Those Others* which appeared in the *Daily Express* of July 23rd.

After a quiet August Conan Doyle took himself off to Southsea for a brief holiday. That said, it was not all play as he delivered a lecture on Spiritualism in Portsmouth on September 7th.

His holiday prior to this lecture was interrupted by the *Express* which contacted him to discuss something in which they felt he would be interested. They were right.

Following the death of his first wife Louise, Conan Doyle had got involved in the case of George Edalji who had been accused of maiming horses in Staffordshire. Conan Doyle had campaigned for his release, pardon and compensation with some success. The *Express* now brought to his attention that a series of postcards had been received in which fresh maiming was threatened.

He declared to the newspaper that he considered it possible that the postcards were simply the work of an imitator[204].

At the end of the month Conan Doyle was discharged from the Volunteer Battalion[205].

---

[204] The *Daily Express* of September 6th 1919.

[205] Pugh, Brian. *A Chronology of the Life of Sir Arthur Conan Doyle.* 3rd Edition. MX Publishing 2014.

"I AM SO HAPPY"

The *Daily Express*, in its issue of October 6th, carried a report of a meeting that had taken place in Wimbledon the previous evening. By describing it as a meeting it is not clear whether it was a lecture or simply a gathering of the like-minded but Conan Doyle was part of this gathering and decided to share with the assembled company, the *Daily Express* and, therefore, the world something of significant importance.

He stated that he had recently heard the voice of his son Kingsley. He described how he had been in a darkened room 'with five men, my wife, and an amateur medium'. He detailed how he had 'bound the medium in six places with string' and had later heard the voice of his son.

The amateur medium in question may well have been one Evan Powell whom Conan Doyle is reported to have seen on September 7th, the same day he had given a lecture in Portsmouth[206]. Kingsley had apparently asked to be forgiven, which Conan Doyle had taken to refer to Spiritualism, which he said was the only difference of opinion they had ever had (Kingsley had not been a believer). Upon receiving said forgiveness Kingsley said 'I am so happy' before fading away.

Conan Doyle naturally knew there would be doubters, but simply said 'I state definitely that I spoke to my son, and that I

---

206 Pugh, Brian. *A Chronology of the Life of Sir Arthur Conan Doyle*. 3rd Edition. MX Publishing 2014.

heard his voice. I would be a most blasphemous liar if what I told you were not true'.

Ten days later Conan Doyle was fending off further attacks against Spiritualism. On this occasion they had come from the church – presumably still annoyed at the suggestion that Jesus had been a medium. *The New York Times* of October 17th reported that the International Church Congress (taking place in Leicester) had railed against Spiritualism and Conan Doyle had been asked his opinion on this during a lecture he delivered in Wolverhampton.

Conan Doyle's response was to simply ask how many of his critics had attended a séance and if they believed that Spiritualism was the work of the devil 'then the devil did not know his job'.

The Wolverhampton lecture was actually entitled *Our Reply to the Cleric*. The cleric in question was presumably one Reverend J.A. Magee to whom Conan Doyle referred, at around the same time, in letters to his mother, as having attacked him and other Spiritualists[207]. Three days after his Wolverhampton appearance, Conan Doyle took the fight to the enemy by repeating the same lecture in Leicester.

November 4th saw Conan Doyle's second Spiritualist book *The Vital Message* reach the shelves. All too predictably the *Daily Express* waded in with its opinion. Its review's subtitle *Sir A. Conan Doyle's weird vision of heaven* very much set the tone for their opinion which focused on the presence of cigars and alcohol in the afterlife and the idea that there was neither a heaven or hell in the sense that most religions taught.

On November 13th the newspaper brought a new type of opponent to the attention of its readers. This new opponent went by the name of Professor Alexander Erskine. Erskine had spoken on the subject of mediums at the Delphic Club on Regent Street the previous day.

---

[207] Lellenberg, Jon et al. *Arthur Conan Doyle: A Life in Letters*. Harper Press. 2007.

Erskine did not rule out the possibility of communication with the dead but stated that 'spiritism…does not constitute real evidence that the spirits of the dead hold intercourse with the living through a spiritualistic medium'. He went on to claim that the medium was always subject to auto-suggestion or suggestion from the assembled company and that it was well known that 'the very presence of a sceptic prevents manifestations'.

Bizarrely, Erskine was more ready to credit some results to telepathy. He highlighted the case of a medium who had told a woman that her son had drowned and would be found in a certain place. Later this had been confirmed to be true.

The answer to this, according to Erskine, was that the boy's subconscious mind had sent concentrated 'dying thoughts' to his mother and that these had been read and relayed by the medium. Erskine concluded 'There was nothing spiritual in this wonderful revelation, but only telepathy'.

This report appeared during a period in which Conan Doyle was conducting a lecture tour in Scotland. He had arrived in Aberdeen two days prior to the *Express's* article and on the day of the article's publication he gave a lecture in Dundee[208].

Presumably the tour in Scotland took place to make up for that which had been planned but not executed for the same time the previous year.

November brought a fresh intervention from the magician Nevil Maskelyne. On the 25th he delivered a lecture of his own on Spiritualism at the Aldwych Club.

'If people reject witchcraft,' he said, 'they must reject spiritualism also, because there is no difference between the two, except that spiritualism has none of the old spells and charms. Telepathy, hypnotism, self-deception, chance and dishonesty can account for everything that has happened in the world of spiritualism'.

---

208 Pugh, Brian. *A Chronology of the Life of Sir Arthur Conan Doyle.* 3rd Edition. MX Publishing 2014.

Not content with this, Maskelyne went on to the subject of Conan Doyle's contact with his son Kingsley. 'What would Sherlock Holmes say about it?' It was Maskelyne's opinion that Conan Doyle had hypnotised himself into believing that contact had taken place and that this sort of thing happened frequently. Surprisingly, Conan Doyle does not appear to have responded to this particular charge. Given that he had already expressed a low opinion of Maskelyne, when the conjurer offered to reproduce the Thomas brothers' séance, he may not have deemed the article worthy of a response.

December began with Conan Doyle revisiting Merthyr Tydfil to deliver another spiritualist lecture, but he was back at Windlesham by the 9th. The rest of the month seems to have been largely taken up with writing letters on the subject of Spiritualism. Letters printed under the titles *I Have Spoken with Spirits*, *Sir A. Conan Doyle on Spirit Photography* and *Conan Doyle's Passionate Defence of Spiritualism* appeared in various national and regional newspapers. His prolific writing on the matter led to many direct responses and Conan Doyle later confirmed to his mother, on December 20th, that he had received both supportive and abusive letters in reply[209].

---

[209] Lellenberg, Jon et al. *Arthur Conan Doyle: A Life in Letters*. Harper Press. 2007.

1920

ENTER HOUDINI

January 1920 began with Conan Doyle engaged in much the same activity as he had ended December 1919. A series of letters on the subject of Spiritualism appeared in *The Times* and *The Evening Standard*. These were roughly split between original remarks and responses by Conan Doyle to questions or attacks from his opponents. If he was frustrated by the constant opposition he certainly did his utmost to hide it.

Aside from this, the year began quietly with a relatively modest number of lectures that took him to places such as Southport, Durham and Harrogate[210]. At around the same time he also, effectively, offered to perform an exorcism.

According to *The Daily Mirror* of January 24th, a family by the name of White, who lived in a poultry farmhouse in East Hertfordshire, had been troubled since the very beginning of the year by a spirit that conveyed messages in Morse code. The family consisted of Mr and Mrs White, their daughter Dorothy and an unnamed son. The son was reported to have been a Morse code instructor in France during the war.

It was the daughter Dorothy who had first heard the sounds but it was the brother who worked out that the spirit was communicating in Morse code. A series of discussions between the spirit, the family and third parties had then taken place. The

---

[210] Pugh, Brian. *A Chronology of the Life of Sir Arthur Conan Doyle*. 3rd Edition. MX Publishing 2014.

understandable position of the sceptic would be to suspect the brother of being the origin of the rapping, but if such a suspicion had occurred it was not mentioned in the article.

The events had been brought to Conan Doyle's attention, it was reported, and he had promised to conduct an investigation. 'In this case,' he said, 'presuming there is no practical joking, it is probably the spirit either of some deceased rustic who knew the daughter, or some soldier pal of her brother, and he talks as he did on earth. I could probably persuade him to go if he is a nuisance'.

The newspaper was not content to leave the story there and sent a representative to the house to test the situation. In its issue of the 30th they were able to report that Dorothy had 'risen to fame as a spirit medium'. The paper's representative, along with a local councillor, named Wren, checked Dorothy's bedroom for any sign of fraud and, when she retired, they took part, with her as medium, in a conversation with the spirit.

When the spirit was asked to send a message 'to mortals through *The Daily Mirror*' the response was 'Tell them they are fools'. Following further questioning the spirit was said to be more than happy to talk to Conan Doyle but firmly rejected the notion that Conan Doyle would be able to convince it to leave the house. It is not clear if Conan Doyle ever followed the matter up.

Around this time Conan Doyle received an unsolicited book entitled *The Unmasking of Robert-Houdin*. The sender (and author) was Harry Houdini. The sending of copies of his book to around two hundred people was his way of introducing himself. Conan Doyle wrote to Houdini to say that he had enjoyed the book despite being irked by some elements of it[211].

This was the beginning of regular correspondence between the two men in which they very swiftly set out their positions with regards to spiritualism. Conan Doyle had started out quite sceptical when he had first got interested in the subject in

---

[211] Sandford, Christopher. *Houdini and Conan Doyle*. Duckworth Overlook 2011.

Southsea. Now he was arguably the movement's most famous and ardent supporter. Houdini, on the other hand, wanted to believe but found himself yet to be convinced.

Their initial exchanges ultimately led to an invitation from Conan Doyle to Houdini for him to come to Windlesham for lunch. The date was set for April 14th[212].

Harry Houdini (c1899)
(Library of Congress/McManus-Young Collection)

---

212 Sandford, Christopher. *Houdini and Conan Doyle*. Duckworth Overlook 2011.

Conan Doyle enjoyed Houdini's company and the feeling was mutual. However, it was destined to founder on Conan Doyle's belief in two things. The first of these was that he could convert Houdini into a believer and the second was his eventual belief that Houdini was actually in possession of supernatural powers. However, all this was yet to come.

The rest of April and May passed with more lectures on spiritualism which took Conan Doyle to the west of England and to Croydon[213]. In the middle of this, Conan Doyle allowed more earthly matters to intrude by refereeing an amateur billiards championship at the Burroughes Hall in St James's Street, London[214].

As May drew to a close Conan Doyle's name appeared again in the *Daily Express*. In its May 27th issue it returned to its position of sceptic and published an account of an interview with Sir Oliver Lodge. Lodge and Conan Doyle were friends and Lodge was easily as much of a believer in Spiritualism as Conan Doyle. Lodge talked about church opposition he had experienced in America, but did not seem concerned with convincing people of the truth of what he was saying. 'People must get their own experience. You must find out for yourself whether it is possible to talk to those who have gone from sight, or get somebody to do it for you'. He went on to remark that a lot depended on whether the people on the other side wanted to communicate.

Lodge also firmly rejected suggestions, made by the church, that both he and Conan Doyle were the unwitting dupes of an 'arch-deceiver'.

In parallel to these events Houdini and Conan Doyle were still corresponding, with the former seeking from the latter the details of mediums that could prove themselves to his

---

213 Pugh, Brian. *A Chronology of the Life of Sir Arthur Conan Doyle.* 3rd Edition. MX Publishing 2014.
214 The *Daily Express* of April 30th listed this as a future engagement of Conan Doyle's.

satisfaction[215]. Conan Doyle provided some names and Houdini duly went to see them. In each case he wrote to Conan Doyle subsequently in sufficiently ambiguous terms that convinced Conan Doyle that the visits had been, at least, partly successful. In reality Houdini had been unmoved by any of them and wrote as such in his private records. If anything, his scepticism was hardening rather than softening and, over time, it would be this that put the greatest strain on his odd friendship with Conan Doyle.

[215] Sandford, Christopher. *Houdini and Conan Doyle*. Duckworth Overlook 2011.

THE COMING OF THE FAIRIES

It was in late June that Conan Doyle became aware of an incident that was to alter the public perception of him in a way the even Spiritualism could not manage. He had made no secret of his unhappiness about constantly being identified as the author of the Sherlock Holmes stories, and his involvement in Spiritualism had not done much to change that. If anything, his new-found vocation led to more mention of Sherlock Holmes, as people struggled to understand how the creator of such a scientific character could have embraced the idea of communicating with the departed.

The irony of the Cottingley Fairies story (as it came to be known) was that it was a very minor series of events to Conan Doyle and he was to repeatedly state how it was very much subordinate to his work with Spiritualism. Yet a good many people remember Conan Doyle as the creator of Sherlock Holmes and the man who believed in fairies. In both spheres of his life – literature and the supernatural – he is remembered primarily for things that he did not personally rate as important.

At this time, Conan Doyle was occupied with preparations for a tour of Australia, a tour designed to promote spiritualism. Given the logistics of such a tour it is surprising that he had any spare time but he certainly made time when the editor of *Light* contacted him to say that some photographs purporting to be of fairies had come to his attention[216].

Arthur and fairies had a history. His father Charles and uncle Richard had almost made a speciality of drawing them, so it was clearly a combination of this and the chance to produce any evidence of a paranormal world that motivated Conan Doyle's interest.

Elsie Wright and Frances Griffiths
(Photographed by Arthur Wright in 1917)

216 Doyle, Arthur Conan. *The Coming of the Fairies*. University of Nebraska Press 2006.

The photographs had been taken some three years earlier by Frances Griffiths and Elsie Wright then aged nine and sixteen respectively. Elsie's father, Arthur Wright, had dismissed the photographs as a prank. He was an amateur photographer himself, knew of his daughter's artistic ability and her experience of working in a photographic studio[217]. If Arthur Wright had had his way the photographs may not have come to light, but his wife Polly believed in their authenticity and, two years later, she showed them at a meeting of the Bradford branch of the Theosophical Society. The exposure the photographs gained as a result led to them coming to the attention of prominent society member Edward Gardner. Gardner conducted an initial investigation, the results of which were enough to convince him that the photographs were genuine or at least worth serious study.

Having learned of the photographs, Conan Doyle made enquiries which ultimately led him to Gardner. He wrote to Gardner on June 22nd and the two men later met. During their meeting it was agreed that Gardner would travel to Cottingley to make further enquiries and Conan Doyle later provided Gardner with a letter to be given to Elsie's father[218].

While the subject of fairies appealed to Conan Doyle on its own merits it also suited him in other respects. By sheer coincidence he had been commissioned by *The Strand* to produce an article on fairies for its Christmas 1920 issue. As he was destined to be in Australia for most of the remainder of the year Conan Doyle intended to write the article before leaving the country. He now found himself in the potential position of having something that would really grab the attention of *The Strand*'s readers.

---

[217] Cooper, Joe. *The Case of the Cottingley Fairies*. Hale 1990.

[218] Three days after his letter to Gardner, Conan Doyle wrote to Houdini to inform him of the first fairy photographs. Houdini appears to have kept his counsel on the subject (Sandford, Christopher. *Houdini and Conan Doyle*. Duckworth Overlook 2011.)

While Conan Doyle continued with his preparations for his tour of Australia, Gardner conveyed his letter to Arthur Wright. It had the desired effect of making Wright more cooperative and in particular it secured his permission for the photographs to appear in Conan Doyle's article. Conan Doyle wrote his piece and submitted it to *The Strand.*

His reason for throwing his weight behind the story was something he explained in the article that he later drafted. If people could be persuaded in the existence of fairies and thus admit 'that there is a glamour and mystery to life' it would be a lot easier for them to accept Spiritualism[219]. To an extent, the Cottingley Fairies were a means to an end.

The need for such means was clear to Conan Doyle from the continuing attitude expressed by the press. The *Daily Express* of July 21st had carried a letter entitled *Spirits and Clothes* in which Conan Doyle's long-standing claim that spirits wore clothes was, once again, questioned. The same questions were constantly being asked and Conan Doyle must have felt that no answer he gave was ever seen as sufficient. It was probably this perception on his part that led to him referring to the need to 'jolt the material twentieth century mind out of its heavy ruts in the mud'.

However, Conan Doyle was not entirely convinced by the fairy photographs at this point. At the beginning of July he had shown them to Sir Oliver Lodge and one Kenneth Styles, a 'fairy authority'; both had doubts. Styles in particular was quoted by Conan Doyle, in a letter to Gardner, as saying 'The more I think of it the less I like it'[220].

On July 29th Conan Doyle, Jean and their children were entertained at London's Holborn Restaurant[221]. There they met, according to the *Daily Express* of the following day, with over

---

219 Doyle, Arthur Conan. *The Coming of the Fairies*. University of Nebraska Press 2006.

220 Cooper, Joe. *The Case of the Cottingley Fairies*. Hale 1990.

221 A photograph of the family either immediately before or after the luncheon appeared in *The Daily Mirror* of July 30th.

one hundred spiritualists, who had gathered to honour their greatest champion and wish him well on his Australian tour.

The *Express* report noted that 'everyone who is any one in spiritualist circles was there' with the notable exception of Sir Oliver Lodge.

Taking its customary mocking stance, the newspaper noted that 'While a "Daily Express" representative was establishing communication with the hors d'oeuvres a spiritualist lady asked, in the sweetest tone imaginable "Are you a medium?"'. The newspaper went on to remark that this was the most commonly heard question at the event. The lunch concluded with a speech from Conan Doyle in which he observed that professional mediums were, at present, the most useful persons in the land. Then, in what was described by one Australian newspaper as unexpected, Conan Doyle said 'I want to take a more direct message than the address and your good wishes. My wife and I have come in contact with the departed dead. We want all to stand up who have been in communication with the departed dead!'[222].

The newspaper observed that 'Men and women sprang to their feet, and remained standing in silent testimony'. It was also reported that of those seated all were men. There 'was not a woman who was not on her feet'.

Conan Doyle was pleased 'You send us forth in good heart, and if we don't do well on the other side, your hands at least are clean'.

Following this, Conan Doyle concerned himself with the final preparations for Australia. On August 13th he set sail aboard the RMS *Naldera* with his family, secretary and maid. His cause (or Crusade) now lay on the other side of the world. Meanwhile the Cottingley investigation was left in Gardner's hands.

---

[222] The newspaper concerned was *The World's News*, a Sydney based newspaper. The issue in question was published some time after the event - on September 18th - the day after Conan Doyle arrived in Australia.

The guests at the lunch at the Holborn
(from The Wanderings of a Spiritualist)

THE 'CHAMPION OF SPIRITUALISM'

Australian newspapers had been taking an interest in Conan Doyle's Spiritualist activities for some time. Many of the country's newspapers had syndicated articles from *The Daily Mirror*, *Daily Mail*, *Daily Express* and some regional newspapers. They had also regularly informed their readers of Conan Doyle's planned tour of their country.

It is not easy to know whether Conan Doyle expected an easier time in Australia, but the articles in the press suggested he was not going to get it. While Conan Doyle spent his voyage lecturing his fellow passengers on the cause, the Australian press was busy providing its readers with opinions on his visit and Spiritualism in general.

The *Windsor and Richmond Gazette*, in its September 10th edition, carried an article which was relatively even-handed, giving both the pro and con sides of the argument. However, it concluded with its author, one Henry Fletcher, saying:

> 'I can not too strongly urge the average person to have nothing to do with it. You would be safer playing with radium or the X-rays.'

He went on to state that it was neither 'kind or advisable' to wake a living person from their sleep and it could be much more harmful to 'prematurely awaken those in the sleep called Death'. This was destined to be one of the kinder articles.

Conan Doyle and his family arrived in Australia on September 17th[223]. His arrival port was Fremantle, which served as the port for Perth in the state of Western Australia.

Unsurprisingly, Conan Doyle was promptly interviewed by the press. In fact, he would later write that he was interviewed three times before he even left the ship[224]. He spoke about his contact with Kingsley and made a point of referring to his dealings with the British press which he did 'bitterly' according to one newspaper[225]. He went on to say that he had long wished to visit Australia and had had the honour of 'seeing the Australian troops break the Hindenburg line'.

The Grand Central Hotel, Adelaide

Following these initial interviews, and, presumably, others, one Perth based evening paper declared that their 'distinguished visitor' 'appears to be a thoroughly normal man mentally'.

---

223 Pugh, Brian. *A Chronology of the Life of Sir Arthur Conan Doyle.* 3rd Edition. MX Publishing 2014.

224 Doyle, Arthur Conan. *The Wanderings of a Spiritualist.* Hodder and Stoughton. 1921.

225 The *Recorder* of September 21st 1920.

By September 21st Conan Doyle and his family were in Adelaide and staying at the Grand Central Hotel. Upon their arrival they were given a welcome letter from the Prime Minister William Morris Hughes[226].

William Hughes (1862-1952)
Prime Minister of Australia (1915-1923)

The next day a letter appeared in local paper *The Register*. Its author, one F. O. Palmerston, sought to inform Conan Doyle of two groups that should be involved in his Spiritualist tour. The two societies in question – The Order of Light and the Spiritual Society of St. John (of which Palmerston was an ex-Vice-President) had, Palmerston stated, '..done excellent work and kept before the public, Sunday after Sunday through

[226] Pugh, Brian. *A Chronology of the Life of Sir Arthur Conan Doyle.* 3rd Edition. MX Publishing 2014.

voluntary workers, the truth of spiritualism - against much opposition'[227].

Palmerston went on to mention a number of names who would probably be prepared to accept an invitation to share the stage with him and support him. One of these names was, curiously, Watson.

It would appear that Conan Doyle either read the letter and promptly acted on it or had already had these names brought to his attention as he lunched with a Dr. Archibald Watson and Dr. William Giles the next day (the 23rd)[228]. It seems reasonably clear, based on what followed, that they discussed how the local spiritualists could assist with his lectures[229]. On the same day, news of Conan Doyle's interviews with the press in Adelaide reached readers in Sydney courtesy of *The Sydney Morning Herald*.

In the *Herald*'s article, Conan Doyle was reported as stating that it was the evidence of the return of the dead of the Great War that had caused him to feel the need 'to come to Australia to let those who had suffered share the joy and comfort that he had derived'. On more earthly matters, Conan Doyle spoke about the England cricket team and proceeded to reveal what he saw as its weak points. Presumably this was useful information for their Australian opponents.

Conan Doyle said very much the same to *The North Western Courier* (published the same day) – minus the cricket. In that paper he concluded by speculating about his reception. 'I need not say I expect, and am prepared for, every form of opposition, but I only ask for a fair hearing and impartial judgement'.

---

[227] In *The Wanderings of a Spiritualist* Conan Doyle would be complimentary about *The Register* as a newspaper.

[228] Pugh, Brian. *A Chronology of the Life of Sir Arthur Conan Doyle*. 3rd Edition. MX Publishing 2014.

[229] In *The Wanderings of a Spiritualist* Conan Doyle wrote that he had held a meeting with Spiritualists in his hotel sitting room. This may well have been the lunch with Watson and Giles.

Conan Doyle was not due to deliver his first lecture until Saturday September 25th so he spent the next couple of days more socially with a visit to the South Australian Museum and lunch with the governor of South Australia[230].

Naturally the Australian press was more than interested in Conan Doyle's first lecture at the Adelaide Town Hall and the *Daily Herald* provided its readers with an account on Monday September 27th.

The article noted several things about the audience. It was observed that it was crowded but also that the audience contained many 'men of high intellectual attainments – lawyers, musicians, doctors, professors, and others'. Presumably following their earlier conversations with Conan Doyle, the local spiritualists were out in force and the various societies, working together, had produced a leaflet, which was handed out, that contained a reprint of one of Conan Doyle's interviews.

The lecture was entitled *The Human Argument* and was one of a series of three he was to deliver in the hall over the course of a few days. The lecture detailed the origins of Spiritualism (with the Fox family in New York), his own early experiences in the late 1880s and the development of the movement in the years since then. To illustrate his personal experience he told the audience of his communication with Kingsley and made the bizarre claim that of all the scientists who had investigated spiritualism not one had come to a negative conclusion and that he could quote professors of universities in support.

He was described, following the ninety minutes of his lecture, as receiving much applause but the newspaper reported there being a 'feeling of disappointment'. This was put down to the fact that the first lecture was the least interesting part and that audiences would be more interested in the second part – entitled *The Religious Argument* which was to be delivered on the evening of the 27th.

---

230 Pugh, Brian. *A Chronology of the Life of Sir Arthur Conan Doyle.* 3rd Edition. MX Publishing 2014.

Adelaide Town Hall
Site of Conan Doyle's first Australian Spiritualist lecture

The second lecture was duly delivered and, once again, the press was eager to report back. This time it was *The Register* which provided some of the best coverage in its issue of Tuesday September 28th.

The aim of the lecture was to illustrate how Spiritualism was compatible with religion and should not be seen as challenging it. 'I do not need faith. I have the knowledge' was one of Conan Doyle's opening remarks and with this he launched into another ninety minute lecture. Conan Doyle's frustration with organised religion came across when he pointed out to his audience that the Roman Catholic Church and Anglican Church had both accepted that psychic research was a blessing but would not accept it as part of their faith. He questioned the attitude of the man '…who plants an apple tree and yet does not want to get apples from it'.

He went on to state that he regretted that Spiritualists had been forced to set up their own church because of this resistance. With what the article described as 'an emphatic sweep of the arm', Conan Doyle declared 'We are the greatest ally that the churches have ever had…and yet how have they met us?' He went on to refer to how opponents used parts of their religious texts to challenge the movement, conveniently omitting to mention other texts that he saw as supporting it.

A perhaps ominous observation by *The Register* was that there was very little applause during this second lecture, although the newspaper did go out of its way to point out that 'the subject did not call for such demonstration'.

On the evening of the article's publication Conan Doyle delivered his third and final lecture *Pictures of Psychic Phenomena*. The *Daily Herald* was on hand to report back in its issue of September 29th. It was noted that he continued to draw large crowds and that, on this occasion, the Governor was present.

Conan Doyle began with an explanation of the functions of a medium and what could be expected at a séance. He tackled the question of fraud by suggesting that many of the people caught playing tricks were genuine mediums who just found, on occasion, they could not produce what was expected of them and thus resorted to tricks – presumably out of a desire not to disappoint. He then made the bizarre statement that the public at large only ever heard of mediums when they were so caught. The hundreds that went quietly about their business did not gain publicity.

This preamble over, he proceeded to show what the article described as 'the most remarkable set of lantern pictures ever seen on the screen'. Conan Doyle personally guaranteed the majority of them as they had either been handled by him personally or he knew intimately the circumstances in which they had been taken.

Photographs were shown of psychoplasm and Conan Doyle even displayed a picture of the naturalist Alfred Russel Wallace, a convert to Spiritualism, with the psychic image of his dead mother. To conclude, he produced a photograph of the ghost of a maid taken by a lady on holiday at an inn in Norwich.

The Register of the same day also covered the event and added that Conan Doyle would repeat his latest lecture on the afternoon of September 30th due to the sheer number of people who were unable to get into the hall.

Conan Doyle took a break on September 29th and visited a nature reserve[231]. It was, however, hardly a private visit as employees of *The Register* newspaper, including its editor Ernest Whitington, accompanied him. While he was engaged in this activity his opponents were starting to gather in the press. Amusingly, these initial detractors were appearing in *The Register*. Amongst them was one Rev. John Blacket who had, according to his letter, been criticised by Conan Doyle for previous opposition to Spiritualism. After quoting Conan Doyle's account of a particular séance, Blacket wondered 'Is not this sort of thing likely to lead to the asylum?'

---

[231] Pugh, Brian. *A Chronology of the Life of Sir Arthur Conan Doyle*. 3rd Edition. MX Publishing 2014.

The following evening, after delivering his repeat performance, Conan Doyle headed to Melbourne arriving there on October 1st. He noted, in his book *The Wanderings of a Spiritualist*, that he had received many messages before he left and one of the most antagonistic had stated 'May you be struck dead before you leave this Commonwealth'.

Adelaide was not yet done with him and, now that he was gone, certain elements launched their attacks. One of the strongest of these appeared on the October 2nd issue of *The Mail.*

Most reports in the press up to this point had been relatively even-handed in their treatment. Even in cases where the reporter was not a believer, the attempt had been made to convey the integrity of Conan Doyle. This was most clearly not the case for *The Mail.*

Conan Doyle was described as 'An Intolerant "Evangel"' who had 'probably made few converts to the "faith"'. His prowess as a lecturer was criticised with the observation that he lacked the power to 'grip or arrest an audience'. The criticisms did not end there. Conan Doyle's criticism of the press, scientists or any 'honest doubters' were all pointed out. 'His style is unreasonably didactic and his method jarring. It is "the Gospel according to Sir Conan" and woe to the unbeliever!'

In common with kinder commentators, the article did not question Conan Doyle's sincerity or honesty but said that there was much in his lectures that 'smacked of the "showman"'.

Previous reports by other newspapers had made clear that the lectures were very well attended and the impression was conveyed that all had been well received. *The Mail* pointed out that many of the attendees it had spoken to had been disappointed that no public séance had taken place, as it was felt that this would be an ideal way to 'clear away suspicion or stimulate thought on the revelation'. The article observed that any South Australians who had 'wondered before he came' had been left 'still wondering'.

The newspaper's parting shot was to give its readers a taste of what Melbourne thought of its new visitor. Quoting from Melbourne's paper *Argus*:[232]

'We cannot welcome Sir Arthur Conan Doyle as an advocate of spiritualism. He represents a force which we believe to be purely evil. But we would join with all good citizens in encouraging more knowledge and education, more courage and endurance, more faith and sacrifice, for these are the corner stones of the life of the people'.

It seemed clear that the Australian tour was shaping up to be very far from the 'unalloyed success' that Conan Doyle later described in his autobiography.

Upon arrival in Melbourne Conan Doyle allowed himself some leisure time. He indulged his love of sport on October 2nd by watching the Victorian football cup at Melbourne Cricket Ground[233].

While he may have been resting, his opponents were not. On October 4th, the day before he was due to give his first lecture, he was attacked by Rev. Father Lonergan from the pulpit of St. Patrick's Cathedral. Conan Doyle was praised for having 'shown some originality' in his fiction but, on the subject of spiritualism, he had demonstrated that 'he had nothing new to talk about'. Spiritualism was dismissed as 'unreal and unstable'

---

232 The *Argus* was criticised by Conan Doyle in his book *The Wanderings of a Spiritualist*. He observed that it published attacks on him and Spiritualism but declined to publish responses to those attacks. He also portrayed the paper as hypocritical by observing that while attacking him it was more than willing to make money by carrying advertisements for his lectures.

233 Pugh, Brian. *A Chronology of the Life of Sir Arthur Conan Doyle*. 3rd Edition. MX Publishing 2014.

and those who devoted themselves to it 'suffered mentally, morally and physically'[234].

On the very day of his lecture Conan Doyle managed to elicit the derision of another Catholic priest in the person of the Very Rev. Father John Barry who declared that the Pope had stated that Catholics were to have nothing to do with Spiritualism[235].

The attacks from the Catholic Church did nothing to affect the popularity of Conan Doyle's lecture. *The Daily News* of October 7th reported that the lecture was crowded and, in what may have been a swipe at the Catholics, Conan Doyle was reported as observing that the Anglican Church was beginning to take an interest in Spiritualism and that progress should be rapid as a result. He also reported, optimistically, that the English press was becoming converted on the matter and that he hoped the Australian press would follow suit. In truth, the press in both countries were displaying very similar attitudes to the subject and not attitudes that were necessarily aligned with those of Conan Doyle.

October 6th saw Conan Doyle attend a luncheon given by the British Empire League in honour of Jean and himself. Even though the main topic of the day was the recent conflict with Germany, Spiritualism still found its way into proceedings. Sir Joseph Cook, while proposing a toast to the visitors, remarked that although he had not studied the subject he believed that Conan Doyle was knowledgeable and sincere.

Conan Doyle, despite being given an apparent opportunity, elected not to talk about Spiritualism on this occasion and confined himself to the subject of the war, declaring that Germany had lost its soul[236].

The next day he returned to the tour in earnest. It was reported, by *Table Talk*'s issue of October 7th, that Conan Doyle was to lecture at the Playhouse that day and again on the

---

[234] *The Argus* October 4th 1920 edition.
[235] *The Daily News* of Perth. October 5th edition.
[236] *The Sydney Morning Herald* of October 7th 1920.

9th. The lectures were to be entitled *Death and the Hereafter* and *The New Revelation* respectively. The former lecture demonstrated that the public fascination with both Conan Doyle and his subject had not dimmed. The *Evening News* of the 8th reported that the audience was 'as large an audience as the Playhouse could comfortably accommodate'.

Conan Doyle spent the time between the Playhouse lectures and the 18th delivering the same lectures in Geelong before returning to Melbourne[237]. During this time the press reaction to his lectures did not really vary. On the 16th *The Australasian* commented on the difference between what it saw as the Conan Doyle of old and the one now present in Australia. 'Sir Conan Doyle has apparently changed his attitude towards the mysterious. Instead of scoffing at mystery, as he did with Sherlock Holmes, he is content to accept it. Instead of reasoning from effect to cause, he is apparently convinced that certain effects are inexplicable on any recognised method of reasoning'.

The Sydney based *Sunday Times* of October 17th offered a more neutral take on Conan Doyle's cause. A correspondent, who went by the initials H.S., argued for open-mindedness and suggested that some members of the Church expected their followers to believe on faith far more than Conan Doyle was expecting.

However, the respite was brief, and the Australian press was back on the offensive by October 18th. The *Evening News* in Sydney ran an article entitled *Conan Doyle's Spirits - "Liars Wizards and Demons"* in which Spiritualism and Conan Doyle were attacked by the Baptist Church. *Spiritualism "Rotten with Fraud"* was the line taken by the *Worker* of October 21st.

On the 28th the Rev. Father Martin wrote a 'review' of Spiritualism in *Freeman's Journal*. 'Let the cobbler stick to his last!' declared Martin thus indicating that Conan Doyle should have stuck to what he was good at. In Martin's opinion this was

---

[237] Pugh, Brian. *A Chronology of the Life of Sir Arthur Conan Doyle*. 3rd Edition. MX Publishing 2014.

writing 'his detective yarns for the amusement of the English-speaking world'. Instead, Martin felt that Conan Doyle had 'left the realm in which he was master for a doubtful science, whose unwilling slave he has become'. On this Father Martin was clearly mistaken. If Conan Doyle was indeed a slave to Spiritualism he was most definitely not an unwilling one.

It is not clear whether or not Conan Doyle was paying any attention to these attacks. If he read any of them he doesn't appear to have responded to them. One possible reason for this was that he had been distracted.

It seems highly likely that following his most recent lecture on October 18th Conan Doyle had received a letter from Edward Gardner with the latest from Cottingley. The letter, which Gardner had written on September 6th, explained that Elsie Wright and Frances Griffiths had taken three more fairy photographs a few days prior to his letter. He enclosed prints and Conan Doyle was clearly very pleased with them. Any small doubts he might have entertained vanished and he wrote back to Gardner on October 21st and confessed that when he had left Gardner to manage events he had felt guilty but that, thanks to the new photographs, Gardner now had a 'complete shield against those attacks which will very likely take the form of clamour for further pictures, unaware that such pictures actually exist'[238].

Conan Doyle was alluding to the fact that his article in which the first fairy pictures would be presented had not yet appeared and that when the images were challenged, as he knew they would be, a riposte of further proof was already there to be deployed against the doubters.

Conan Doyle was careful to remind Gardner where his personal priorities continued to lie. 'The matter does not bear directly upon the more vital question of our own fate and that of those we have lost, which has brought me out here'.

---

[238] Doyle, Arthur Conan. *The Coming of the Fairies*. University of Nebraska Press 2006.

The middle of November saw Conan Doyle reach Sydney. While there was naturally interest in Conan Doyle himself the Sydney press did something unusual by showing an interest in Jean. The Sydney based *Sunday Times* of November 14th carried an article written by 'Onlooker'.

The article was complimentary in so far as it went out of its way to paint Jean as more than a mere satellite of her husband. Attention was drawn to her 'keen intellect' and her modernity. That said it was made clear that she had adopted the more traditional approach of abandoning her own interests to follow those of her husband and in order to be a mother.

The one thing absent from the article was direct quotes from Jean. This oversight was remedied by a similar article that appeared on the 15th in the pages of *The Sydney Morning Herald*. The article made plain that for many years Jean's biggest source of sorrow was that she did not share her husband's interest in Spiritualism. The war had changed this with the death of her brother and now she was as strong an adherent as her husband.

The reporter who interviewed her at Petty's Hotel[239], where the family was staying, had asked about the children's exposure to Spiritualism to which Jean had stated 'It is good for children to be brought up as spiritualists. It is good that they should know that dear ones who have passed on have not gone out of their lives, that they are ever ready to help from the other side'.

She went on to bemoan the practice of teaching children to believe in 'hell fire and purgatory'.

Conan Doyle was due to give his first lecture in Sydney the same day as the *Herald*'s article was published. His performance was judged the next day in the pages of *The Sydney Morning Herald*'s November 16th issue.

Conan Doyle was suffering with a sore throat, which was not altogether surprising, bearing in mind the sheer amount of talking he had been doing. Having to constantly make himself

[239] In *The Wanderings of a Spiritualist* Conan Doyle described Petty's Hotel as 'an old-world hostel with a very quiet, soothing atmosphere'.

heard to large audiences had clearly taken its toll. The report however stated that despite some 'huskiness' no one had trouble hearing him.

This lecture was another performance of *The Human Argument* and did not vary from prior performances elsewhere until the very end where the report referred to some objections that had been raised by one Rev S. G. Fielding. Fielding had apparently claimed that séances led to insanity and depravity. Conan Doyle pointed out to his audience that this accusation had arisen out of a comment made by a Dr. Forbes Winslow who had claimed that eleven thousand people were in asylums as a result of spiritualism. A claim that Dr. Winslow had later retracted[240].

The following day support for Conan Doyle came from an unexpected source. *The Richmond River Express and Casino Kyogle Advertiser* of November 16th carried an article entitled *A Startling Sermon* in which the Rev. J. Frederic Sanders, Congregational minister at Manly, was reported as having delivered a sermon during which he had praised Conan Doyle and told his congregation to expect a 'wonderful message' from him. Like Conan Doyle before him, Sanders drew parallels between the actions of Christ and mediums and endorsed Conan Doyle's idea of hell as a waiting room for Heaven saying 'It seems to me to be a very reasonable idea'.

Sanders' message apparently left many of his congregation 'dumbfounded' and, after leaving, they were described as having 'found their tongues'. The implication given in the article was that they were not of the same mind as their minister.

The controversial sermon must have been delivered on November 14th as the nearest Sunday to the date of the article. On this same day Conan Doyle boarded a ferry that travelled to

---

[240] Conan Doyle would later write that his first lecture in Sydney had been briefly interrupted by a protestor who had called him the Anti-Christ several times before being removed. This did not appear to get a mention in reports (from *The Wanderings of a Spiritualist*).

Manly with the intention of paying it a visit. He was reported as not getting off the ferry[241]. His reason for this was that, as he got closer, he could see nothing worth getting off for. In an interview later that day he admitted that he had subsequently learned that he had not, so to speak, seen Manly's best side and that he now understood where he needed to go to truly appreciate it.

Between November 15th and 20th Conan Doyle delivered his programme of lectures. On the 17th he delivered his lecture *The Religious Argument* and this prompted a meeting the following night, also at the Town Hall, of a group called Christian Evidence Propaganda[242]. One of the attendees, Mr W.T. Forshaw questioned Conan Doyle's courage by remarking that he had declined to take part in a public debate on Spiritualism. According to Forshaw, Conan Doyle 'had not the courage to back up his cult; he was anti-Christian; he was not prepared as an honest man to defend his position in public'. The president of the organisation, David Simpson, admitted to being persuaded that spirit communication was real but declared that the Bible prohibited anyone taking part in such communication. He, like Forshaw, wanted Conan Doyle to participate in a public debate and called upon Spiritualists to encourage Conan Doyle to do so.

Conan Doyle remained unmoved and laid out his reason for this in his book *The Wanderings of a Spiritualist*. Referring to Simpson's constant demands for a debate, he stated that a debate was 'out of the question, since no debate is possible between a man who considers a text to be final, and one who cannot take this view'.

On November 19th yet another article mocking Conan Doyle appeared in the *Daily Observer*. Under the heading *Touchy Topics of the Day*, Conan Doyle was described as 'lecturing on spooks and spookology'. The newspaper, like many observers, expressed surprise that the creator of Sherlock Holmes had

---

241 Sydney's *The Daily Telegraph* of November 15th.

242 *The Sydney Morning Herald* of November 19th carried the story.

become a 'spiritualistic gospeller' and further observed that the 'millions of readers for whom he has provided many a pleasant hour will feel glad that the yearning to commune with the dead did not seize him twenty years ago'.

Around this same time Conan Doyle received a challenge that he decided to accept. A Sydney photographer named Mark Blow (who had been mentioned at the Christian Evidence Propaganda meeting) had claimed that he could reproduce a spirit photograph with the promise that he would pay twenty-five pounds to a charity if he failed. Conan Doyle offered to match the sum if Blow succeeded. They met at the offices of an evening paper with the editor of the paper acting as referee.

According to Conan Doyle, Blow asked many questions about the circumstances in which Conan Doyle's photographs had been produced to which he was given answers. Conan Doyle then repeated the challenge that Blow was to reproduce similar photographs under the same conditions and produced some photographic plates from his own pocket for Blow to use.

Blow allegedly demanded that he be allowed to produce his photographs under conditions of his own choosing. Conan Doyle declined saying the conditions had to be the same and that 'the whole test lay in the conditions'. The impasse led to the challenge falling through which only reinforced Conan Doyle's belief that agreeing to challenges in general was foolish[243].

On November 23rd Conan Doyle elected to correct his oversight in relation to Manly and took his entire party off to the Manly Pacific Hotel[244]. While there he visited the church of Rev. Sanders and addressed the congregation[245]. It is not known how his address was received.

---

243 Doyle, Arthur Conan. *The Wanderings of a Spiritualist*. Hodder and Stoughton. 1921.

244 Pugh, Brian. *A Chronology of the Life of Sir Arthur Conan Doyle*. 3rd Edition. MX Publishing 2014.

245 Doyle, Op. cit.

If Conan Doyle needed reminding that his religious allies were few it continued to be provided courtesy of the press. The day prior to Conan Doyle's departure for Manly a Rev. H.B. Hewett described him as a 'Deluded Man'[246]. On the same day as he travelled to Manly *The Sydney Stock and Station Journal* referred to much of what was spoken about Spiritualism as 'twaddle' and that Conan Doyle had demonstrated that he was 'no exception to the twaddle rule'. A Presbyterian Minster by the name of Finlay Brown said, in *The Sydney Morning Herald* of November 24th, that the word spiritualism was being misused and that the correct word to be used in connection with Conan Doyle's lectures was that of 'Necromancy'.

On November 25th an important event occurred back in England. *The Strand* published the first article concerning the Cottingley Fairies[247]. Given the nature of what the article suggested the press was keen to comment. One of the first newspapers to do so was Conan Doyle's regular foe the *Daily Express*. In its piece it gave the basics of *The Strand*'s article and quoted Conan Doyle's statement of confidence in the photographs.

In the absence of Conan Doyle himself the newspaper spoke to Gardner who immediately revealed that further 'still more wonderful' photographs had since been taken under 'absolute test conditions'. In a statement that must have made readers suspect trickery Gardner stated that 'The photographs can only be obtained by the girls themselves working together…Nobody else can take the fairies'. In accordance with previously laid out plans to protect the girls, their names had been changed to Iris and Alice.

This attempt at protecting the girls was soon demonstrated to be not only a waste of time but a tactic that backfired. In an article ultimately published in January 1921 *The Westminster Gazette* noted that 'Sir Conan does not know Yorkshire people, particularly those of the dales, because any attempt to hide

---

246 *Riverine Herald* November 22nd.

247 The article was entitled *Fairies Photographed.*

identity immediately arouses their suspicions, if it does not go so far as to condemn the writer for his lack of frankness'.

This 'lack of frankness' had led to the majority of locals dismissing the article altogether and less than a month after *The Strand*'s publication the *Daily Express* was running further articles in which the true names of the girls now featured[248].

Back in Australia Conan Doyle's focus was on his last Sydney based lecture. He had elected to respond to some of his critics and did so on the afternoon of Saturday November 27th. In his lecture (again at the Sydney Town Hall) he accepted the possibility of faked spirit photographs and fake mediums but made it clear that this was not evidence of all photographs and mediums being fakes which is what many opponents had been suggesting. When conducting investigations himself with a new medium he deployed every possible test, as his default position was not to trust them. However, he added, 'I also do not trust theologians who make up committees of investigation. No check is ever put upon them'[249].

Conan Doyle had no more Australian lectures to deliver following the 27th. He filled the remaining time before his departure for New Zealand relaxing in Manly and at a farewell reception given to him in Sydney's Town Hall by local Spiritualists[250].

Conan Doyle departed Australia, leaving his family in Manly, on December 2nd. Was his reception in New Zealand to be any different?

---

248 *Daily Express* December 23rd 1920.

249 *The Sydney Morning Herald* November 29th 1920.

250 Pugh, Brian. *A Chronology of the Life of Sir Arthur Conan Doyle.* 3rd Edition. MX Publishing 2014.

FIFTEEN DAYS & EIGHT LECTURES

Naturally the press in New Zealand had been taking an interest in Conan Doyle as he made his way across Australia. His proposed schedule was clearly known and letters about his arrival in New Zealand had been appearing in newspapers since at least November.

The Christian voice of opposition was in force as a letter to *The Marlborough Express* of November 25th illustrated. A letter to the editor made mention of Conan Doyle's remark that Churches should be helping him instead of showing opposition.

'It would be well for Christian people to realise that no follower of Jesus Christ can have anything to do with modern "spiritualism"…'. The letter was signed CHRISTIAN which underscored a point that Conan Doyle made in his book *The Wanderings of a Spiritualist* to the effect that attacks against him tended to come from two groups – Christians and materialists – the only marked difference between the two groups being that the Christian attacks were generally anonymous and those from materialists were signed.

He travelled aboard the *Maheno* with his companion Mr Carlyle Smythe and arrived in Auckland on December 6th. Due to what can only be described as red-tape with a preceding ship, Conan Doyle was not able to actually reach his hotel until the

7th which did not give him a great deal of time to settle in and prepare for his lecture at the Town Hall[251].

What little time he did have was reduced still further by, what Conan Doyle described as, a 'peremptory demand from six gentlemen'. The gentlemen in question were photographers and they demanded to see the negatives of the photographs that Conan Doyle displayed as part of his lectures. Conan Doyle later wrote that other photographers had distanced themselves from this group of six and had described them as 'self-advertising busybodies who had no mandate'. This was backed up to a certain extent when a photographer named W.H. Bartlett wrote to the *New Zealand Herald* to say that reports that he was one of the six photographers were false and he wanted any reports to that effect corrected[252].

Needless to say Conan Doyle refused the request. He did so not only because of his experience with photographic challenges in Sydney but also because he did not possess the negatives as they, in most cases, remained with the person who had taken the picture.

The response of the photographers to this refusal was to restate their challenge in the press along with their feelings about Conan Doyle's refusal to cooperate. One of the six, named Victor R. Millard, wrote a letter to the *New Zealand Herald* and it was reproduced in the *Otago Daily Times* of December 9th.

In the letter Millard went on at some length about how people were being expected to accept the genuineness of the photographs purely on Conan Doyle's word. Not content with that, Millard got personal, stating of Conan Doyle, 'Here is a man, who, by force of character, succeeds in dominating the minds of people and nations, is banqueted, decorated, and worshipped as a good man by spiritual communities wherever he treads'. Millard concluded by saying that if Conan Doyle

---

[251] Doyle, Arthur Conan. *The Wanderings of a Spiritualist*. Hodder and Stoughton. 1921.

[252] The *New Zealand Herald* December 9th 1920.

agreed to the challenge it '...would be at least something in return for the few hundreds of pounds he will relieve the city of, and justify his power which we emphatically deny'.

Conan Doyle later wrote that 'one gets used to being indirectly called a liar, and I can answer arguments with self-restraint which once I would have met with the toe of my boot'[253].

It was not the only challenge. The other came from a conjurer who called himself Carter the Great. Carter challenged Conan Doyle to produce a ghost under test conditions and offered to pay one thousand pounds to charity if Conan Doyle was successful. Conan Doyle dismissed the challenge on the pure and simple grounds that he had never personally claimed to be able to produce a ghost and that therefore the challenge was 'easy money' for the conjurer. It must have also crossed his mind that the conjurer's aim could well have been publicity.

Despite all these events he was ready and able to deliver his first lecture in the Auckland Town Hall on December 7th. He followed this, the next day, with his lecture on spirit photography. As was becoming customary, the lectures enjoyed capacity audiences. The *New Zealand Herald* of December 9th was complimentary about Conan Doyle's sincerity, remarking that even the strongest doubter would leave the hall 'in the spirit of "I wonder"'.

When he later wrote up events, Conan Doyle noted that an ex-medium later lectured in the same hall 'with the most terrifying revelations' and expressed disappointment that his schedule had prevented him attending[254]. He also noted that said ex-medium had subsequently not done very well.

In fact, the case for the opposition was put by two separate speakers, both claiming to have been mediums. The first event, which took place on the evening of the 9th was a lecture by one

---

253 Doyle, Arthur Conan. *The Wanderings of a Spiritualist*. Hodder and Stoughton. 1921.
254 Ibid.

E.H. Portere on the production of spirit photographs[255]. Portere had certainly done his utmost to get noticed. Advertisements for his, effectively, anti-spiritualist lectures appeared alongside those for Conan Doyle's pro lectures. In one advertisement he claimed 'You owe it to your soul's self to hear me'. Of Conan Doyle he stated 'He has not been in personal touch with the unseen - I have'[256].

It was later reported that the lecture could not be taken seriously as a response to Conan Doyle and that it would only appeal to non-believers – in other words Portere was preaching to (and only to) the converted.

Clearly pushing a Christian agenda, he talked of demons and the many former spiritualists who now occupied asylums. Described by reports as indulging in 'rambling discourse' he invited people to trust in God and rely on their priests. One audience member told him to 'shut up' and a number of people walked out – a proportion of these with decidedly amused faces[257].

The following night it was the turn of one Mr Wesley Richards. The *Auckland Star* of December 11th reported that the hall was 'just about full' and it is not unreasonable to suspect that this had something to do with the reaction to the lecture of the previous night. Richards, like Portere, put much down to the malign influence of demons and talked at length about what mediums suffered and that Conan Doyle understood nothing about said suffering. Unlike his predecessor, Richards was not reported as suffering any heckling. The *New Zealand Herald* of the same date reported that the event suffered from a lot of 'coming and going' with people leaving before the end and others arriving after proceedings had commenced.

By this time it was the day of Conan Doyle's first lecture in Wellington. He had arrived on the 10th and the *Dominion* newspaper of the previous day had reported that the Mayor of

---

[255] The *New Zealand Herald* December 9th 1920.

[256] The *New Zealand Herald* of December 7th 1920.

[257] The *New Zealand Herald* of December 10th 1920.

Wellington had suggested the idea of a Civic Reception to Conan Doyle for the day of his arrival. Conan Doyle had respectfully declined. This decision was almost certainly down to his schedule which was both hectic and brief.

One of the first things he was interviewed about upon his arrival was the Cottingley Fairies. Conan Doyle summarised the events but made clear his priorities by stating 'That is not related to Spiritualism. It is a separate line of development entirely'[258].

He was far more concerned with his first lecture in the capital and this was covered by the *Evening Post* of December 13th. The newspaper reported that around three thousand people attended and that Conan Doyle had conducted the entire lecture without the need for a chairman and without any form of introduction. The *Dominion* of the same day went further, reporting that the Town Hall was full to capacity.

Predictably, in Conan Doyle's wake came the lectures by the opposition. On Sunday December 12th one Rev. S. Beckingham was reported as admitting that there was something in Spiritualism but that he did so with 'certain reservations' and described the practices 'as empty as a hollow gourd'[259].

December saw Conan Doyle's last appearance in Wellington. Once again reports made plain that his lectures had not suffered for all the condemnation directed at them by members of the Church. The *Evening Post* of December 14th said that the audience for the second lecture was larger than the first and that many people were forced to stand due to the lack of available seating.

It seems likely that part of the reason for this overcrowding was the fact that Conan Doyle had reduced his lectures in number from three to two for the duration of his time in New Zealand. This was touched on by the issue of *Press* that had appeared on December 13th.

---

258 *Ashburton Guardian* December 14th 1920.
259 *Dominion* of December 13th 1920.

In a short article it said that Conan Doyle's short stay in the country was due to 'unforeseen circumstances'. This seems like a bit of dramatic licence on the part of the press as Conan Doyle certainly alluded to no problems and knew how brief his visit to New Zealand would be before he had even arrived.

December 15th saw Conan Doyle arrive in Christchurch[260]. That day's issue of *Free Lance* noted that it had taken some considerable time to get Conan Doyle to tour Australasia and that, so far, he was out of pocket because he tended to hand all profits over to local 'Spiritualistic organisations'.

Conan Doyle was, arguably, not in the best of moods at this point in his tour. His spirit photographs were again under attack; this time from one Mr P. Virtue who had questioned why a spirit would clearly display injuries sustained in life. Conan Doyle decided to address this with a letter to the *New Zealand Herald* and this was published on the day of his arrival in Christchurch. Wounds, he said, appeared on the images of spirits 'for evidential purposes, to insure that we recognise the person'. This suggestion was, unsurprisingly, mocked by Virtue in a reply that appeared three days later.

Conan Doyle probably did not see this response as, by this time, he had delivered his two lectures and was on his way to Dunedin. Some contributors to the press were well disposed towards him prior to his arrival. An anonymous letter to the *Otago Daily Times* was published on the 15th and strongly suggested that people 'close their ears somewhat to the din of blind prejudice raised by worthy but timid men who fear to seek truth in ways they do not understand…'. Three days later the same newspaper reminded its readers that Conan Doyle would be speaking at His Majesty's Theatre and that it was expected that his lectures would be as crowded there as they had been everywhere else on his tour.

Naturally the Church had done its best to poison the ground in advance of Conan Doyle's arrival. The December 18th issue

---

260 Pugh, Brian. *A Chronology of the Life of Sir Arthur Conan Doyle.* 3rd Edition. MX Publishing 2014.

of *Press* carried an attack from one Bishop Brodie. The line taken was all too predictable. Under the title *A Blasphemy Nurtured in Fraud* the Bishop referred to the Pope's ban on Catholics involving themselves with Spiritualism and suggested that those who ignored this would find themselves heading in the direction of the lunatic asylum.

Another article in the same newspaper attempted to undermine Conan Doyle by saying that there was nothing new in Spiritualism and the only thing that was new from Conan Doyle was his 'fairy gospel'. Its author Rev. W. Ready went on to say about Conan Doyle, with respect to the Cottingley Fairies, 'I fancy he is merely trying to "pull our legs" and is laughing up his sleeve at the readiness of his infant followers to swallow anything he might say'.

Despite this, Conan Doyle delivered his two lectures on December 20th and 21st. The *Otago Daily Times* of the 22nd reported on the latter and, in common with most reports, remarked on the large crowds and Conan Doyle's impressive arguments. Unlike some previous occasions, this lecture had a chairman in the person of Rev. Hector Maclean who was probably one of the most generous of Conan Doyle's religious opponents. Maclean openly acknowledged the differences between his position and that of Conan Doyle, but said that he was sympathetic towards 'every earnest seeker after truth' and that Conan Doyle 'fulfilled that description'. In fact, Maclean had claimed that this opinion was not just his but that of many ministers in the city. Based on the comments from most of his brother clerics it seemed a bold claim.

On Christmas Eve, Conan Doyle departed New Zealand for Australia. A hectic two weeks were behind him and he must have been relieved to be heading back to his family.

THE END OF AN ERA

Conan Doyle arrived back in Melbourne on December 27th[261]. Upon his arrival he headed directly for Sydney where he was to re-join his family. The reunion took place on the 30th when Jean and the children returned from an excursion to the Blue Mountains.

On the same day as this reunion Conan Doyle lost his greatest confidant. His mother Mary, the mam, died at her home in Sussex. Conan Doyle revealed some of his thoughts soon after in his book *The Wanderings of a Spiritualist*. He acknowledged her lack of sympathy and understanding for his Spiritualist mission but noted 'She understands now'.

---

[261] Pugh, Brian. *A Chronology of the Life of Sir Arthur Conan Doyle*. 3rd Edition. MX Publishing 2014.

1921

FAREWELL AUSTRALIA

The most significant opening event of 1921 was the funeral of Conan Doyle's mother Mary. She was laid to rest in the churchyard of St Luke's, Grayshott alongside her first daughter-in-law Louise and grandson Kingsley. The decision to bury her in Grayshott was presumably motivated purely by the existing Doyle presence rather than any particular attachment to the area. The gravestone was a Celtic cross and the words 'To know her was to love her' concluded the text upon it.

It must have upset Conan Doyle that he was not able to attend his mother's funeral regardless of the solace he found in Spiritualism. It seems likely that he was in a poor frame of mind and that this was perhaps due to a combination not only of his mother's death but also the negativity he had encountered (especially from the press) during his tour. Whatever mood he was in and regardless of its cause, he was about to make a mistake that would overshadow his last few weeks in Australia.

Conan Doyle and his party arrived in Brisbane on the 7th or 8th of January[262]. A few days prior to this he had written to the London based *International Psychic Gazette* with a view to summarising his thoughts on Australia and its reaction to his message. The contents of his letter were considered so

---

[262] Pugh, Brian. *A Chronology of the Life of Sir Arthur Conan Doyle.* 3rd Edition. MX Publishing 2014.

newsworthy that they found their way into Australian newspapers just as he was arriving in Brisbane.

The gravestone of Conan Doyle's mother Mary in St Luke's Churchyard. (Author's Collection)

He spoke of what he viewed as a press boycott in which he felt his opponents had been given more room to express their views than the pro-Spiritualist camp. He put this down to an 'ignorant want of proportion' and 'moral cowardice'. He went on to call the Australian press 'backward' in their view of the subject and concluded by saying 'It is the want of liveliness and the spiritual deadness of this place that gets on my nerves'[263].

He went on to attack the Presbyterian Church for praying that he would not reach Australia and said that if they had genuinely believed their prayers would be effective it would make their actions 'near to murder'.

His outburst made it into many papers (and was quoted slightly differently in almost all of them) and during the course of January his views and the reactions to them found their way across Australia.

The Presbyterian Church was quick to defend itself. In the *Northern Star* of January 10th it 'declined to seriously notice' Conan Doyle's 'alleged' statement. *The Northern Miner* of the same date carried details of an interview held with Conan Doyle the previous day in which he had been challenged to explain his outburst and how he squared it with his public displays of satisfaction with the tour.

In what can only be described as damage limitation, Conan Doyle said that his complaints about the press mainly applied to Melbourne and the newspaper *Argus*. He had been impressed with the attitude to Spiritualism in Sydney and across New Zealand.

However, this was too little too late and the collective Australian press wanted its say. *The Horsham Times* of the 11th said that if Conan Doyle had not found his message as well received as he had hoped it was not because of ignorance but the fact that Australians were '...almost wholly free from the superstitious instinct'. In response to Conan Doyle's remark about the country's 'spiritual deadness' getting on his nerves, the newspaper remarked that the 'average Australian opinion of the great novelist in his new role would make far more interesting reading'.

---

[263] *Mayborough Chronicle, Wide Bay and Burnett Advertiser* January 8th 1921.

By far the strongest reaction came from *The Catholic Press* on January 13th. The title *Doyle, The Spook-Raiser – His Twaddle about Australia* clearly indicated its agenda. 'There is nothing so amusing as the pompous ass who gets annoyed because his fellows will not take him seriously…'. This was followed by comments to the effect that Australians had long ago learned to see through tricks and 'when a plausible stranger comes to them with a bag of mysteries they suspect him'.

The same paper also tackled Conan Doyle's complaints about the press, alleging that he was only unhappy with Melbourne because they would not give him the same coverage as he had enjoyed elsewhere. After a collection of further similar remarks they concluded by saying that nobody in the country was likely to be much interested in Conan Doyle's planned book of his time in Australia.

The anger and commentary generated by Conan Doyle's assessment of Australia did appear to affect the number of newspapers that reported on his lecture in Brisbane. His first lecture in the city was given on January 10th and, while many newspapers continued to run with the reactions to his Australian assessment, a report did manage to find its way into the following day's issue of *The Brisbane Courier*.

The newspaper observed that the majority of the audience were middle-aged or elderly and suggested that Conan Doyle had delivered his lecture free from any form of interruption or dissent. It also noted that the lecture, as with others, had been well attended. The same pattern was repeated with his lecture on spirit photographs which took place the following day and was covered by the same paper.

It appeared therefore that Conan Doyle's outburst had offended the press, certain religious groups and individual commentators but the average man in the street had not been moved one way or the other. The report on the second lecture concluded by stating that, due to the shipping strike, Conan Doyle was unable to go to Tasmania as he had planned and that he would therefore give an additional lecture in Brisbane. It was duly reported that there was 'heavy booking' for this unexpected lecture[264].

On the same day as his spirit photography lecture Conan Doyle laid the foundation stone of the first 'Spiritual Church' of Australia. During his speech at the ceremony he took the opportunity to advise his fellow Spiritualists not to demonstrate 'uncharitableness toward other religions, for there were many ladders to heaven'[265].

On the same day that Conan Doyle gave his unexpected extra lecture in Brisbane another attack on spirit photographs appeared in the latest edition of the *Worker*.

In what was presumably a display of sarcasm, Conan Doyle was initially referred to as 'Sherlock Doyle' and was, yet again, challenged to produce one photograph that was not a fake. If he was able to do so the author of the article promised, again with more than a hint of sarcasm, '..to proclaim my entire, absolute and unswerving faith in Spiritualism, providing I am not called upon to practise religious exercises with household furniture, in a subdued light, or receive inconsequential messages from dead friends which throw about as much intellectual light on the really important questions of human existence as a firefly would through the murky midnight of Woy Woy tunnel'.

The tirade continued, 'Better the hottest Scotch hell that ever burned in pulpit imagination than the colorless, aimless kind of disembodied consciousness which Spiritualism has discovered in darkened back parlors'.

Throughout the tour, with the exception of the odd article, the opinions of Jean had not been reported in the Australian press. The newspaper *The Queenslander* decided to address this in its issue of January 15th. It is tempting, if a touch cynical, to

---

264 *The Brisbane Courier* of January 13th.
265 *The Register* of January 12th.

wonder if this was a move driven by the family to earn some good press. The interview was probably conducted the previous day when Conan Doyle visited the Redbank Plains apiary[266].

'I shall always think of Australia as a place of hospitality and flowers' Jean was reported as saying. Everyone from shop assistants to waitresses had been helpful and friendly. She praised Australian women in particular for an absence of snobbishness. The rest of the article was little more than a biography dealing with her family and her interest in Spiritualism.

Two days after the article was published, Conan Doyle and his party were back in Sydney en route to the Blue Mountains. During their time there the Brisbane based newspaper *Worker*, in its January 20th issue, attempted a summing up of Conan Doyle's impact in the country.

It started out with an even-handed attitude condemning both Conan Doyle and the church. The former was criticised for his comments on the Australian press and his comments on the country's spiritual deadness. The latter was criticised for its attacks on Spiritualism.

The newspaper then made a comment which flew in the face of pretty much all reporting to date. It alleged that Conan Doyle's lecture on spirit photographs had '...got very badly on the nerves of the public in each city where he delivered it'.

According to the article, the second lecture '...consisted of dreary and unconvincing stories' and '...strained credulity to impossible limits'. The conclusion drawn was that the good reception Conan Doyle had enjoyed was more to do with his fame as an author and that anyone less 'celebrated' would not have been received so well[267].

The final event of note in January took place on the 30th when Conan Doyle and his family attended the weekly service

---

266 Pugh, Brian. *A Chronology of the Life of Sir Arthur Conan Doyle.* 3rd Edition. MX Publishing 2014.

267 With the benefit of historical hindsight, it can be said that there is a strong ring of truth to this assessment.

of the Stanmore Spiritualist Church. At its conclusion Conan Doyle summed up his tour. He announced that, after all expenses, the tour had concluded with a profit in the region of seven hundred pounds. Of this he proposed to hand one hundred to the editor of the *Harbinger of Light*, a Melbourne based Spiritualist magazine, for propaganda purposes. The decision to single out a Melbourne paper for this help clearly had its roots in the increased resistance that Conan Doyle felt, rightly or wrongly, that he had experienced there. No such grant was offered to any other periodical. Fifty pounds was given to the Spiritualists of Brisbane and, after various other gifts, he estimated there would be five hundred pounds left. This sum he intended for the Spiritualists of Australia to use largely as they saw fit.

'I thank all Australia,' he said, 'for its goodness to us. You cannot go through a great country arguing and fighting your way as we have done without occasionally being rubbed the wrong way…I have no ill-will to anyone in this continent'.[268]

February 3rd saw Conan Doyle and his family on board the SS *Naldera*. They left Adelaide en route to Perth. Perth's *The Daily News*, in its February 10th issue, reported that Conan Doyle would be giving a lunch-hour lecture at His Majesty's Theatre at 1pm. The idea behind this was to make it as easy as possible for people to attend. It was an unplanned lecture arranged without his knowledge by local spiritualists. The press interviewed Conan Doyle on the morning of the 11th and it was at this point that he confirmed the unscheduled nature of the lecture[269]. The lecture, despite its hasty arrangement, was a success although it was noted that mainly women attended[270].

---

[268] *The Sydney Morning Herald* of January 31st 1921.
[269] *The Daily News* of February 11th 1921.
[270] *Kalgoorlie Miner* of February 12th 1921.

Following the lecture Conan Doyle made haste to board the *Naldera* and left Australia.

Conan Doyle works on his book The Wanderings of a Spiritualist (Taken from the book itself)

An article appeared in *The Sunday Mirror* in Perth on the 13th. It stated that 'Chief Spook Doyle' had sent them (the newspaper) a message. The message was clearly not from Conan Doyle and contained phrases such as 'I have been a humble instrument in impregnating Australia from end to end with vital and novel truths.' It concluded by quoting prices for the forthcoming book (presumably also false) and ended with 'S'long you big-hearted boneheads'.

HOLMES ON SCREEN, STAGE AND PAGE

In March, Conan Doyle and his family reached Marseilles in France[271]. At around the same time, Conan Doyle's second article on fairies appeared in *The Strand*. It elicited very much the same sort of comments as the first, and public opinion on the matter did not really shift in any direction.

Conan Doyle was probably not too concerned as he had other distractions. Upon his arrival in Marseilles he had visited some battlefield sites[272]. Following this it had been his intention to head to Paris en route to England. His plans were interrupted by the death of his brother-in-law E.W. Hornung.

Hornung was in France at St. Jean de Luz and had succumbed to influenza. It is hard to conceive the pain felt by Conan Doyle's sister Connie at the loss of both her husband and son in a relatively short space of time. Conan Doyle attended the funeral and *The New York Times* reported on the death in its April 8th issue noting that, thanks to Hornungs's marriage to a sister of Conan Doyle, '…the great detective, Sherlock Holmes, and the great thief, Raffles, became, in a sense, brothers-in-law'.

On the subject of Sherlock Holmes, *The Daily Mirror* of March 23rd carried a one-page advertisement for a series of fifteen films known as *The Adventures of Sherlock Holmes.*

---

271 Pugh, Brian. *A Chronology of the Life of Sir Arthur Conan Doyle.* 3rd Edition. MX Publishing 2014.
272 Ibid.

Produced by The Stoll Film Company Limited and directed by Maurice Elvey the films starred Eille Norwood as Sherlock Holmes.

Eille Norwood (1861-1948)

In a move which appears, to cynical eyes, to be ensuring as wide a release as possible, the advertisement stated that the films would be shown '…in every Cinema of repute' and would-be viewers were invited to ask their local cinema owner for details of where they could view the series.

Conan Doyle had signed the deal back in 1920 entitling Stoll to produce forty-six short films[273].

By mid-April Conan Doyle was back in England and was delivering his now well-honed lectures at the Queen's Hall in London. Aside from this activity, April was a relatively quiet month which would probably have been a welcome relief after such a sustained period of travel.

May 2nd saw the performance of a one-act Sherlock Holmes play entitled *The Crown Diamond* which took place at the

---

[273] Zecher, Henry. *William Gillette: America's Sherlock Holmes.* Xlibris 2011.

Bristol Hippodrome. It was presumably a try-out as the *Daily Express* of the 12th reported that the play was to also be performed in London and it would mark the London debut of actor Dennis Neilson-Terry.

The Times of May 10th carried a notice to the effect that Conan Doyle had instructed the firm Messrs. C. Bridger and Son of Haslemere to sell his former Surrey home Undershaw.

The striking aspect was that it was made plain that 'a very low price would be accepted' in order to ensure a swift sale. The advertisement achieved the desired result with the *Farnham Herald* of the 14th announcing that the house had been sold for four thousand pounds – a fraction of what it had cost to secure the land and construct the house back in 1897.

Why sell the house at such a loss, why the sudden need to be rid of it? It is clear that Jean had no fondness for the house. It would have been too strong a link to her husband's past and first family. However, if the house had bothered her that much she would surely have found a way to encourage her husband to sell it sooner.

It seems plausible that Conan Doyle had rented Undershaw out in the interim purely to keep some money coming in before handing the house over to Kingsley. Kingsley's death in 1918 would have brought an end to that idea. Perhaps Conan Doyle's hectic schedule had meant 1921 provided the first opportunity since Kingsley's death for the house's future to be considered.

We do not know whether or not it crossed Conan Doyle's mind to offer the house to Mary but if he had done so she would almost certainly have declined. For Mary, Undershaw was the site of many sad events and invoked memories she had little desire to relive.

Towards the end of the month Conan Doyle's account of his travels in Australia, *The Wanderings of a Spiritualist*, began serialisation in *The Weekly Dispatch* and would run until mid-

July[274]. Aside from this, June, July and August were decidedly quiet months.

It could well have been during this quieter time that Conan Doyle allowed his mind to wander back to his detective. *The Crown Diamond* was certainly not enjoying the success of its eleven year old predecessor *The Speckled Band*. After its one week run in May it had enjoyed another week in late August but it simply was not matching the other's reception. Conan Doyle was keen to make more money from it and decided upon a novel approach.

Having adapted a number of his written efforts for the stage, he now hit upon the idea of reversing the process. He took the script for *The Crown Diamond* and turned it into a short story. One thing he clearly did not do was spend a great deal of time on the process and it showed. The resultant story *The Adventure of The Mazarin Stone* was the second (and last) Sherlock Holmes story to be told in the third-person. This approach was clearly as a result of its stage origins and, for the same reason, events took place largely in one room.

The artistic duties fell to A. Gilbert who had illustrated Holmes's last outing in *His Last Bow* back in 1917. He produced a series of illustrations that were, arguably, superior to the narrative. The story was set for the October issue of *The Strand*.

Continuing on the Holmes theme, September 28th saw Conan Doyle attend a dinner at the Trocadero in London hosted by the Stoll Film Company. It was reported by both *The Daily Mirror* and *Daily Express* of the following day that Conan Doyle had given a speech in which he had talked about the tendency of some readers to confuse him with his detective and how, at an event in New York, the audience had been disappointed when he appeared because they had been expecting someone cadaverous covered with needle marks.

---

[274] Pugh, Brian. *A Chronology of the Life of Sir Arthur Conan Doyle*. 3rd Edition. MX Publishing 2014.

Illustration for The Adventure of the Mazarin Stone by A. Gilbert

At the beginning of October, Sherlock Holmes's latest story became available. At the same time, his creator returned to matters Spiritualist with a series of lectures which took him to places such as Warrington and Nottingham. In the midst of this he was taken to task by his old sparring partner Stuart Cumberland with regards to his (Conan Doyle's) assertion that clairvoyants could help in the solving of criminal cases – in particular those involving missing persons[275]. Conan Doyle

[275] The *Daily Express* of October 22nd 1921.

seems to have let this wash over him on this occasion as he does not appear to have responded.

One earthly thing that he did do during November was to resign as Deputy Lieutenant of Surrey. This was announced in the *Gazette* of the 29th and it is a wonder that he did not do it long before[276]. He had not been a resident of Surrey for fourteen years and it is surprising that he had not been asked to relinquish the role. The only use his position had been to him in those fourteen years was to give him a plausible excuse for his custom uniform for visiting the front during the war.

A few days before this announcement, undergraduates at Cambridge University decided to use Conan Doyle as a means of playing a practical joke. A report of events found its way into the pages of the *Daily Express* of November 25th.

A considerable number of placards went up in the University town advertising that Conan Doyle would attend a meeting of the Anglo-American Psychological Society at the Cambridge Guildhall on November 24th at 8.30pm. It was said that Conan Doyle was to speak on 'the visualisation of materialisation'.

The advertising was successful and the Cambridge Guildhall was 'packed' according to the *Express* article. When 9pm came and went with no sign of any speakers the audience began to get restless. At this point an undergraduate emerged onto the stage with a banner which, when unfurled, read 'Sir Arthur Conan Doyle has failed to materialise'.

Following a pause, during which the audience awoke to the fact that they had been hoaxed, there was uproar followed by the demand 'We want spirits'. The paper reported that this demand was answered by 'a sepulchral voice' which replied 'Whisky'. Ultimately the only way for the management to disburse the crowd was to gradually turn out all the lights. The originators of the hoax went undiscovered. If Conan Doyle had any thoughts on this (or even knew of it) they are not known.

---

[276] Pugh, Brian. *A Chronology of the Life of Sir Arthur Conan Doyle.* 3rd Edition. MX Publishing 2014.

Given the seriousness with which he took the subject he is not likely to have been too impressed if he had known.

December passed largely uneventfully. The rest was required as the following year would see the Conan Doyle family return to the United States.

1922

BACK TO AMERICA

1922 began with a serious investigation that was, perhaps, worthy of Sherlock Holmes. In 1921 Portland Prison in Dorset had been converted into a Borstal[277] and troublesome boys from other Borstals were transferred to it. At some point, presumably towards the end of 1921, a number of boys had attempted suicide and the Home Secretary had asked Conan Doyle to visit and assess the situation. It is not clear exactly when this visit took place, or why he was asked, but Conan Doyle allegedly reported back to the Home Office that he considered the suicide attempts to be in the nature of a practical joke[278].

On the evening of January 3rd a night warder saw clouds of smoke coming from a cell window. He entered the cell to find its occupant writhing on a burning bed. It was determined that he had meddled with the gas light and set fire to his bedding deliberately in order to give himself injuries that would admit him to hospital and thus get himself out of the cell.

The *Daily Express* reported the story in its issue of the 4th and cast doubt on Conan Doyle's assessment and suggested that something had to be amiss with the running of the institution if it moved boys to such measures.

Conan Doyle does not appear to have been involved with the matter any further after this report. He had plenty to occupy

277 Today we would know these as youth prisons or detention centres.

278 Portland Prison was, prior to its conversion, one of the prisons in which George Edalji had been incarcerated.

him at this point. He was about to head to Scotland for a short series of lectures and he had two pieces due to be published in *The Strand*.

The first of these was the latest Sherlock Holmes story – *The Problem of Thor Bridge*.

Sergeant Coventry, Holmes and Watson at Thor Bridge (Illustration by A.Gilbert)

A vast improvement on its immediate predecessor, the story was published across the February and March issues of *The Strand*. It was also to be the last story illustrated by A. Gilbert although he continued to work for the magazine until at least 1924.

The second of Conan Doyle's *Strand* items was entitled *The Book I Most Enjoyed Writing* which would be published in March[279].

Matters relating to Spiritualism were still very prominent. Back in October of 1921 the editor of the *Sunday Express* – James Douglas – had spent a weekend with Conan Doyle at Crowborough. Douglas was conducting his own personal investigation into Spiritualism and spent the weekend discussing the subject with Conan Doyle. He was also reported as having experienced automatic writing[280].

Given his past experience of the newspaper it is a wonder that Conan Doyle agreed to the idea at all. Any hope he may have entertained of a fair hearing was dashed in the *Daily Express* of January 20th in which Douglas's conclusions were summarised as 'devastating to those who believe in this strange religion'.

Two days later Douglas's opinion was published and was fairly damning. Conan Doyle was permitted a right of reply the following week in which he said, of Douglas, 'Your reasoning power is not on a par with your intelligence'[281].

The Daily Mirror of February 8th reported that Conan Doyle was giving a series of lectures in Glasgow which were due to end on the 9th with the display of a series of photographs 'demonstrating recent psychic revelations'.

His book *The Wanderings of a Spiritualist* had made it to the United States and was reviewed by *The New York Times* in its issue of February 19th. The review did not really come down on one side or the other. At one point the book was praised with the assessment that it was 'difficult for even the cynic to read these pages with anything but sympathy' but it was later described as 'an informal notebook, in haphazard sequence…in

---

279 Pugh, Brian. *A Chronology of the Life of Sir Arthur Conan Doyle.* 3rd Edition. MX Publishing 2014.

280 *Daily Express* of October 22nd 1921.

281 Later quoted in the *Daily Express* of February 4th.

which cricket and football tumble in between ectoplasmic flows'.

Conan Doyle was, by this time, planning a trip back to the United States. The main purpose of the visit was to continue his lectures on Spiritualism but it would also give him the opportunity to meet with Houdini. Houdini, for his part, had maintained a correspondence with Conan Doyle. One of the many letters that had awaited Conan Doyle upon his return from Australia had been from Houdini and Houdini would regularly write to Conan Doyle to seek his opinion on a medium or a séance[282].

When Houdini learned of Conan Doyle's planned visit he immediately wrote to suggest that the family stay with him. Conan Doyle declined on the grounds that he had to stay somewhere public for the purposes of his role[283]. This presumably meant that he needed to stay somewhere like a hotel to facilitate access for reporters. It may also have stemmed from a desire not to impose.

The New York Times of March 19th reported on Conan Doyle's imminent arrival. The only useful fact they provided was that Conan Doyle was to arrive on April 8th. The rest of their article was little more than a summary of Conan Doyle's life which would have been familiar to many people already.

The same newspaper reported Conan Doyle's departure from England on April 2nd aboard the *Baltic*. It also announced Conan Doyle's intention that any profits from the tour would be donated to 'the cause of psychical research'.

Conan Doyle arrived in the United States one week later. *The New York Times* of the day reported that his first lecture would be on Wednesday April 12th at Carnegie Hall. It further reported that a box would be placed at the entrance to the hall into which people could place questions. A selection of these

---

282 Sandford, Christopher. *Houdini and Conan Doyle*. Duckworth Overlook 2011.

283 Ibid.

would be answered by Conan Doyle at the conclusion of the lecture.

The Conan Doyle family in New York 1922
(Library of Congress, Prints & Photographs Division, [reproduction number, e.g., LC-B2-1234])

Two days before the lecture Conan Doyle met with reporters en masse at the Hotel Ambassador. His thoughts were summarised by *The New York Times* on the 11th. There was nothing much that was not already known to anyone who had followed Conan Doyle's Spiritualist career to date. He spoke of marriage in the afterlife, the absence of physical pain and how he felt that Spiritualism complemented rather than opposed religion.

Doyle Foresees A Finer Religion was the title of *The New York Times* article of April 13th which covered Conan Doyle's debut American lecture. Many of his three thousand five hundred strong audience were reported as being those in mourning for 'war bereavements' and Conan Doyle assured them that their loved ones were waiting for them in the form that they had known them in life. 'We are standing on a vast ocean of psychic knowledge,' said Conan Doyle, 'but some of us are only ankle deep, and we would have you on the shore see what we have seen and know'.

The lecture contained one element which, with historical hindsight, seems rather amusing. Not long after the commencement of the lecture the audience was startled by a series of, what were described as, 'shrill whistles'. The article reported that some of the people on the stage had heard the noise and wondered if it was some 'manifestation of a spirit somewhere in the audience'. It turned out to be a noise caused by an elderly man as 'he hoisted an apparatus to aid his faulty hearing'.

The following evening Conan Doyle gave a lecture at Brooklyn's Academy of Music. In it he suggested that people were more likely to find happiness than sadness in the next world and that theologians of the past had been too hard on the human race.

He went on to remark that husbands and wives only met in the afterlife if they had been well suited in life. If they had not been they were destined to find a partner in the next life to whom they would be best suited[284].

The New York Times, whilst not as adversarial as many newspapers, was clearly not pro-Spiritualism. In its issue of April 10th it published an editorial entitled *Such a Man on such a Mission*. Its bias against Conan Doyle was sufficient to invite criticism. A man by the name of Edward Beck wrote to the newspaper to take it to task for its attitude.

'As far as we know,' he wrote, 'there are two theories possible regarding "spiritualistic" phenomena. One is that they are caused by beings called spirits, the other that they are caused by a force subject to our own wills. Neither theory has been substantiated hence either must be admitted as a possibility. Men of the calibre of Sir Arthur and others should not be held up as victims of brain deterioration because they accept the one that to us seems the wrong one. They may be right'[285].

On April 16th Conan Doyle visited an amateur medium by the name of Ticknor[286]. On that same day the Rev. F.W. Stacey of Middletown declared, in his Easter sermon, that he thought it was a pity that Conan Doyle was wasting his time on Spiritualism as he had told his audiences nothing that they could not have found out from the Bible[287].

Outside of the clergy there was another man who had little sympathy for Conan Doyle's mission. New York's mayor John Francis Hylan had no time for Spiritualism and made this very clear at a dinner to celebrate the tenth anniversary of the Broadway Association at the Hotel Astor on April 19th.

'You have no doubt been reading in the papers,' he said, 'that the creator of Sherlock Holmes, Sir Arthur Conan Doyle, is in a new line of business, and from all reports the shekels are

---

284 *The New York Times* of April 14th 1922.
285 *The New York Times* of April 15th 1922.
286 Pugh, Brian. *A Chronology of the Life of Sir Arthur Conan Doyle*. 3rd Edition. MX Publishing 2014.
287 *The New York Times* of April 17th 1922.

rolling in to him as fast as when he told how easy it was for the famous detective of fiction to get out of tight places'. Carrying on in the same vein he went on to say '...the lure of the unknown is always fascinating and there will always be a large audience to listen to airy nothings'.

New York Mayor John Hylan

His mocking earned him only 'scattering applause' according to *The New York Times* of the following day and he left the event soon after.

Following further appearances at Carnegie Hall, Conan Doyle left New York on the 22nd. His destination was Boston and a lecture at its Symphony Hall on the 24th. After this he made his way to Washington.

Towards the end of April he received a challenge from the American scientific community. The President of Bates College, Clifton D. Gray, stated that while Conan Doyle's lectures had box office value they would not stand up in the laboratory. 'When he can bring on a phial containing a bit of ectoplasm it will be time to listen to him'. Making clear that he believed this would not happen he added 'Let him write more Sherlock Holmes stories'[288].

If Conan Doyle heard of this challenge he ignored it. The beginning of May saw him back in New York and lecturing again at Carnegie Hall. In the lecture he gave on May 7th he made mention of a photographer called William Hope. Hope, who operated in Crewe, had claimed to be able to produce spirit photographs and Conan Doyle had subsequently endorsed his results. Many of Hope's images now formed part of Conan Doyle's New York lectures. *The New York Times* noted, in its issue of the following day, that one of the photographs was of W.T. Stead the famous writer and contemporary of Conan Doyle who had died on the *Titanic*.

Shortly after this lecture Conan Doyle and Jean found the time to visit Harry Houdini at his home[289]. Houdini would have taken great delight in showing Conan Doyle his library of psychic books which the latter had expressed a desire to see[290]. They would also have discussed Conan Doyle's lectures, one of which (at least) Houdini had allegedly attended covertly[291]. Even if he had not attended, Houdini would have read about them and saved the newspaper reports in his files. We can be fairly certain that Hope's photographs would have been discussed.

While Conan Doyle was confident of their authenticity, it seems clear, and hardly surprising, that Houdini was not. His friend, and psychic investigator, Harry Price had already conducted an investigation of Hope on behalf of the Society for Psychical Research. He made it clear that, in his opinion, the

---

288 *The New York Times* of April 29th 1922.

289 Pugh, Brian. *A Chronology of the Life of Sir Arthur Conan Doyle*. 3rd Edition. MX Publishing 2014.

290 Sandford, Christopher. *Houdini and Conan Doyle*. Duckworth Overlook 2011.

291 Ibid.

photographs were fake[292]. This only increased the gulf that was forming between the Society and Conan Doyle, who was growing increasingly unhappy at what he saw as its opposition to his position and beliefs. He wrote to Houdini later in the year stating 'I am sure now that there was trickery [by] the investigators'[293]. Conan Doyle was so certain of this that he later sought legal advice on the possibility of getting Harry Price evicted from rooms that he rented from the London Spiritualist Alliance. Price later wrote 'Arthur Conan Doyle and his friends abused me for many years for exposing Hope'[294] and Conan Doyle wrote to *The Evening Standard* (on August 9th) to lay out what he considered to be the flaws in Price's investigation[295].

Not long after their meeting, Houdini extended an invitation to Conan Doyle to attend the annual banquet of The Society of American Magicians at New York's McAlpin Hotel[296]. Naturally the event was covered by the press and, as usual, Conan Doyle stole the show.

Following an introduction to the assembled company by Houdini, Conan Doyle spoke of his fondness for conjurers. They were performing a valuable service by unmasking fake mediums – which he referred to as 'human hyenas'. The only problem he had with them was when they launched from attacking fake mediums into attacking Spiritualism as a whole. When a conjurer does so 'he deals in a subject which he does not understand'.

Conan Doyle then put away his soapbox and decided to turn the tables on the assembled magicians. He announced that he

---

292 Sandford, Christopher. *Houdini and Conan Doyle*. Duckworth Overlook 2011.
293 Ibid.
294 Ibid.
295 Gibson, John Michael and Green, Richard Lancelyn. *Letters to the Press*. Martin Secker & Warburg Ltd. 1975.
296 Pugh, Brian. *A Chronology of the Life of Sir Arthur Conan Doyle*. 3rd Edition. MX Publishing 2014.

had some film footage to show them. He stated that it was 'psychic' in nature but, aside from this, he gave no further introduction and made it clear he would take no questions afterwards. It is amusing to speculate as to how the magicians would have felt being in the dark. Houdini, as in the dark as his fellow magicians, would have undoubtedly appreciated the showmanship.

The film Conan Doyle showed was, in fact, early footage from a movie of his book *The Lost World* which was in production. What *The New York Times* later referred to as 'Prehistoric brutes' were shown fighting each other and the assembled company was stunned[297]. It certainly trumped all the magic tricks they had performed prior to Conan Doyle's speech.

Conan Doyle promptly wrote a letter to Houdini to explain events. 'The purpose was, simply, to provide a little mystification to those who have so often and so successfully mystified others.' He went on to state, 'The dinosaurs and other monsters have been constructed by pure cinema, but of the highest kind, and are being used for "The Lost World" picture which represents pre-historic life upon a South American plateau'.

Conan Doyle concluded his letter to Houdini with a cheeky request that he knew would not be agreed to, '…confidence begets confidence and I want to know how you got out of that trunk'[298].

The amusement Conan Doyle had enjoyed at the expense of the magicians subsequently backfired. One Herbert Dawley laid claim to the patents behind the dinosaur technology and said that it had been 'pirated' from him. This led to an alarmed statement from the film's producer, Catherine Curtis, that she had been assured that all appropriate rights had been secured.

---

[297] *The New York Times* of June 3rd 1922.

[298] *The New York Times* of June 4th 1922.

She requested immediate meetings with all concerned parties, including Conan Doyle[299].

The New York Times of June 7th reported a flurry of legal actions. Dawley made a claim for ten thousand dollars in damages for patent infringement against Conan Doyle. He followed this up with a separate action for ten times that amount against one Watterson Rothaker (who held the film rights to *The Lost World*) for producing the footage. The third action was initiated by Catherine Curtis, also against Rothaker, presumably on the grounds that she had invested on the understanding that all necessary rights had been secured.

The press caught up with Conan Doyle, who was now enjoying a period of rest in Atlantic City. He refused to comment[300]. For reasons that are not entirely clear Dawley did not pursue his legal actions[301].

Conan Doyle did not have time to dwell on matters legal. Instead he had an attack to respond to. The attack in question came from one P. Wilson who had written an article entitled *Elucidating Conan Doyle*[302]. In the article he attempted to explain Conan Doyle and his actions to date to the reader. Wilson's method for doing this was to provide a basic biography that spoke of Conan Doyle's artistic background and how it ran in his family. 'Doyle was not bred of stolid or unimaginative stock – far from it. His mind worked in mysteries....Conan Doyle's spiritualism, when you know his antecedents, thus ceases to be quite so surprising as it has often appeared'.

Wilson's article continued, running through the key moments in Conan Doyle's life – his schooling at Stonyhurst, study in Germany and finally to Edinburgh University. From

---

299 *The New York Times* of June 6th 1922.

300 *The New York Times* of June 6th 1922.

301 Nollen, Scott Allen. *Sir Arthur Conan Doyle at the Cinema.* McFarland & Co Inc. 2004.

302 A copy of Wilson's article found its way into *The New York Times* of June 18th.

there it moved onto the meeting between Conan Doyle and Joseph Bell and the eventual creation of Sherlock Holmes. Based on all of this Wilson delivered a conclusion. 'The truth is that Doyle has always been intellectually dependent. He visits the arctic regions and at once proclaims them the world's next health resort. He listens to a few speeches by Joseph Chamberlain and promptly stands for Parliament as a tariff reformer'.

Wilson was clearly painting Conan Doyle as a man easily swept up in the moment and inclined to abandon causes as quickly as he adopted them. Referring to spiritualism, Wilson continued, 'This is his mood today. But we have no guarantee that the mood will continue…if we accept his present gospel, we may find tomorrow that he has passed on his way to yet another equally infallible, though different, revelation'.

Across three pages, the article continued to both explain the triggers for Conan Doyle's actions and then criticise them. Conan Doyle's belief in spirit photography was mocked with the line 'To base one's belief in a future life on the lens of a Kodak is… a hazardous enterprise…'.

The article then moved onto attacking spiritualism in general and deployed points that were hardly original. Despite this absence of originality, Conan Doyle was clearly infuriated by the article in a way that he had not been by countless other attacks and wrote a response from his hotel on June 16th. In it he declined to respond to any of the personal attacks but did take Wilson to task for stating, amongst other things, that mediums he had recommended had been convicted of fraud – a suggestion he strongly denied. His letter was later published in *The New York Times* of June 22nd.

The day after writing his response to Wilson's attack, Conan Doyle and his family were joined by Harry and Bess Houdini and the two men resumed their conversations about all matters relating to Spiritualism - Conan Doyle eager to convince and Houdini sceptical but equally eager to believe.

The following day, June 18th, was, however, the beginning of the end of their friendship. Conan Doyle sought out Houdini and told him that Jean wanted to conduct a séance, through the medium of automatic writing, with the aim of making contact with Houdini's late mother. The sequence of events leading up to the séance varied in subsequent accounts with Conan Doyle later asserting that the séance was his idea rather than that of his wife and, later still, stating that the séance was conducted at Houdini's request and that Jean had been averse to the idea. Bearing in mind how sensitive Conan Doyle must have been following the attack on his character and beliefs by Wilson the notion that the séance was, in reality, Jean's idea, perhaps motivated by a desire to lift her husband's mood, seems plausible.

The séance was conducted in Conan Doyle's hotel suite without Bess present on the grounds that it could adversely affect the results[303]. Houdini, according to Conan Doyle's later account, gave little if anything away during the séance while Jean spoke to his dead mother and wrote page after page of responses down. At the conclusion Houdini left the room, according to Conan Doyle, without comment.

Later, back in New York, the two men met again and Conan Doyle came away with the impression that Houdini's scepticism had been swayed by the séance. In reality he could not have been further from the truth. Regardless of the impression he gave in public Houdini was far from convinced. One of the principal reasons for this was the fact that his mother had communicated with him in English – a language she had never spoken. It was probably only because of his belief in the sincerity of Conan Doyle and Jean that he had not reacted angrily or made public the reasons for his continued scepticism.

Conan Doyle in the meantime was preparing to leave the United States aboard the *Adriatic* and his interactions with the press had, on occasion at least, drifted away from Spiritualism

---

303 Sandford, Christopher. *Houdini and Conan Doyle*. Duckworth Overlook 2011.

onto more earthly matters. For example, in the days since the séance he had praised the sport of baseball and professed the belief that it could become established in England if publicised properly[304]. He also held out hope of further adventures for Sherlock Holmes saying 'I may write of Sherlock Holmes again but only if some very strong idea takes hold of me'[305].

One final event commanded Conan Doyle's attention before he left the United States. He and his entire family were invited by the Houdinis to be among the guests at their twenty-eighth wedding anniversary party at New York's Carroll Theatre[306]. Houdini's motivation for this has to be wondered at. The consummate showman had been repeatedly upstaged by Conan Doyle in terms of publicity and to Houdini that must have hurt. Added to this had been the events of the recent séance but, for reasons best known to himself, he was not admitting his true feelings about that event to anyone.

On June 23rd Conan Doyle and his family headed back to England on board the *Adriatic*[307]. They arrived back in England in early July and from that point until September the family appears to have enjoyed a relatively low profile. There can be little doubt that some of this time was used by Conan Doyle to complete his written account of his American tour and gather together and write up his material relating to Cottingley.

---

304 *The New York Times* of June 19th 1922.

305 *The New York Times* of June 23rd 1922.

306 Sandford, Christopher. *Houdini and Conan Doyle*. Duckworth Overlook 2011.

307 Pugh, Brian. *A Chronology of the Life of Sir Arthur Conan Doyle*. 3rd Edition. MX Publishing 2014.

THE PUBLIC RIFT OPENS

On September 1st *The Coming of the Fairies* was published by Hodder and Stoughton. Within it Conan Doyle presented what was, essentially, a fairy dossier. The background to the whole affair, material provided to *The Strand*, the letters between Gardner and himself and reactions to the story in the press were all joined together with a commentary.

The *Daily Express*, in its issue that day, adopted its usual irreverent tone in its response to the publication. 'There can now be no doubt about fairies. Sir Arthur Conan Doyle has written a new book about them, he prints their photographs. Some have hair done in the Parisian manner. One is "bobbed"'.

The mocking continued. 'Yet this is nothing. Sir Arthur Conan Doyle publicises reports from "Mr. Sergeant," a former officer of the Tank Corps, who went to Cottingley, in Yorkshire, where the fairies were seen by "Frances" and "Elsie" in 1920. "Mr. Sergeant" saw the fairies himself. That settles it.' The use of quotes around the names was bizarre as it suggested that the names were pseudonyms when, by this time, the names of the girls, at least, were widely known.

Later in the article Conan Doyle was quoted saying that Mr. Sergeant had long had the gift of clairvoyance. To this the newspaper had scoffed 'If a clairvoyant who has been in the Tank Corps cannot see real fairies, who can?'

Two days later Conan Doyle's account of his travels in America began serialisation in *Lloyd's Sunday News* over a period of several months[308].

Ever since he had publically declared himself to be a Spiritualist, and had commenced lecturing, Conan Doyle had come in for criticism and outright attack. The two main sources of these attacks had been the scientific community and the religious community (branches of Christianity in the main). With the latter Conan Doyle had always gone to great lengths to suggest that Spiritualism was not an opponent to religion but a companion or even support. October 15th 1922 saw a slight change in this.

The evening of that day saw Conan Doyle at a meeting of the Marylebone Spiritualist Association held in the Aeolian Hall in New Bond Street, London. His speech made clear not so much an opposition to Christianity but his increasing frustration with the attacks that emanated from it. He asserted that the reason Christianity had spread throughout the world two thousand years previously was because it had been accompanied 'by a perfect whirlwind of spirit-power'. This power, he went on to assert, had been lost by the Church since then and it had lost its impetus as a result.

'The Churches must come to us for the spirit-power they have lost. We do not want an amalgamation. We are far bigger than they. We have the knowledge which will illuminate all the Churches of the world. Every Church wants to know where its dead go and what becomes of them. We know with certainty. If the Churches will come to us humbly we will help them'[309].

The cooperative Conan Doyle offering help to the Church appeared to have been replaced by a Conan Doyle that was demanding that the Church come and ask him nicely or remain stagnant.

---

308 Pugh, Brian. *A Chronology of the Life of Sir Arthur Conan Doyle.* 3rd Edition. MX Publishing 2014.

309 The *Daily Express* of October 16th 1922.

October witnessed the private differences of opinion between Conan Doyle and Houdini really launch into the open[310]. It is hard to determine the exact trigger for this event. The two men were well aware of each other's position and respected it. It is hard to blame the séance in Atlantic City for this turn of events. It was no doubt distressing for Houdini and even more so when he determined it to be fake, but the séance had been some four months previously.

The particular battle ground seems strange. Conan Doyle had been quoted, whilst in America, on the subject of radio and how it could be a means by which spirits could communicate with the living. It had been reported more than once and Houdini would have been aware of it for some time, as he was in the habit of collecting and filing as many reports on spiritualist matters as he could.

But he now used this subject in an article entitled *Ghosts that Talk-By Radio*. In the article he was quick to declare his respect for Conan Doyle but, at the same time, he declared that if he were to hear spirit voices over the radio he would prefer to do so in a laboratory. He concluded by stating 'If there are mediums who are not fraudulent, I have yet to see them'[311]. This was a fairly public statement to the effect that he believed the séance conducted by Jean in Conan Doyle's presence was fake. Just in case this was not clear, he followed it up in another article that same month by declaring that over the course of twenty-five years and hundreds of séances he had 'never seen or heard anything that could convince me that there is a possibility of communication with the loved ones who have gone beyond'[312].

---

310 Sandford, Christopher. *Houdini and Conan Doyle.* Duckworth Overlook 2011.
311 Ibid.
312 Ibid.

Houdini had also written about his doubts as to the existence of ectoplasm, the substance that mediums often produced at séances. Needless to say, Conan Doyle was convinced of its existence and saw it as physical evidence of the connection between the real world and the spirit world. As recently as October 1st an article about his belief (or reaffirmation of his belief) had appeared in *The New York Times*.

Under these circumstances it is hard to imagine that Houdini would not have realised how his articles would be interpreted by Conan Doyle. He just had to sit back and wait for the response.

In the meantime it is highly likely that he would have read *The New York Times*' review of Conan Doyle's book *The Coming of the Fairies* which appeared in its October 22nd issue. The vast majority of the article was a summary of the book's main points. The opinions upon it were largely confined to the last two paragraphs. The writer of the review declared himself to be unsure as to whether he believed in fairies or not but the review would suggest that he was leaning towards the negative. 'Are there fairies or not?. If the reader is under ten years of age he or she is apt to need small proof, but those people who have reached wiser years must settle the problem to their own satisfaction in their own way'.

Having said this, the reviewer made plain that Conan Doyle wrote in such a pleasant way as to render the book an enjoyable read even for those who were not believers. His main regret was that Conan Doyle had not taken a more direct hand in events rather than leaving most of the legwork to Gardner.

As October drew to a close Conan Doyle's opinion was sought by *The Daily Mirror*. It was upon a subject that was close to his heart (or it had been at one time) that was not concerned with either the spirit-world or that of literature.

The arena in this instance was that of boxing. The Bishop of Willesden – William Willcox Perrin – had declared that it was 'appalling that a disgusting fight between two men should be recognised'. Perrin had later revised this statement to make clear that his objection was primarily to the large professional fights that had knock-out blows where men were punched to the point where they could no longer stand.

Conan Doyle's fondness for the sport was well known and this no doubt prompted the *Mirror* to contact him for his opinion. He responded by telegram to declare that it was a national sport and that if it were banned it would simply go underground where conditions would be a lot worse. In Conan Doyle's opinion Perrin's objections would be eliminated if referees did their jobs properly and stepped in to stop fights before they reached the stage to which the Bishop alluded[313].

Conan Doyle undertook a series of Spiritualist engagements during November. Some were lectures and some were simply speeches at non-Spiritualist events[314]. One of the presumably more tense engagements took place on November 14th when he attended a meeting of the Society for Psychical Research in London[315]. Given the SPR's involvement in the investigation into the spirit photographs of William Hope, and its conclusions of fraud which Conan Doyle rejected, the event could not have been a pleasant one.

Not long after this Conan Doyle learned of Houdini's latest comments on matters spiritualist and his assessment of the mediums he had met to date. Unsurprisingly Conan Doyle took exception to the suggestion that his wife had not conducted a true séance. In a letter dated November 19th he made clear that he was upset and, in effect, challenged Houdini to explain the fact that he had not raised any objections to his face at the time. Houdini's response was to say that he had been too overcome at the time and had only reached his conclusions later based on the fact that his mother could not communicate in English[316].

---

313 *The Daily Mirror* of October 26th 1922.

314 Pugh, Brian. *A Chronology of the Life of Sir Arthur Conan Doyle.* 3rd Edition. MX Publishing 2014.

315 Ibid.

316 Sandford, Christopher. *Houdini and Conan Doyle.* Duckworth Overlook 2011.

Conan Doyle was often mocked for taking things on trust. It is hard to imagine him taking Houdini's explanation in the same fashion on this occasion. He was a man of honour, even in the eyes of his opponents, and it is fair to assume that he would have expected Houdini to bring any complaints to him directly rather than splash them around in the press. The fact that this had been done after he had left the United States – effectively when his back was turned – must have left a bad taste in his mouth. In Conan Doyle's eyes at least, their relationship had moved from a respectful difference of opinion to one of distrust. It seems that Houdini was genuinely blind to the level of offence he had given to the man he claimed to respect.

In November an event occurred which did nothing to improve relations between the two men. The US journal *Scientific American* offered two thousand five hundred dollars to the first medium to produce a visible manifestation to the satisfaction of a panel of five judges[317].

Conan Doyle had no objection to the investigation as he held the journal in high esteem but he did object to the prize money. His opinion found its way into the November 25th edition of *The New York Times* under the heading of *Doyle offers help in psychic inquiry.*

'Of course it is very satisfactory to see a journal of the standing of The Scientific American taking an interest in psychic matters. Most newspapers can give pages to sport but refuse to publish a word about the most important phenomena...'.

On the subject of the prize money, Conan Doyle was unambiguous. 'I don't understand the necessity or wisdom of publically offering prizes for conclusive psychic manifestations

---

317 Sandford, Christopher. *Houdini and Conan Doyle.* Duckworth Overlook 2011.

or psychic photographs. That is a direct invitation to the rogues of two continents.'

Aside from his fear that a cash incentive would bring all the worst people out of the woodwork, Conan Doyle also failed to see the need when, in his opinion, there was already substantial 'indubitable' evidence.

Houdini's position as the star of the anti-Spiritualist movement was briefly challenged at the beginning of December when the spotlight moved to a Catholic priest named Father Charles M. de Heredia[318].

In a meeting of New York's Catholic Club on December 3rd Heredia claimed that there were genuine mediums but that they readily admitted their inability to control their powers. He also admitted his belief in psychical phenomena but stated that it was not currently possible to identify whether such things were caused by devils or spirits.

That said he launched into a mock séance. 'Everything that I am going to show you now is lies, all lies'. According to *The New York Times* he kept his audience laughing with his mockery of pro-Spiritualist figures such as Oliver Lodge and Conan Doyle. He pretended to get in touch with Lodge's dead son Raymond and got him to communicate by knocks 'that hell was a nice place and there was plenty of whisky there'. This was a clear poke at Conan Doyle's assertion that many of life's pleasures existed in the spirit world.

He followed this by deploying conjuring tricks to levitate tables, and also performed some automatic writing. He refused to explain any of his tricks but repeated that it was 'lies, all lies'.

On December 10th *The New York Times* carried details of another letter from Conan Doyle to the editor of the *Scientific American.* The preamble to the letter noted that the prize on offer was five thousand dollars. Whether this apparent increase was due to a prior lack of interest or a mistake was not clear.

---

[318] This is how Heredia's name was written in *The New York Times* of December 4th 1922. Occasionally it was written as Carlos.

From Conan Doyle's opening it would appear that his previous letter had been interpreted as some kind of challenge to the journal and he was keen to correct this. 'I had no idea of issuing a challenge to you. My complaint was that so many of our bitter critics, such as this Mr. Black, are quite ignorant of the subject which they treat. I am, however, delighted that you should take it up, and would do my best to assist you'.

He went on to repeat his fears about the existence of a cash prize and suggested that the money would be better spent sending a representative of the journal around the world to visit mediums and gain experience. He also stated that any investigators needed to be open-minded and he recommended a series of books that he felt any would-be investigator should read in advance of any investigation.

On the same day as his letter appeared in *The New York Times* Conan Doyle and his family sat down to a séance at Windlesham. This was, by now, a fairly regular occurrence but this séance was to be special. A spirit by the name of Pheneas took possession of Jean[319].

Pheneas was to be a regular presence from this point onwards and became, effectively, a member of the family. One of his first pronouncements was that the family should return to America in 1923. This was hardly a stunning revelation however, as Conan Doyle had already announced his intention to return in a wire to *The New York Times* almost a month earlier[320]. Pheneas' comments ranged in subject from the domestic to international but were always taken very seriously

---

319 Pugh, Brian. *A Chronology of the Life of Sir Arthur Conan Doyle.* 3rd Edition. MX Publishing 2014.

320 The occasion for this wire had been his initial reaction to the *Scientific American* plan to offer a prize for the first confirmed manifestation. (*The New York Times* of November 25th 1922).

by Conan Doyle. His belief in Pheneas was such that a book would ultimately be published.

The last few weeks of the year were uneventful. *The Case for Spirit Photography* was published on the 14th[321] and, on the 29th, an amusing article appeared in the *Daily Express* in which a young girl called Margery claimed to have seen fairies in Alton, Hampshire. The newspaper did not pass comment but took the opportunity to remind its readers of Conan Doyle's claims two years previously.

---

[321] Pugh, Brian. *A Chronology of the Life of Sir Arthur Conan Doyle.* 3rd Edition. MX Publishing 2014.

1923

THE NEW PAGET?

January opened with, as might be expected, more matters Spiritualist. There was a lecture to the London Spiritualist Alliance on Psychic Photography, a lecture in Luton and the Annual General Meeting of the Society for Psychical Research.

In the middle of the month Conan Doyle denounced as a slander a book that purported to be about the afterlife of Lord Kitchener. Billed by the *Daily Express* as a 'spiritualist book' it must have pained Conan Doyle to read excerpts and come to the conclusion that this was one more thing likely to damage the cause rather than assist it[322].

The cause of Spiritualism came in for further mockery on January 16th. A Mr. Gustav Adolf Hummeltenburg had recently died leaving the sum of three thousand pounds to the London Spiritualist Alliance for the purpose of founding a college for the training of mediums.

The executors of his estate had asked the courts to legally declare whether or not the bequest was 'a good charitable gift' - which was their personal view. Representatives of the Great Ormond Street Children's Hospital were present (along with representatives from other charities) to argue against the gift. The reason for this was that the hospital was to be one of the beneficiaries of the residue of the estate and if the bequest to the Alliance was annulled it would mean more money would come to them and the other charities.

---

[322] The *Daily Express* of January 13th 1923.

A Mr. Vaisey, who spoke for the hospital, argued that it was as impossible to train mediums to communicate with spirits as it would be to train an athlete to jump over St Paul's Cathedral. He went on to say 'The onus is admittedly on Sir Arthur Conan Doyle and those with him to show that spirits can be communicated with and they have not done it'.[323]

The judge, Mr Justice Russell, was clearly not pro-spiritualist stating sarcastically, 'I can understand a man being trained for all terrestrial occupations, but I would also like to see a curriculum for the training of spiritualistic mediums'.

According to *The Daily Mirror* of January 17th, an affidavit from Conan Doyle was read out to support the Alliance's claim to the bequest but it appeared to make little impression on the judge. He made it clear that legal decisions to date had largely declared that mediums were 'rogues and vagabonds'. He therefore struggled with the idea that the bequest could be seen as charitable. In an attempt to underscore his point he asked the counsel for the executors 'What about a trust for people with red hair?' to which counsel responded 'It would be a good charity'. No allusion was made in the report to Conan Doyle's Sherlock Holmes story *The Adventure of the Red-Headed League* so it is not clear whether the judge's remark was deliberate or coincidental (although the former seems likely). Despite the Judge's clear leanings the case was adjourned.

The month closed with the news, in *The Daily Mirror* of the 26th, that Conan Doyle's play *Fires of Fate* was to be filmed. The newspaper reported that casting had taken place and the cast and crew were to head for Cairo shortly. The estimated cost of the production was stated to be thirty thousand pounds.

Towards the end of February Conan Doyle was due in Torquay to lecture on *The New Revelation.* Shortly after he arrived there he learnt of a suspected poltergeist case in Gorefield near Wisbech in the Cambridgeshire fens. He wrote a letter to the affected family which they received on the 21st. *The*

---

323 The *Daily Express* of January 18th 1923.

Daily Mirror, which was already following the story, reprinted his letter in its issue of the 22nd.

The poltergeist activity centred around the young daughter of a farmer named Joseph Scrimshaw. The spirit's main activities concerned the movement and damage of furniture.

Conan Doyle's letter was decidedly strange. After the initial expressions of sympathy, his advice was '…send your daughter for a rest and change. Then open all your windows. Ventilate well and you will find the phenomena, after a day or two, will cease altogether'. The advice seemed to be much the same as it would be for a bad smell.

On the same date as the letter was received, the press maintained a night-time presence at the Scrimshaw farm. According to the *Mirror* the ghost decided to take a night off as nothing happened. The gathered members of the press were not content with this and managed to persuade Scrimshaw to admit a party of local spiritualists to conduct a séance on the 23rd.

This was an altogether more productive event according to the reports. One of the spiritualists, Henry Simpson, detected the presence of several spirits. Another member of the party, Hugh Lacey, determined that one of the spirits – a clean shaven man with black hair – used to ride a coal black mare when alive. The *Mirror's* reporter, presumably with his tongue in his cheek, asked Scrimshaw whether this could be Dick Turpin and Scrimshaw agreed that it could be. This was seized on and the newspaper's title for the article in its issue of the 24th became *Dick Turpin as a Furniture Mover*.

The Society for Psychical Research sent a representative – named Dingwall – and he went from room to room in the farm accompanied by the reporter. He declared it likely that the farmer's daughter was a medium but that his full report would be made only to the Society and 'may not be published for fifty years'. When pressed on Conan Doyle's opinion he only stated 'I have not considered Sir Arthur Conan Doyle's letter'. His lack of consideration for Conan Doyle's opinion may well have had its roots in the fact that Conan Doyle had publicly criticised

Dingwall's professionalism in 1922 for, what Conan Doyle saw as his misguided endorsement of Harry Price's investigation into the Hope spirit photographs[324].

In March *The Adventure of the Creeping Man* was published in *The Strand*. It featured the Holmes debut of artist Howard K. Elcock[325]. Howard Keppie Elcock had been born in Glasgow in 1887 and was thirty-six at the time of publication. During his career he illustrated *Pearson's Magazine*, *Collier's* and *The Royal Magazine*. Like many other artists of the time he had produced drawings to illustrate stories and articles about the war but he was clearly prepared to turn his hand to anything, making drawings to illustrate the activities of spiritualists such as Daniel Dunglas Home and tourism posters for various train companies such as London Transport and the London and North Eastern Railway.

It is not clear what brought him to the attention of *The Strand* as a potential illustrator but he would illustrate more Sherlock Holmes stories than anyone since Sidney Paget. His ultimate story count was seven which, although it paled next to Paget's total, was more than his nearest rival Frank Wiles who would illustrate four and A. Gilbert who illustrated three[326]. Elcock was effectively *the* Sherlock Holmes artist from 1923 to the end of 1926.

Hot on the story's heels was the publication, in book form, of *Our American Adventure,* Conan Doyle's account of his visit to America the previous year[327]. The timing meant that people who had not had a chance to read any form of serialisation of

---

324 Gibson, John Michael and Green, Richard Lancelyn. *Letters to the Press*. Martin Secker & Warburg Ltd. 1975.

325 Whitt, J.F. *The Strand Magazine 1891-1950 A Selective Checklist.* 1979.

326 Frank Wiles probably produced more actual illustrations thanks to being the artist for the serialised *The Valley of Fear*.

327 Pugh, Brian. *A Chronology of the Life of Sir Arthur Conan Doyle.* 3rd Edition. MX Publishing 2014.

his trip would now be able to learn about it just as he was about to embark on his next visit.

Conan Doyle and his family caught the train from Waterloo to Southampton on March 28th to connect with their ship *Olympic*. At Waterloo they were photographed by *The Daily Mirror* for inclusion in their issue of the 29th.

The Conan Doyle family arrived in New York on April 3rd. Two days later came the news that Lord Carnarvon, the fifth Earl, had died in Cairo. He had become famous as the sponsor of Howard Carter's excavation of the tomb of Tutankhamun. His death triggered rumours of a curse on the Pharaoh's tomb. These appeared to originate with a lady by the name of Marie Corelli who had claimed that 'the most dire punishment follows any rash intruder into a sealed tomb'. This she had apparently gleaned from a rare book in her possession.

The New York Times, faced with this supernatural story, took the opportunity to put the idea to Conan Doyle for publication in their issue of April 6th. He, in their words, 'was inclined to support' the idea - at least to an extent. 'One does not know what elementals existed in those days, nor what their form might be'. He went on to highlight a couple of examples including a mummy in the British Museum which had caused trouble for everyone who had come into contact with it.

Conan Doyle spent the next ten days largely in New York. Aside from the lectures he was scheduled to present he also learned that he had the latest round of a legal battle to contend with. *The New York Times* of the 11th reported that an application had been made to the State Supreme Court, the previous day, to take Conan Doyle's testimony in a suit brought by William Gillette. Gillette, backed up by the brother of Charles Frohman, had objected to the films starring Eille Norwood that had been produced by Stoll films[328]. The claim being made was that the dramatic rights to Sherlock Holmes had been given to Gillette and Charles Frohman and it was

---

[328] Zecher, Henry. *William Gillette: America's Sherlock Holmes*. Xlibris 2011.

these rights that had led to Gillette's Sherlock Holmes play in 1899 and the film version in 1916. The first attempt to block distribution on these grounds had been made the previous year. It was reported that the defendants (presumably Stoll Films) had stated that Gillette had never obtained film rights and '...his dramatic rights are limited to The Sign of Four'.

Mention of *The Sign of Four* was apt as it was the next and last Stoll film to be released. The cinema correspondent of the *Daily Express* was clearly impressed with the film. In the edition of the newspaper published on May 2nd he praised Eille Norwood's Holmes as more 'rugged' than the version of the detective depicted by John Barrymore. Displaying more than a touch of jingoism the correspondent observed 'This British triumph of polished technique and skilful mystification makes the average American film-thriller look like a factory throw-out'.

On May 7th the paths of Conan Doyle and Houdini crossed again when both found themselves staying at the Brown Palace Hotel in Denver[329]. Their ongoing duel had not let up and was becoming increasingly bizarre, with them exchanging very public blows through the press while retaining relatively cordial relations in their private correspondence. It was a situation that Conan Doyle recognised could not possibly last.

The two men spent time together when their schedules permitted it and they revisited the issue of the séance with Houdini's mother, with Conan Doyle endeavouring to clear up points that Houdini had taken issue with – the most notable being the English communications from his mother[330]. He was clearly wasting his time – Houdini's position was as unshakeable as his own.

Conan Doyle spent the rest of May moving swiftly from place to place. From Denver he went to Salt Lake City and from

---

[329] Pugh, Brian. *A Chronology of the Life of Sir Arthur Conan Doyle*. 3rd Edition. MX Publishing 2014.

[330] Sandford, Christopher. *Houdini and Conan Doyle*. Duckworth Overlook 2011.

there to Los Angeles. During this period he took time out to visit some cinema studios and talk with the actors Douglas Fairbanks and Mary Pickford. It was during this same month that *The Daily Mirror* informed its readers that Conan Doyle was on the point of publishing his memoirs. It was notable that the writer of the short article expressed the hope of reading about Conan Doyle's school years, medical career and early storytelling but expressed no interest in Spiritualism[331].

The end of May brought Conan Doyle to San Francisco where he was due to give a lecture on June 2nd[332]. Before this could take place newspapers in both the United States and Britain were carrying reports of his declaration that he had received a message from the spirit of Lord Northcliffe, the late owner of both *The Daily Mail* and *The Daily Mirror* who had died in August of 1922. The spirit message stated that the world was heading towards a 'catastrophe' that would make the recent war appear 'insignificant' unless there was a 'wave of spiritual reform'[333].

It is not too clear when or where this message was received although Conan Doyle did attend a séance with one Mrs Inez Wagner on May 24th while in Los Angeles[334]. The newspaper reports declared that Conan Doyle had been told that the aforementioned catastrophe would occur in his lifetime.

He spent the following few days touring various towns and cities in the western United States. His last stop was Seattle on June 12th before he then sailed to Canada[335]. Even during this part of his tour he continued his private and public exchanges with Houdini.

---

331 *The Daily Mirror* May 12th 1923.

332 Pugh, Brian. *A Chronology of the Life of Sir Arthur Conan Doyle.* 3rd Edition. MX Publishing 2014.

333 The *Daily Express* of June 1st 1923.

334 Pugh, Op. cit.

335 Pugh, Op. cit.

He remained in Canada until around July 4th. Not long afterwards he was reported as staying in the vicinity of Loon Lake in California where he later gave a lecture[336].

On July 24th the *Daily Express* published a short article entitled *The Detective in Fiction* in which it was observed that regardless of the state of the economy the detective story would always find a market. Sherlock Holmes was credited as triggering the rise in the genre's popularity although Poe's Dupin was justly credited as the first of the breed. The article's author reminded his readers that Conan Doyle had been accused by 'American critics' of plagiarism when Holmes had become popular.

After stating that this was unfounded, due to Holmes being clearly based on Joseph Bell rather than Poe's Dupin, the journalist suggested that Bell (in reality) and Poe (in fiction) may have both built their systems of deduction on a work written by Voltaire entitled *Zadig* or *Destiny* in which a man named Zadig determined the appearance and movement of a missing horse and dog by means of examining their tracks.

By the time this idea emerged Conan Doyle and his family were preparing for their return to England. They departed the United States aboard the *Adriatic* on August 4th[337].

---

[336] Pugh, Brian. *A Chronology of the Life of Sir Arthur Conan Doyle.* 3rd Edition. MX Publishing 2014.

[337] Ibid.

A MAN DECEIVED?

Conan Doyle and his family arrived back in England on August 13th[338]. They appeared to spend the remainder of the month in a fashion that ensured they remained out of the press. In September it was Jean who ended the family's press holiday and made it to the pages of *The Daily Mirror*.

At some point during her travels with her husband she had come to the conclusion, presumably based on experience during those travels, that men were better domestic servants than women. The article stated that, following her return from America, all the servant positions at Windlesham had been taken by men. The implication of the article was that between mid-August and mid-September (when the article was published) she had given notice to all the female staff at Windlesham and had replaced them with men. This undertaking went some way to explaining the family's relatively low profile since their return.

In the article, entitled *Men as "Maids"*, Jean was quoted as saying 'The experiment is a decided success. I have proved that men are far more efficient than girls and far more conscientious. Of course, men need training, and the women who employ them must exercise patience while teaching them. They are very quick to learn, however. I think men should be given a chance in the training schools instead of many of the

[338] Pugh, Brian. *A Chronology of the Life of Sir Arthur Conan Doyle.* 3rd Edition. MX Publishing 2014.

flighty girls who go there'. She concluded by advising other women to follow her example[339]. It is tempting to wonder whether the decision to remove female servants from the house was really to do with efficiency or whether it was more to do with removing perceived competition.

Back in the United States, the prize money for the first successful medium to satisfy the committee of the *Scientific American* was still available and a contender came forward who was considered worthy enough to report in the British press.

The Rev. Josie Stewart had been encountered by Conan Doyle during his American tour and was described, by the *Daily Express*, as 'the spiritualist pastor of the First Independent Church at Cleveland.' She had impressed Conan Doyle to such an extent that he had personally brought her to the attention of the magazine as a candidate. Given his opposition to the idea of a prize this was rather surprising.

Stewart had apparently impressed the judges on October 16th with a display of automatic writing at an open air séance. It was, however, pointed out that no less than three earlier tests at the offices of the magazine had failed before Stewart had suggested the open air event.

The *Express'* correspondent described how, at the open air séance, Stewart had been given some blank cards on which there later appeared spirit writing. The *Scientific American* issued a statement following this event 'Mrs Stewart made out a prima facie case. We were sufficiently impressed to proceed further. We have not caught the medium in any blatant fraud and the writings produced were apparently on our own cards'[340]. It later transpired that Stewart had been pre-preparing cards[341].

Back in Britain, Conan Doyle found himself in a potentially embarrassing situation. In March of 1919 he had attended a

---

339 *The Daily Mirror* of September 11th 1923.

340 The *Daily Express* of October 18th 1923.

341 Sandford, Christopher. *Houdini and Conan Doyle.* Duckworth Overlook 2011.

séance at the home of P.T. Selbit. At the time, this séance's location had been kept secret from the public and the medium had been referred to in the press as 'The Medium in the Mask'[342]. Conan Doyle had not declared whether or not he had been convinced by the medium but had gone so far as to say that the séance itself was 'very clever'.

Selbit had decided to repeat the event, using the very same medium, and invited Conan Doyle, Jean, the editor of *Light* and a few others to a house in Long Acre, near Covent Garden. The date for the séance was November 7th.

During the course of the séance a luminous cloud was seen to issue from the medium's side and float around the room. This was followed by other displays of the medium's power which included the identification of items sealed into a box before she had entered the room.

Following all of this, the medium called for the lights to be turned on and Selbit then announced that the entire séance was a fake, that this had also been the case in 1919 and that Conan Doyle had clearly been deceived on both occasions.

Conan Doyle, in response, stated, correctly, that he had not pronounced the medium to be genuine in 1919 and refused to be labelled as a man deceived. Clearly angry, he then turned to Jean and said 'it's time we went' following which they did exactly that. Given his history with the *Daily Express* on matters relating to Spiritualism (and the 1919 séance in particular) he cannot have been too surprised when the event's agenda was revealed[343].

The rest of the year passed relatively uneventfully, the only item of note being that Conan Doyle's Sherlock Holmes play *The Crown Diamond* was performed again at London's Coliseum. However, it is also possible that Conan Doyle was preparing his next Holmes adventure for the public, as it was to be published at the beginning of 1924.

---

342 See the earlier chapter CHALLENGE AND COUNTER CHALLENGE in the year 1919.

343 The *Daily Express* of November 8th 1923.

1924

VAMPIRES, CLIENTS AND GARRIDEBS

The January issue of *The Strand* contained *The Adventure of the Sussex Vampire*[344]. It had been almost a year since the publication of the last Holmes story but, despite the long gap, Howard Elcock retained his position as illustrator. Despite his atmospheric illustrations, the story was rather poor and clearly indicated Conan Doyle's production line attitude towards the Holmes stories. However, it was destined to become famous for a statement from Holmes on the subject of the supernatural - 'The world is big enough for us. No ghosts need apply'.

Given Conan Doyle's ambivalent and, occasionally, resentful attitude to Holmes, attributing this statement to him very much satisfied Conan Doyle's agenda. It suited him to portray his great detective as a sceptic – one of the very people with whom he found himself in perpetual conflict.

His literary output continued in February with the publication of his account of his latest trip to the United States – *Our Second American Adventure*. He also paid tribute to his father Charles by mounting an exhibition of his works at the Brooke Galleries in London.

344 Pugh, Brian. *A Chronology of the Life of Sir Arthur Conan Doyle*. 3rd Edition. MX Publishing 2014.

March and April were quiet months during which one of Conan Doyle's most notable activities was to attend the Amateur Tennis Championship at Queens on April 24th[345].

On the very same day as Conan Doyle was enjoying the tennis an interesting article appeared in the pages of *The Daily Mirror*. In the section *Today's Gossip* the correspondent, known as 'The Rambler', observed that work was being carried out on Conan Doyle's old home Undershaw in Surrey. The house was being 'greatly enlarged' and it was noted that it was 'now a private hotel'. No information was given as to when the work was expected to be complete.

On May 20th Conan Doyle's adversary the *Daily Express* noted that Conan Doyle was to deliver a radio broadcast that night on 'Psychic Developments'. Two days later *The Daily Mirror* informed its readers of Conan Doyle's sixty-fifth birthday. In the very short biography it dwelt on his brief medical career before reminding people (as if it was necessary) that he had gone on to write the Sherlock Holmes stories. There was no mention of his Spiritualism related activities.

June saw the death of Conan Doyle's sister Constance, the widow of Willie Hornung. This event, in addition to being sad, effectively also brought to an end any meaningful connection between the Doyles and the Hornungs as Constance was the last link.

July and August were quiet months but September saw Conan Doyle's name linked again to Tutankhamun and Egyptian curses. The *Daily Express* of September 13th carried the news of the suicide of Egyptologist H.G. Evelyn-White. Evelyn-White was in Egypt at the time of the tomb's discovery but had no other connection with it. Despite this, he had convinced himself that he was a victim of a curse connected with manuscripts in his possession. The newspaper simply could not resist dragging Conan Doyle's earlier talk of elementals into the article, despite the fact that this death had no

---

[345] Pugh, Brian. *A Chronology of the Life of Sir Arthur Conan Doyle*. 3rd Edition. MX Publishing 2014.

connection with the famous pharaoh, and the Egyptologist had not believed himself to be affected by any curse connected to the tomb.

Very shortly after this, Conan Doyle wrote to the newspaper[346]. His subject matter was not Egypt but the famous ship the *Mary Celeste* (which he referred to as the *Marie Celeste*) which had been found mysteriously abandoned some fifty years earlier.

A man by the name of Captain Lucy had come forward with a story that he had supposedly learned from a man by the name of Triggs. Triggs had claimed that the *Marie Celeste*, on which he was serving as boatswain (the crewman in charge of rigging, anchors etc.), had come upon a derelict ship (name unknown) during its voyage. Members of the crew had boarded it to discover that it contained a substantial amount of money. The decision had been taken to appropriate the money and this was later distributed between the captain and senior crew only. The entire crew of the *Marie Celeste* then transferred to the derelict vessel and sailed on, thus leaving the *Marie Celeste* to be discovered some days later[347].

Conan Doyle considered the story an 'extreme improbability'. In his opinion it simply moved the mystery 'from one ship to another'. He also questioned the likelihood of the crew of the ship, who had not shared in the money, staying quiet for fifty years and never telling 'a story which everyone wished to know, and which involved no criminal confession on their part'. He also questioned why a 'decent captain' would ruin his career by such an act and thus effectively consent to going into permanent hiding.

Three days later Conan Doyle's autobiography *Memories and Adventures* was published by Hodder and Stoughton. The *Daily Express* of that day (September 18th) was very

---

[346] The *Daily Express* of September 15th 1924.

[347] Unsurprisingly the story was reported worldwide. The source in this instance is the Australian newspaper the *Western Argus* of September 30th 1924.

complimentary, stating that Conan Doyle's 'remarkable career' could hardly be matched for its 'variety and romance'. The reviewer, with astounding understatement, remarked 'We judge from this book that at the present period in his life the thing that gives him most pleasure is the study of the occult, and it is with pride that he says that he has already travelled more than 50,000 miles and has addressed 300,000 people on this subject'.

Then, with equally stunning foresight, the reviewer stated 'Whatever he may himself think, we can assure him that he will go down to posterity as the inventor of "Sherlock Holmes", which presents that particular facet of his mind which appeals to the popular imagination all round'.

The *Express* had not lost its interest in approaching Conan Doyle concerning the next world but he was finally demonstrating a measure of caution. The newspaper approached him seeking his opinion on a range of messages purporting to be from the late explorer Sir Ernest Shackleton. In the column *The Talk of London* which appeared in the September 30th issue it was reported that Conan Doyle had written back on the subject to state that he had received several communications that had also purported to be from Shackleton but that none of them were 'evidential'.

Continuing on the theme of messages from beyond, the *Express*, in its issue of October 4th, carried an article on life after death for pets entitled *Barking Dogs in the Beyond* in which Conan Doyle was quoted as saying 'All our pets, of every sort- and very especially dogs- are with us in our next life. The bond of affection is one which survives death'.

October was quite a busy month for publications. The 5th saw the publication *Do the Dead Still Live?* in the *Sunday Pictorial*. The 15th saw a contribution along the same lines from Conan Doyle appear in the book *Survival* along with contributions from Sir Oliver Lodge[348].

---

[348] The *Daily Express* of October 15th 1924.

Conan Doyle was busy at the time working on his next Professor Challenger novel *The Land of Mist*[349]. This was destined to be his 'Psychic Novel' and this epithet was already established in the public domain. On October 30th *The Daily Mirror* gently mocked him by stating 'Conan Doyle's psychic novel will be full of high spirits'. He was not singled out for such treatment. In a reference to the General Election, which had been held the previous day, the newspaper also commented 'The elections are over, but struggles for seats will continue on the tubes' – a reference to the London Underground.

Five days earlier the latest Sherlock Holmes adventure *The Adventure of the Three Garridebs* had appeared in *Collier's* (it would appear in *The Strand* the following January illustrated by Elcock). At the beginning of November *Collier's* followed with *The Adventure of the Illustrious Client* (February 1925 in *The Strand*). At around the same time Conan Doyle found himself in the unusual position of being on the receiving end of some praise from the church in the person of the Bishop of London.

On November 2nd the Bishop spoke at All Saints' Church in Haggerston, Hackney. He announced that he had read the book *Survival* and was pleased that the 'scientists' behind it had reached a firm belief in the existence of an afterlife even if they had arrived at that conclusion via a different route to the church[350].

On the 9th Conan Doyle and others of like mind attended the Queen's Hall in London for the Spiritualists' Service of Remembrance. According to *The Daily Mirror* of the following day Conan Doyle recounted a story about Admiral Togo of the Imperial Japanese Navy and how he had communicated with his dead sailors following the Russo-Japanese War and told them the result. Another speaker, the Rev. G. Vale Owen, informed the assembled company that he had been in contact with no less than thirty-seven dead soldiers who had informed

---

349 Pugh, Brian. *A Chronology of the Life of Sir Arthur Conan Doyle*. 3rd Edition. MX Publishing 2014.

350 *The Daily Mirror* of November 3rd 1924.

him that all the buildings destroyed in the war had been re-erected in the spirit world. Conan Doyle also declared that spirits were a part of their present proceedings and were circling above them in the hall[351].

December saw Conan Doyle close the year with a series of Spiritualist services held at the County Hall, Spring Gardens in London. The first of these services took place on the 7th and Conan Doyle took the opportunity to announce that a new church was to be founded in the capital that would act as a halfway house between Spiritualism and the Church of England[352]. Another service was held a week later[353].

Conan Doyle elected not to spend Christmas (or at least some of it) in England. By the 27th he was in Grindelwald in Switzerland[354].

---

351 The *Daily Express* of November 10th 1924.
352 *The Daily Mirror* of December 8th 1924.
353 Pugh, Brian. *A Chronology of the Life of Sir Arthur Conan Doyle.* 3rd Edition. MX Publishing 2014.
354 Ibid.

1925

BOOKSHOP, BELFAST AND THE LAND OF MIST

January 1925 commenced at a pace for Conan Doyle. He returned from Switzerland in the middle of the month and by the 21st he had been elected president of the London Spiritualist Association[355].

While he had been out of the country a rather bizarre letter entitled *Conan Doyle's Chance* appeared in the pages of the *Daily Express*. Someone who signed themselves as 'My Dear Watson', residing in Baker Street, drew the attention of the newspaper's readers to the mysterious vanishing of a Miss Cameron who worked as a typist in London and whose fiancé lived in Crowborough. The letter's author suggested that, as it had been 'many years since we read breathlessly of the adventures of that super-detective', Conan Doyle should make use of the 'thrilling story at his own front door' and let Holmes 'assist in solving a mystery after his own heart'[356]. It was in decidedly poor taste to ask Conan Doyle to base a Sherlock Holmes story around a vanished woman whose fiancé was a relatively close neighbour. This would-be Watson was also somewhat in error as people in England had read the last Holmes story *The Adventure of the Sussex Vampire* exactly one year previously (hardly 'many years' ago) and were about to read *The Adventure of the Three Garridebs* and *The Adventure*

[355] Pugh, Brian. *A Chronology of the Life of Sir Arthur Conan Doyle.* 3rd Edition. MX Publishing 2014.
[356] The *Daily Express* of January 13th 1925.

of the Illustrious Client in the pages of *The Strand* over the course of the following two months[357].

The major news at the end of January was that Conan Doyle was, in the words of the *Daily Express*, to become a 'shopkeeper'. Both the *Express* and *Mirror*, in their issues of January 27th, alerted their readers to Conan Doyle's establishment of his 'Psychic Bookshop and Library' at a short distance (eighty yards according to both newspapers) from Westminster Abbey. The bookshop had been built behind a hoarding, according to the *Mirror*, and its purpose had been 'a well-guarded secret until yesterday'. Conan Doyle had apparently boasted that it would quickly become known as the 'shop nearest the Abbey'. It was also noted that an envelope had been affixed to the frontage upon which had been written, in Conan Doyle's own hand, 'Letters will be taken in next door'.

According to the *Express* the shop consisted of 'a spacious saleroom and showroom fitted in oak with three counters and tiers of bookshelves, and a large basement capable of accommodating a vast amount of stock'.

The *Express* continued with the story in its next day's issue. It reported that Conan Doyle hoped to open the bookshop the following week and that it would contain a special room set aside for those seeking 'spiritualistic knowledge'. Conan Doyle stated 'Lady Conan Doyle will take a close personal interest in the bookshop and give it her regular attention. She will have a special room on the premises where she can be consulted by mourners. We shall be able to place inquirers in touch with those who can help'. Assuming this to be the same special room for those seeking knowledge it very much appeared that Jean was being set up as something akin to a Spiritualist Consultant.

---

[357] Elsie Cameron was ultimately found dead on her fiancé's property in what became known as the 'Chicken Run Murders'. Conan Doyle took an interest but the fiancé, Norman Thorne, was ultimately hanged.

Conan Doyle was realistic about the commercial prospects of his new venture. 'I do not anticipate that the bookshop and library will be a commercial success, at any rate at first. I am opening it as a hobby, much as other men might run a yacht'.

Conan Doyle (seated), Mary Conan Doyle (far right) and two bookshop staff in The Psychic Bookshop and Library (The Collection of Georgina Doyle)

February saw the shop finally open for business. It also saw the release in New York of the film of *The Lost World* and, on the literary front, Conan Doyle finished work on *The Land of Mist*[358].

The subject of Oscar Slater arose once more at around this time. A letter, written on white tissue paper, from Slater to Conan Doyle had been smuggled out of the former's prison by a fellow prisoner on the occasion of his release. Conan Doyle took up the case once again with the Secretary for Scotland, but although an invitation to discuss it in person was extended, it was made clear, in advance, that his appeal was rejected.

Conan Doyle was angry and disclosed the matter to the press along with his response to the invitation: 'As your decision is announced I can see no object in an interview. I need not say I am disappointed. I have done my best to set this injustice right. The responsibility must now lie with you'[359].

The *Daily Express* of March 11th carried an interesting article regarding a Czech playwright named Dr. Karel Capek. Capek had come to Britain on a visit in 1924. Following a tour of the country he had produced an account of his visit entitled *Letters from England.* One of the objects of Capek's visit was clearly literary tourism as he had made a point of arranging to see H.G. Wells and of going to Baker Street. Of the latter he remarked 'There is not the slightest trace of Sherlock Holmes there, it is a business thoroughfare of unexampled respectability, which serves no higher purpose than to lead to Regent's Park, which, after a long endeavour, it almost manages to achieve'. It was noted that this news would be a blow to Prague based Conan Doyle enthusiasts of whom there were, according to the article, 'a great number'.

After a relatively quiet April, May saw Conan Doyle take his Spiritualist message to Belfast. By the time he and Jean arrived in Belfast on May 10th the local press had been talking about the visit for some time. The *Belfast Telegraph* of March 28th had been one of the earliest newspapers to give the month

---

358 Lycett, Andrew. *Conan Doyle: The Man who Created Sherlock Holmes.* Orion. 2007.

359 The *Daily Express* of March 5th 1925.

in which the first lectures would be delivered[360]. As the date drew closer, specific lecture dates began to appear in many of the local newspapers with the exception of the *Irish News* which refused to carry any advertisements for any of Conan Doyle's lectures.

Conan Doyle and Jean stayed in the Midland Station Hotel. His first engagement was not until the 12th so he had the 11th to himself. His reaction to an article on his visit that appeared in the *Northern Whig and Belfast Post* of the 11th would have been interesting to witness.

It would have been clear to Conan Doyle that the newspaper was not pro-spiritualist. It began by observing that his creation of Sherlock Holmes and his work as a war historian were just as much of a pull for audiences as his interest in Spiritualism. 'Were the apostle of spiritualism of today not the creator of Sherlock Holmes of yesterday probably he would have fallen flat enough in the former capacity, so far as the great majority of the public are concerned'[361]. The newspaper concluded by observing, of Spiritualism, 'In the main these beliefs appear to be too vague and general to be very harmful. The pity of it is when some spiritualists allow themselves to be cozened of their money by so-called mediums and those who exploit the latter'.

The 12th saw Conan Doyle as the principal guest of honour at the luncheon of the Rotary Club of Belfast. This was a purely literary event and Conan Doyle acknowledged this following the meal. The *Belfast Telegraph* of the same day reported that Conan Doyle, accompanied by much laughter and applause, 'rejoiced' at having the chance to meet with the 'leading citizens of Belfast' on a platform that was less 'contentious than that which he would occupy for the next two days'.

Sherlock Holmes also received a mention with Conan Doyle acknowledging that Sherlock Holmes had been, from a financial viewpoint at least, 'a valuable asset'.

---

360 *Sir Arthur Conan Doyle's 1925 Visit to Belfast.* Research notes compiled and supplied by Oscar Ross.

361 Ibid.

The following evening saw Conan Doyle get back to the matter in hand – Spiritualism. He gave his first lecture in the Ulster Hall on 'The New Revelation'. It ran along much the same lines as the lectures he had given countless times before. He explained how he had first come to the subject and made his way through to the topic of ectoplasm[362]. The Rev. R.W. Seaver, who presided over the meeting, made it clear that, despite his position, he was presiding in his own capacity and not as the representative of the church. Seaver was clearly a supporter of Spiritualism and made it plain he considered that current Religion was simply not up to the task any more.

News of the lecture found its way into the May 14th issues of the *Belfast News-letter* and *Irish News*. Neither really offered an opinion on the subject. The former provided a straight report without comment and the latter simply observed that there was a large attendance and that Lady Conan Doyle had been presented with a bouquet by a young lady during proceedings.

The following day saw Conan Doyle give his lecture 'The Proofs of Immortality'. He began by dealing with a few audience questions before eventually arriving at the subject of Spirit photography which, once again, did not vary from past presentations in other countries and this had an effect on how his entire visit was ultimately judged. The *Northern Whig*, in its issue of May 18th observed that many of the people who had attended the lectures were 'sadly disappointed. Sir Arthur told them little that they had not heard or read before'.

The editor of the *Belfast Telegraph* drew a line under the entire subject and informed his readers that he would carry no more discussion on the subject of Spiritualism. However, on the 19th, he made an exception to this rule for Conan Doyle himself. Conan Doyle and Jean had left Northern Ireland, in all

---

[362] *Sir Arthur Conan Doyle's 1925 Visit to Belfast*. Research notes compiled and supplied by Oscar Ross.

probability on the evening of the 15th[363], but he had written a letter to the newspaper to sum up his feelings about his visit.

He expressed his gratitude for the 'fair hearing' that he felt he had been given but, in a parallel with his experience in Australia, he noted that one newspaper (the *Irish News* although he did not name it) had refused to advertise his lectures and that his two lectures had been picketed by opponents who had distributed 'abusive handbills'. He took the opportunity to point out to anyone who had seen a copy that its 'assertions' were 'grotesque inventions'.

The editor of the *Telegraph* added a footnote to the letter to point out that his printing of the letter did not mean that he was opening the matter up for 'general discussion'.

May 20th saw a report in the *Daily Express* that Conan Doyle and Sybil Margaret Thomas, Viscountess Rhondda were to open a psychic exhibition at the Caxton Hall in Westminster that very day.

Of special interest were 'three waxen "gloves"' which had been allegedly taken from the hand of a materialised spirit. A reporter from the newspaper had interviewed Conan Doyle the previous day and had naturally asked more about, what the article later referred to as, the 'eerie exhibits'.

'The spirit,' said Conan Doyle, 'when it appeared at a séance, was asked to dip its hand into a bowl of melted paraffin wax. After it had done so, it vanished, leaving on a table a wax glove. The glove is so small at the wrist that no human hand could have been withdrawn from it'.

The article went on to state that a number of spirit photographs would be on show including a number that Conan Doyle had himself exhibited as part of his lectures. It was not

[363] *Sir Arthur Conan Doyle's 1925 Visit to Belfast.* Research notes compiled and supplied by Oscar Ross.

clear whether these were Conan Doyle's photographs or copies, but given that he was opening the exhibition the former seems quite likely.

The Viscount and Viscountess Rhondda
(Library of Congress)

The film of *The Lost World* premiered in London at the New Gallery Kinema in Regent Street[364] on June 12th. It was reviewed in the *Daily Express* of the following day under the heading *Nightmare Beasts in a Film.*

The newspaper's cinema correspondent was clearly impressed, describing the film as a 'notable addition'. A set-piece fight between two dinosaurs was described as a 'magnificent bit of realism' even though their movements were also described as 'occasionally a trifle mechanical'.

In conclusion, the film was assessed to be 'a masterpiece of creative film genius, and should be a "gold mine" for its fortunate owners. The extraordinary resources of the screen for making the incredible credible have never been more skilfully demonstrated'. This assessment may well have been shared in scientific circles as the film had a special screening at the British Museum on the 19th[365].

July saw the story's latest successor, *The Land of Mist*, begin its serialisation in the pages of *The Strand*. It would run monthly until March of 1926. The month also saw the expansion of Conan Doyle's Psychic Bookshop to support a museum. The issue of *Light* published on July 4th carried a letter from Conan Doyle in which he let it be known that he intended to establish a museum in the basement of his bookshop. He expressed the hope that it would become 'a powerful propaganda centre'[366].

In his letter he requested that readers of the magazine 'give, lend or sell' exhibits to him. He noted that he currently had, on loan, the 'two wax gloves lent me by the Psychic College' and

---

[364] Kinema was how it was listed in the June 11th issue of the *Daily Express*. The spelling is derived from kinematic and was the forerunner of the modern word - cinema.

[365] Pugh, Brian. *A Chronology of the Life of Sir Arthur Conan Doyle*. 3rd Edition. MX Publishing 2014.

[366] Gibson, John Michael and Green, Richard Lancelyn. *Letters to the Press*. Martin Secker & Warburg Ltd. 1975.

'the Garscadden collection of photographs'. The wax gloves were presumably those previously on display at the Caxton Hall. A few weeks later, in August, a representative of the *Daily Express* visited the museum and was given a tour by Conan Doyle[367]. Amongst the items described as being on display, which included 'ghostly fingerprints', were some plaster casts of hands. These casts had been taken from the aforementioned wax gloves that had been lent to Conan Doyle. It was not clear whether the original wax gloves were still in the museum at the time of the tour but if the casts were now a feature it would suggest that the gloves had been returned to the Psychic College. Conan Doyle added some detail stating that the séance at which the original wax impresses had been achieved had taken place in Warsaw conducted by a medium named Franek Kluski.

Conan Doyle had hoped that his museum would become a 'propaganda centre'. It is arguable whether or not it managed this but it certainly became an information centre – a fact that caused Conan Doyle to comment in a letter to *The Daily News* on December 9th.

He noted that inquirers who came to the museum generally knew nothing of Spiritualism and often came with prejudices on the subject. Conan Doyle likened it to someone coming to a geological museum, knowing nothing of the subject and then seeing fit to lecture the curator 'upon the order of fossils'[368].

---

367 The *Daily Express* of August 19th 1925.
368 Gibson, John Michael and Green, Richard Lancelyn. *Letters to the Press*. Martin Secker & Warburg Ltd. 1975.

PARIS AND BIGNELL WOOD

September saw Conan Doyle attend the International Spiritualist Congress in Paris[369]. According to the *Daily Express* of the 7th, the Congress commenced on the evening of the 6th in the hall of the 'Société des Savante' (or Learned Society). Conan Doyle had been appointed president of the congress and addressed the audience in French. The audience included scientists and fifteen nations were represented.

The newspaper interviewed Conan Doyle before he spoke and he was characteristically direct about his aims. 'For years we have battled against a campaign of lies. Now thousands of people all over the world are beginning to realise that Spiritualism is a matter of the utmost importance. They say "but you have no proof". I can only reply that we have proof in abundance. They are here for every one to test for himself'.

The congress continued for a week and was very popular. *The Daily Mirror* of September 9th noted that 'thousands' were unable to gain admission to the hall where Conan Doyle spoke and it was not an isolated incident.

On the 13th a lecture on spirit photography was due to be given by Conan Doyle at the Salle Wagram. Conan Doyle had chosen this venue as it was, apparently, the largest hall available in Paris. The lecture was fully subscribed and, half an hour before Conan Doyle was due to speak, the hall was full

---

[369] Pugh, Brian. *A Chronology of the Life of Sir Arthur Conan Doyle*. 3rd Edition. MX Publishing 2014.

and the Paris police placed it under guard with the doors locked.

This proved to be completely inadequate and the hall was later stormed by around four thousand people who also wanted to hear Conan Doyle, resulting in the police being completely overpowered[370].

In its already mentioned issue of the 9th, *The Daily Mirror* had also noted that a Sherlock Holmes play was being performed in Paris that week, in English, and that Conan Doyle had attended one performance and 'delighted the many people in the audience with a speech'.

Conan Doyle's great detective was clearly in his mind at this time. Whether he had gone to the play in Paris because Sherlock Holmes was occupying his thoughts or whether his thoughts about Holmes had been triggered by the play is not clear, but it was evident that new written adventures were on the cards. The *Daily Express* of the 16th broke the news to its readers that Conan Doyle had confided to 'a friend' that he would 'revive Sherlock Holmes, should an appropriate plot be forthcoming'. He was quoted as saying 'All my time in recent years has been given to "spiritism," for which I have not accepted a penny remuneration. It is therefore necessary to spend some time earning a living'.

That 'time earning a living' would see the Canon of Sherlock Holmes stories completed and published in less than two years.

Conan Doyle was back in England at the beginning of October. He wasted no time in launching himself back into the local fray. The *Daily Express* had run a series of articles by ten authors, including Conan Doyle, under the heading *My Religion*. In

---

[370] These events were reported in *The Daily Mirror* issues of September 14th and 15th.

successive editions, the newspaper had carried short pieces by the relevant authors (including Rebecca West, Henry Arthur Jones and Israel Zangwill) in which they wrote of what religion meant to them. Conan Doyle decided to take them on.

His chosen venue was the Grotrian Hall (formerly the Steinway Hall) in London on October 4th and the event was covered in the *Daily Express* of the following day. Conan Doyle, when his turn to speak came, began with praise for the *Daily Express*. Given the way the newspaper had opposed and mocked Spiritualism it is a wonder that Conan Doyle was content to give it any time at all. Despite this he praised the newspaper for carrying the articles before criticising the other contributors to the series. Arnold Bennett was dismissed as 'all negative' Rebecca West's contribution was dismissed for not offering any guidance and Israel Zangwill, described as 'my friend' by Conan Doyle, was dismissed as 'equally ignorant' as the other contributors. 'Mr Zangwill was crying for civilised men to find "the next religion." The idea that we, the ridiculed spiritualists, may have found it has never entered his head'.

All of the articles, along with responses from various 'eminent divines' would later be published as a book on October 27th by Hutchinson and Co[371].

In the middle of October, Conan Doyle was staying at his flat in Buckingham Palace Mansions, when he learned of the recent court appearance of one Mme. "Estelle" who had been fined twenty pounds for the charge of fortune telling following a sting where two policewomen had pretended to be mourners and had come to the lady seeking consolation.

Conan Doyle was angry and wrote to the editor of the *Daily Express*. 'Sir, Is it not time that the prosecution - or rather the persecution - of clairvoyants and mediums should cease?'. Referring to the sting he stated 'The whole proceeding is repugnant to one's sense of justice, and is foreign, to the spirit of British law, which has never encouraged the "agent provocateur"'.

---

[371] The *Daily Express* of October 26th.

He went on to note that he knew another medium who had been the subject of two similar police stings and that the fines were 'far higher than for personal assault or for aggravated cruelty to an animal'[372].

In its issue of the 21st, the *Daily Express* published a range of responses to Conan Doyle's letter. One customer of Mme. "Estelle", named Alice McQueen, had nothing but praise for the clairvoyant and announced that she had been in court ready to stand as a defence witness. A man from Bristol questioned why the clairvoyant could not sense 'the approach of the wives of police officers in disguise'. Finally, a writer from Brighton suggested that if it was illegal to tell fortunes 'it must surely be illegal to have fortunes told' thus suggesting that the police should be held to account for instigating the fortune telling in the first place.

It was around this time that Conan Doyle was adding to his property portfolio. He purchased Bignell Wood, a cottage in the New Forest, as a present for Jean although it was also suggested that their spirit guide Pheneas had been the instigator of the purchase. The cottage certainly became something of a retreat for the family and was perhaps one they very much needed.

November 8th saw Conan Doyle at the Queen's Hall in London. The occasion was the Spiritualists' Day of Rememberance. In front of three thousand Spiritualists, Conan Doyle, in the words of the following day's *Daily Express*, 'administered verbal chastisement' to members of the clergy who had denied 'the geographical idea of heaven'.

'The day will come when we shall have to hold a protest meeting against the heretical and unscriptural language of the bishops of the Church. It is hard for us to stand by in silence when we see those who ought to be guiding the people teaching them that which is heretical and untrue.'

---

[372] The *Daily Express* of October 17th.

Bignell Wood in the New Forest. The Conan Doyle family retreat (The Collection of Georgina Doyle)

The man singled out as the principal opponent was the Bishop of Liverpool who had, according to Conan Doyle, 'warned us off'. 'I give the Bishop of Liverpool a public challenge. Can he, in all the world, point to any power which God gave to man which is not to be used? If he would have the courtesy to do me the honour, I would come to Liverpool and debate the subject on a public platform with him'. Judging by his known movements, his gauntlet was not picked up by the Bishop.

The end of November saw Conan Doyle defending himself against yet another accusation that he had been hoaxed. Two years previously it had been suggested that he had been taken in by the 'medium in the mask', now he was being accused by a Boston scientist, Dr. W.F. Prince, of being taken in by 'spirit photographs' that Prince had declared to be fake.

One of the many photographs that Conan Doyle had exhibited during his American lecture tour was of some firemen who had died in a Chicago fire. Prince declared that the spirits in the photographs had been 'furnished' by 'the upper two-fifths of Murillo's "Holy Family" which is in the National Gallery…'.

Conan Doyle had allegedly referred to this photograph as the most remarkable he had ever seen. On the 23rd the newspaper located Conan Doyle at the Old Bailey in London with its Recorder, Sir Ernest Wild, and asked him about the matter.

'I exhibited forty-five pictures at my lectures in America, and Dr. Prince objected to one,' said Conan Doyle. 'I thought it was doubtful, so I withdrew it and mentioned the fact to my audience. What I said of the photographs referred to was that they were "the most artistic I had seen". On examining them I wrote to "Light," about a month ago, pointing out that the "extras" were from well-known pictures, and that the mediumship was suspicious'.[373]

---

[373] *The Daily Mirror* of November 24th 1925.

December was a relatively quiet month until the immediate days before Christmas. The old suggestion made by members of the clergy that spirits were not really spirits but demons was restated by a Rev. Dinsdale Young in the pages of the December 23rd issue of *The Daily Mirror*. In the same newspaper the vicar of St Paul's in Covent Garden, London shared this view but instead of consequently regarding Spiritualism as 'an unmitigated evil', which was the opinion of his fellow vicar, Rev. Young instead suggested that the business of Spiritualism be left to 'skilled and qualified investigators such as Sir Oliver Lodge and Sir Arthur Conan Doyle'.

The *Daily Express* on Christmas Eve printed a letter from Conan Doyle that was loosely connected to the *Mirror*'s theme. Conan Doyle confirmed that 'No message should be accepted unless it satisfies the judgement and reason of the recipient'.

1926

KEEPING A LOW PROFILE?

January 1926 opened quite modestly with three Spiritualist speeches and ended, on the 27th, with a lunch event at the Savoy to commemorate the centenary of the death of French lawyer Jean Anthelme Brillat-Savarin who had found fame as a gastronome.

The remainder of the first half of the year was relatively quiet with Conan Doyle making scarcely any impact in the press. Life was far from boring however; there were additional Spiritualist events and involvement in the Amateur Billiards Championship but nothing that really excited press interest.

Sherlock Holmes, however, was making an impression in the press if only in an amusing way. A company called Ronuk, based in Sussex, was using Holmes and Watson as a means to sell its furniture polish and other household products. Its advertisements featured drawings of Holmes and Watson examining floors and furniture with Holmes observing that the quality of the polish was a clear indicator that a Ronuk product had been used. Each advertisement ended with the statement *With apologies to Sir A. Conan Doyle.* It was not entirely clear whether they were apologising for the quality of the Holmesian deductions or the use of the characters[374]. The illustrations that

[374] The firm Ronuk was later to become part of the British firm Ronseal.

accompanied the advertisements were simplistic but showed skill. They were signed "Riley Streets".[375]

The low press profile ended suddenly at the beginning of June. On the 3rd the *Daily Express* carried an article announcing the publication of *The History of Spiritualism.* It seems reasonably clear that it was the work on this book that had, to some extent at least, caused Conan Doyle's low profile up until that point. The main purpose of the article was not to herald the publication of the book but to announce Conan Doyle's explanation for so-called 'spirit raps'.

The answer was, what he termed, ectoplasm rods. According to the article, he had stated '...raps are caused by a protrusion from the medium's person of a long rod of a substance having certain properties which distinguish it from all other matter'. He went on to state that French physiologist Charles Richet had coined the term ectoplasm and it was rods of this substance that were capable of conducting energy, in Conan Doyle's words, '...in such a fashion as to make sounds and strike blows at a distance'. To Conan Doyle this theory neatly explained all 'ringing bells, jangling tambourines, swaying tables and dancing crockery'.

Towards the end of July Conan Doyle became involved in a truly bizarre legal case. The case in question was reported on by *The Daily Mirror* of July 22nd and concerned copyright. The case was brought against Frederick Bligh Bond, the noted psychical researcher and member of the Society for Psychical Research, by one Geraldine Cummins and it concerned a work that Bond intended to publish entitled *Chronicles of Cleophas.* Cummins, who was able to perform automatic writing, had been approached by Bond to communicate with the spirit world. She had subsequently made contact with a spirit named Cleophas who had dictated to her a history of early Christianity. It was this that Bond now proposed to publish.

---

375 The editions of *The Daily Mirror* published on March 10th and 23rd.

Charles Richet (1850-1935)
(Bibliothèque nationale de France)

The issue at stake was the ownership of the copyright of the work. Bond claimed it belonged to him as the communication was addressed to him and Cummins claimed it was hers as she had written it down.

Frederick Bligh Bond (1864-1945)

The automatic writing sessions had commenced in May of 1925 and had continued through until July of the same year. The issue of ownership had clearly arisen subsequent to this. The newspaper reported that Bond had, in January 1926, consulted Conan Doyle over the matter and Bond's defence counsel wished to draw the court's attention to the response received.

It seems clear that Conan Doyle had sided with Miss Cummins (or at least had not sided with Bond) as Bond's counsel, Mr Moritz, stated 'Sir Arthur seems to have taken a violent view with regard to this matter, and plunged into it in a partisan spirit. He has taken up a certain attitude which makes anything he said with respect to the case worthless'.

No further details of Conan Doyle's contribution to the case were given in the report and the case was adjourned.

THE CASE FOR AND AGAINST

July and August of 1926 were quiet months, the main highlight, if it could be so called, being Conan Doyle's participation in the Wright Cup Handicap billiards tournament. Conan Doyle lost in the final heat to a Mr J.T. Evans[376].

In September the Sherlock Holmes story *The Adventure of the Three Gables* was published in the American magazine *Liberty* and in *The Strand* a month later. For the latter Howard Elcock once again provided the illustrations. The story was clever but was, in many respects, similar to *The Adventure of the Second Stain*, in that it concerned a document which the principal female character needed to secure in order to avoid a scandal. Isadora Klein is one of the most formidable female antagonists that Sherlock Holmes faces but ultimately, like Lady Hilda from *The Second Stain* she is confronted in her home by Holmes and loses the battle of wills with him.

Liberty also saw the initial publication, in its October issue, of *The Adventure of the Blanched Soldier*. This, again, appeared in *The Strand* a month later. Between these two events, on October 31st, occurred the death of Harry Houdini.

---

376 Pugh, Brian. *A Chronology of the Life of Sir Arthur Conan Doyle*. 3rd Edition. MX Publishing 2014.

Houdini had died in the days following an event where he had agreed to receive a series of stomach punches from a student named Whitehead[377].

One of Howard Elcock's illustrations for The Adventure of the Three Gables

Conan Doyle was naturally asked to comment and, diplomatically, went out of his way to gloss over the differences between himself and the late escapologist. When Houdini's widow offered to send him some Spiritualist books from her

[377] Sandford, Christopher. *Houdini and Conan Doyle*. Duckworth Overlook 2011.

late husband's library Conan Doyle refused. His reason for refusing was a practical one, he knew that he would eventually have to write about Houdini and he wanted to be able to write without feeling under any obligation to the family[378].

His reason for wishing to avoid any such obligation would become clear when his book *The Edge of the Unknown* was published in 1930. In the book he stated that one of Houdini's biggest problems had been his vanity which, eventually, became 'more amusing than offensive'. Conan Doyle also commented on Houdini's 'passion for publicity' stating 'Even when he laid flowers upon the graves of the dead it was in the pre-arranged presence of the local photographers'. He also believed, unsurprisingly, that it was Houdini's desire for publicity that had driven his campaign against Spiritualism.

One thing, however, was certain. Houdini's presence would be felt from beyond the grave, although not necessarily in the manner which Conan Doyle hoped for.

As the year drew to its close two Sherlock Holmes stories found their way into the hands of the public. In November the story *The Adventure of the Lion's Mane* was published in *Liberty* and, in December, *The Adventure of the Retired Colourman* appeared. As before, *The Strand* published each story one month behind[379]. As they read these adventures, the public were blissfully unaware that they were now only two stories away from the end of Sherlock Holmes.

---

378 Sandford, Christopher. *Houdini and Conan Doyle*. Duckworth Overlook 2011. Bess Houdini later offered Conan Doyle a portfolio from her husband's collection that contained sketches by Conan Doyle's father Charles. This was accepted.

379 Pugh, Brian. *A Chronology of the Life of Sir Arthur Conan Doyle*. 3rd Edition. MX Publishing 2014.

Between the two stories there was a change of illustrator. *The Lion's Mane* was the last, in *The Strand*, to be illustrated by Howard Elcock and, when *The Retired Colourman* was published, it was *The Valley of Fear*'s illustrator Frank Wiles who returned to the task of bringing Holmes's adventures to life.

At this time Conan Doyle was devoting more and more energy to his Psychic Bookshop. *The Daily Mirror* of December 4th observed that he was present in the shop 'daily' and could be seen '...attending to the wants of customers'.

Conan Doyle seems to have been in a combative frame of mind at this time. This was demonstrated, on December 7th, when a letter written by him was published in that day's *Daily Express*. The subject of the letter was tax 'shirkers'.

He had observed that hotels along the south coast were 'half empty' while those on the Riviera were filling up fast. He asked if there was not some 'moral obligation', in times of economic pressure, for people with money to holiday within Britain thus ensuring that they helped the economy. He moved on from this to attack the 'shirkers' who lived in the Channel Islands or abroad in order to escape taxation. He suggested that those who did so should have their names black-listed in the *Gazette* before having their citizenship revoked if they did not mend their ways.

Was it pure patriotism that drove him to write on the subject or was he in such a frame of mind because of recent opposition in matters psychic? The latter is certainly possible as the Cottingley Fairies and their authenticity were once again being questioned.

In a letter to American psychologist Carl Murchison of Clark University, Massachusetts dated December 11th Conan Doyle made reference to remarks made by one Joseph Jastrow, another psychologist, that had appeared in a newspaper[380].

In the newspaper's report Jastrow had stated that the fairies had been cut out from a magazine. In his letter to Murchison,

---

[380] Possibly *The New York Times* of November 30th.

and after covering some other subjects, Conan Doyle turned to Jastrow's comments regarding Cottingley. He was clearly irritated and pointed out to Murchison that the photographs had 'met all criticism' and that the 'young girls' had been vindicated in terms of their honesty. He concluded by stating that every expert called upon to examine the negatives had 'testified to their reality'.

Joseph Jastrow (1863-1944)

Murchison clearly passed the letter to Jastrow who wrote back, to Murchison, on January 5th 1927. He was clearly in as combative a mood as Conan Doyle, describing the whole event as a 'preposterous story about fairy photographs.' He went on to state that, as far as he was concerned, the pictures were clearly set up and that 'the mark of the shears in cutting them out appears definitely'. Contradicting Conan Doyle's final statement Jastrow stated that almost everyone who had examined the photographs had, in fact, rejected them as 'ridiculous'[381].

[381] The letters from Conan Doyle and Jastrow were collated by Murchison into a book entitled *The Case For and Against Psychical Belief* (1927). The book presented essays and letters from believers, non-believers and those as yet undecided. In the same book an excerpt from Harry Houdini's work *A Magician Among the Spirits* showed that the great escapologist shared Jastrow's opinion of the photographs. Houdini drew attention to the claim of a candle making firm - Messrs. Prince and Sons - that the fairies featured in the photographs were an 'exact reproduction' of the fairies they had featured in an advertisement for night lights.

1927

THE CANON COMPLETE

January was a quiet month but it closed with the penultimate Sherlock Holmes story *The Adventure of the Veiled Lodger* being published in *Liberty*. Frank Wiles, once again, provided the illustrations when the story reached *The Strand* in February.

February was a much busier month. Conan Doyle was summoned to the Sussex Petty Sessions to answer for the behaviour of his two dogs who had been accused of 'worrying sheep' at the end of January. Unlike the similar case some years previously with his dog Roy, Conan Doyle lost the case but got away lightly receiving an order to keep the dogs under control[382].

February 25th saw Conan Doyle at the White City for the British Industries Fair. He was there to represent the Raphael Tuck printing company of which he had been a director for many years. In this capacity he met King George V who was visiting the fair with Queen Mary. The King was very pleased to see him and reminded Conan Doyle that he was still in possession of a menu that Conan Doyle had signed for him at a dinner when he had been Prince of Wales[383].

At the beginning of March *The Adventure of Shoscombe Old Place* was published in *Liberty*. The very last Sherlock Holmes adventure was a clever story and a worthy one to end on. As

---

382 Pugh, Brian. *A Chronology of the Life of Sir Arthur Conan Doyle*. 3rd Edition. MX Publishing 2014.
383 *The Daily Mirror* of February 26th 1927.

usual, it was published in *The Strand* the following month. At the time of the story's US release Conan Doyle's attention could not have been further removed from literature. The *Daily Express* of March 1st reported that he was showing a keen interest in tests the newspaper was organising of 'jumping balloons' which were designed to be worn by pedestrians with the aim of making them lighter.

Conan Doyle laid claim to the basic idea but further claimed that he had never expected to see it put into practice. The practicality of the balloon being tested by the newspaper was questionable given that it was eighteen feet in diameter.

The rest of March passed quietly with the exception of the publication of *Pheneas Speaks*. This was a collection of messages received from Pheneas since he had begun communicating with the family through Jean.

April was a good deal busier. Following the middle of the month, when Conan Doyle and Jean took a short holiday in Exmouth, matters Spiritualist returned to the fore. According to the *Daily Express* of the 25th, Conan Doyle laid the foundation stone of a new Spiritualist Church in Kingston on the 24th and announced that there were now five hundred Spiritualist Churches in Great Britain with the same number under construction. On the 28th, according to the next day's *The Daily Mirror*, he spoke at the dedication of another Church in Southwark Bridge Road and lightly mocked the many men that he knew to be believers in Spiritualism who refused to openly admit it for fear of endangering their careers.

In May Conan Doyle made two addresses on Spiritualism. The first of these was at the Grotrian Hall and the second at The New Spiritualist Church in Surbiton[384]. In parallel, entries were appearing in the personal columns of newspapers in which the Psychic Bookshop was offering, post free, copies of *Pheneas Speaks* at 2s 9d and 3s 9d. These, presumably, being paperback and hardback editions. The wording of the advert was amusing.

---

[384] Pugh, Brian. *A Chronology of the Life of Sir Arthur Conan Doyle*. 3rd Edition. MX Publishing 2014.

'It has been said that nothing valuable comes through in Spirit circles. Test it by reading PHENEAS SPEAKS as reported by Sir A. Conan Doyle'[385]. Given the use of his title, which he tended to omit in literary matters, it seems unlikely that Conan Doyle put the advertisement together himself.

June 16th saw the publication of *The Casebook of Sherlock Holmes*. Anybody looking forward to fresh adventures in the future was soon put in their place by an article in that same day's *Daily Express*.

LAST GOOD-BYE OF SHERLOCK HOLMES was the title and the article began by quoting Conan Doyle's preface to the book in which he stated that Sherlock Holmes was running the risk of becoming 'one of those popular tenors who, having outlived their time, are still tempted to make repeated farewell bows to their indulgent audiences'. He went on to express the vain hope that 'some more astute sleuth with some even less astute comrade may fill the stage which they have vacated'.

Many other sleuths would indeed follow Holmes but if Conan Doyle was hoping that his characters would fade he was destined to be disappointed. On the same day as his words were quoted in the *Daily Express* one of its reporters travelled to Windlesham to get him to expand on his preface.

The interview took place in the study where the reporter noted that the walls were lined with books, with some twenty shelves devoted to Spiritualism. He also noted that the way the room was arranged, with boxing gloves and dumbbells on the floor, created 'an atmosphere of sympathy and manliness…that gives poor Sherlock Holmes a pat on the back'.

In response to the request to talk about Holmes, which he surely must have realised was the purpose of the visit, Conan Doyle replied 'Oh, I hate the old man. I am afraid I cannot tell you very much about him'. He then proceeded to make every effort to demonstrate Holmes's proper place in his affections.

---

385 *The Daily Mirror* of May 26th 1927.

'I was tired of Sherlock Holmes from the beginning,' he stated, but conceded that it was 'an excellent way for a struggling young man to get a foothold and to get money'.

There were, however, clearly aspects of having created Sherlock Holmes in which Conan Doyle took great pride. He noted that in France a department of the police in Lyons was named after him and not Holmes – the Salle Conan Doyle. He also showed the reporter a signed photograph of the chief of the Lyons police under which had been written 'To the illustrious father of Sherlock Holmes – Sir Arthur Conan Doyle. Homage and admiration. – Edmund Lockard'.

Conan Doyle concluded by expressing the hope that there was a paradise for fictional characters and that Sherlock Holmes was now there. 'He is an old man now, perhaps ninety, and he is sitting reading in a sunny field. Dr. Watson approaches him and says "My dear Holmes, I have lost my pipe. I wonder if you could help me find it. Where do you think it could be?"

"I haven't the slightest idea," replies Sherlock Holmes comfortably, and he sits down to read "The White Company"'[386].

On July 3rd Conan Doyle was back at the Grotrian Hall in London talking about the next life. During the course of his speech he made the statement 'Great Britain is just as dear to God as was Judea'. He made the point that man-made dogma was responsible for turning people away from religion and that it was the Spiritualists that were endeavouring to 'get back to Christ'[387].

---

[386] The article was published in the Daily Express of June 17th 1927.
[387] The *Daily Express* of July 4th.

THE CONVICT RELEASED

At the end of July the *Daily Express* carried a story about Oscar Slater. William Park, a Glasgow based journalist, had written a book entitled *The Truth About Oscar Slater*. It contained a preface by Conan Doyle and was published by his Psychic Press – presumably one of the very few titles of a non-Spiritualist nature.

The book purported to contain information about a new witness whose testimony, if heard, would not only be enough to see Slater cleared but would provide sufficient information to give the investigation new leads.

In his preface, Conan Doyle was blunt. He stated that there was little that could be done for Slater who, at fifty-eight years old, was going to find it hard to resume his life but 'for the credit of British justice, for the discipline of the police force, and for the teaching of officials that their duty to the public has to be done, a thorough public enquiry should be made into the whole matter'[388].

It is hard to know whether Conan Doyle seriously thought that this would help Slater. His preface made it reasonably clear that he saw more benefits for the British justice system than he did for Slater himself. However, the *Daily Express*, so often the source of the mockery that Conan Doyle endured in matters Spiritualist, declared itself very much the believer and supporter of what he was attempting to achieve. In its issue of the 28th the

[388] The *Daily Express* of July 25th 1927.

newspaper stated that it regarded it 'as a duty to demand an inquiry. The public conscience must be roused and free this innocent man from prison before he dies and British justice is dishonoured'.

It did not take long for this new campaign to make progress. The very next day, the newspaper carried an article entitled *Slater Case – Inquiry to be Held.* In the article it was announced that the Scottish Office had seen a copy of Park's book two days previously and had decided not only to look at the new facts contained within it but also to examine the handling of the original case.

The next day the matter was raised in the House of Commons and the Lord Advocate, William Watson K.C, claimed that the case had been considered repeatedly by the present Secretary of State for Scotland as well as his predecessors.

This was put to Conan Doyle by a *Daily Express* reporter. Conan Doyle was dismissive, pointing out that only one inquiry had been made in 1914 and had only taken place '…on account of the agitation I was making at that time'. He dismissed that inquiry as '…a greater scandal than the original Oscar Slater scandal. You cannot cover one scandal by referring to another one'.

He went on to pose, through the newspaper, two questions to the Lord Advocate, the second of which was the most pointed. 'Does he think that such a verdict of murder should be returned when, from first to last, no connection was ever shown between the murdered woman and the accused?'

In conclusion he once again expressed the belief that British justice had more to gain than Oscar Slater. 'Poor Slater is already hopelessly done for. No one can restore the vanished years, but his martyrdom will bear some result if it saves the public from the danger of similar miscarriages'[389].

---

[389] The *Daily Express* of July 30th 1927.

At the beginning of August an article entitled *Ghost of the Moat* appeared in the *Daily Express*. In it Conan Doyle described how a medium by the name of Mrs Wickland had assumed the personality of 'a ghostly ostler' who inhabited a moated grange in Sussex.

However, as the article went on it revealed that Mrs Wickland had not only adopted the personality of the spirit but had taken on its appearance as well. As Conan Doyle stated 'Before our eyes she changed in an instant into a heavy-faced, sullen old man with bent back and loose, senile lips'.[390]

Such an account naturally attracted opinions and the newspaper was able to carry some of these in its next day's issue. Sir Oliver Lodge naturally believed, declaring it to be 'a reasonable thing'. A Dr. Stanford Read, described as a nerve specialist, put it down to a condition known as 'hysterical identification' and also pointed out that similar effects could be produced through hypnotism.

The story carried on in the same newspaper on the 6th. This time it was the turn of the newspaper's readers to offer their opinions and, on this occasion, there was some mockery. A writer from Bournemouth went so far as to say 'Sir Arthur Conan Doyle's story proves too much. It proves not only the survival after death of the corporal body of the ostler, but the survival of his clothes. An immortality that is shared by a man's breeches and striped vest is hardly worth making a fuss about'.

Other readers, whose letters were published or referred to in later editions of the newspaper attacked Conan Doyle for trying to make people believe what was described as 'spiritualistic nonsense'[391].

In the same month Conan Doyle resumed his speeches. At the Grotrian Hall he spoke of the literary men who had

---

390 The *Daily Express* of August 4th 1927.
391 The *Daily Express* of August 9th 1927.

communicated via mediums. A similar speech was given at the same location at the beginning of September, during which Conan Doyle spoke of a communication with Charles Dickens. Evidently Dickens expressed sadness that he had not been able to finish the story *Edwin Drood* but confirmed that the character had not died[392].

At the end of September, on the 23rd, the October issue of *The Strand* was published and commenced the serialisation of Conan Doyle's adventure *The Maracot Deep*. An advertisement in the *Daily Express* on the day of publication described it as 'even more thrilling and exciting than Conan Doyle's masterpiece, "The Lost World"'.

Readers were promised sea-monsters and an underwater city in the story which, according to the editor, was Conan Doyle's finest.

Towards the end of October Conan Doyle came out in favour of euthanasia. On Saturday October 22nd one Albert Edward Davies had been acquitted of murdering his three-year-old daughter who had been in the final stages of tuberculosis.

Davies had been accused of drowning his daughter in the bath but a 'medical witness' at the trial at Chester Assizes had declared that the girl had in fact died of shock upon being placed in the bath.

In what the newspaper described as a 'startling suggestion', Conan Doyle had stated 'I think that if there were a law that three medical certificates justify the putting away of any person who is in a hopeless position as regards life and death it would be a very great improvement. It would only be humanity and common sense'[393].

---

[392] *The Daily Mirror* of September 5th 1927.

[393] *Killing to End Suffering* from the *Daily Express* of October 24th 1927.

Conan Doyle's position on this is not too difficult to comprehend. He would have undoubtedly been influenced by his experience with his first wife Louise and also by the comfort he took in his belief that death was not the end.

November brought the news that Oscar Slater was to finally be released from prison. Both the *Daily Express* and *The Daily Mirror*, in their editions of the 11th discussed the issue, with the *Mirror* stating that the Secretary of State for Scotland had announced, the previous day, that Slater would be released on licence 'as soon as suitable arrangements could be made'.

While the *Mirror* largely confined itself to the facts of the case, the *Express* took a large amount of credit for the situation, stating 'One of the chief reasons for the decision to release Oscar Slater is the recent action of the "Daily Express" in persistently demanding a reconsideration of his case by the Scottish authorities'. Up to this time the newspaper had a point, but its next statement was tenuous at best. 'An investigation carried out by the "Daily Express" revealed the gravest suspicion that Slater had suffered a miscarriage of justice and was an innocent man, and it was obvious his release could not be long delayed'.

Anything the newspaper's 'investigation' had uncovered had likely already been raised by Conan Doyle's prior campaign and William Park's recent book, the latter of which had really triggered recent events.

Slater finally walked from Peterhead Prison on November 14th[394]. For Conan Doyle, the remainder of the year passed quietly.

---

[394] Pugh, Brian. *A Chronology of the Life of Sir Arthur Conan Doyle.* 3rd Edition. MX Publishing 2014.

1928

FLOOD DAMAGE

1928 opened badly. *The Daily Mirror* of January 28th reported that Conan Doyle's Psychic Museum, situated in the cellar beneath his bookshop, had been damaged by flooding. Many pages of automatic writing had been rendered illegible and many books and photographs had been effectively destroyed by the water which had reached the height of nearly four feet.

'Fortunately we have copies of nearly all the manuscripts,' said Conan Doyle, 'and it should be quite possible to rebind some of the books, but much of the matter destroyed is quite irretrievable'.

Perhaps in an effort to do him a good turn, the newspaper reminded its readers that the museum was free to enter and contained 'many interesting things'.

In February Conan Doyle published *A Word of Warning* which was described as a 'bitter tirade' against organised Christianity by the *Daily Express* of February 20th. He dismissed such Christian elements as the virgin birth, Holy Communion, Baptism and Confession. The latter in particular was denounced as a 'perverse and dangerous' practice. He questioned, by way of example, why 'a young woman should tell her secret thoughts to a celibate of the opposite sex'. 'It is difficult to say whether it is the man or the woman whose delicacy suffers most'. It was arguably his most robust attack against the Church to date.

Five days later the *Daily Express* announced that Conan Doyle had joined its 'staff of weekly contributors' to the

Sunday Express and would be submitting an article under the heading of *Spiritualism Week By Week.* Conan Doyle's willingness to work with a newspaper who more mocked him than supported him is astounding. It seems that said mockery was viewed, by him, as a price worth paying for access to a newspaper as a means to convey his message. He was certainly not afraid to come at the subject from all angles. The *Daily Express* of March 10th announced that the next edition of its sister paper would contain 'a strong article on "Fraudulent Mediums"' written by Conan Doyle.

On Sunday March 25th Conan Doyle made a speech on Spiritualism at the Grotrian Hall. Now this was not unusual but, as the *Daily Express* of the 28th pointed out, one of the people who joined him on the platform was very much worthy of mention.

The man, who was described by the paper as 'distinguished' and 'grey-haired', was none other than William Gillette. According to the newspaper, very few people even knew he was in London and he had, apparently, 'just come over for the round trip'.

Why was Gillette sharing the platform with Conan Doyle? Some of their last exchanges had been over the Sherlock Holmes film rights where they found themselves on opposing sides. His presence on the platform suggested that any ill-feeling from that period had been overcome.

If Gillette had spoken it would certainly have been reported so we are forced to assume that he was no more than a guest but it is possible, even probable, that his sharing the platform with Conan Doyle would have been viewed as an endorsement of Spiritualism. The notion would have certainly surprised anyone familiar with Gillette's more recent work. The previous year had seen Gillette publish a book entitled *The Astounding Crime on Torrington Road.* This book had featured mediums who were eventually revealed to be frauds[395]. Conan Doyle accepted

---

[395] Zecher, Henry. *William Gillette: America's Sherlock Holmes.* Xlibris 2011.

that there were fraudulent mediums so is not likely to have been upset by this unless he had believed Gillette to be labelling all mediums as such.

A perfectly plausible reason for Gillette's appearance was Sherlock Holmes. Gillette was not exactly broke but his generosity to others had left him in need of a cash boost. It had been suggested to him that he revive the Sherlock Holmes play and tour the United States[396]. He was in two minds about it and perhaps he discussed the idea with Conan Doyle during his visit. Given that Conan Doyle would have, presumably, been owed royalties from such a venture, the subject was a very likely one to arise between them.

In April, however, Gillette requested that the idea be shelved. This decision may have been entirely his own but it could also have been influenced by the opinion of Conan Doyle.

May began with the news that Conan Doyle's books continued to be popular with young boys. The *Daily Express* of May 5th announced that Conan Doyle, John Buchan and Edgar Wallace were, according to the Carnegie UK Trust, the top three writers for boys although it was also noted that 'Books of the detective-adventure type such as "Bulldog Drummond," seem to be equally popular with boys and girls'.

Three days later, *The Daily Mirror* reported that Conan Doyle had purchased 'a picture painted under psychic influence'. The picture, painted by one Captain Will Longstaff, was not insignificant. It measured nine feet by four feet, six inches and was reported to symbolise the spirits of the dead 'filing past their own gravestones'. When the painting had been purchased and for what sum were not detailed[397].

At the end of the month the same newspaper announced that *The Daily News* would, from June 1st, publish a series of articles under the umbrella heading *Where are the Dead?*.

---

[396] Zecher, Henry. *William Gillette: America's Sherlock Holmes.* Xlibris 2011.

[397] *The Daily Mirror* of May 8th 1928.

Conan Doyle and Oliver Lodge were listed as amongst the contributors. Later that same month, on the 24th, Conan Doyle made an address at the Grotrian Hall under the same title[398].

Between these two events was the latest chapter in the case of Oscar Slater. Friday June 8th saw his appeal against his conviction opened in Edinburgh in the very same court where he had previously been condemned. The *Daily Express* article of the following day reported that the court laid the groundwork for proceedings before adjourning to the following day. No mention of Conan Doyle was made in the article although some sources claimed that he attended[399].

Amusingly, Conan Doyle did feature in the same newspaper but only in connection with the publication of the second edition of his book *The Coming of the Fairies.* The new edition contained further eye witness accounts along with new photographs from Devon and Germany but the newspaper said that the sceptic 'will possibly remain a sceptic still' as the new testimony was, in its reviewer's opinion, less convincing than that which had appeared in the first edition.

On June 11th Conan Doyle had a meeting in London with Slater. Slater had been told that he would not be allowed to speak in his own defence at his appeal. He feared some kind of conspiracy and expressed to Conan Doyle his desire to bring a complete halt to proceedings.

Slater had clearly not kept this idea to himself as the *Daily Express* was able to report on it in its issue of the 14th and state that it was common knowledge in Glasgow. The newspaper naturally made contact with Conan Doyle who stated that 'I think he [Slater] is worried by all that he has gone through. When he found that he could not give evidence he imagined that there was a foolish conspiracy against him, and he declared that he was going to do this foolish action'.

---

[398] Pugh, Brian. *A Chronology of the Life of Sir Arthur Conan Doyle.* 3rd Edition. MX Publishing 2014.

[399] Ibid.

Conan Doyle went on to say that he had pointed out to Slater that the appeal would go on without him whether he liked it or not. Although he described Slater's actions as foolish, Conan Doyle is likely to have been very angry at Slater's position. He already had a fairly low opinion of Slater's character and it was clear that, from Conan Doyle's point of view, this was just as much about the reputation of British justice as it was Slater's wrongful conviction.

The appeal resumed on July 9th and Conan Doyle attended. It continued for a few days and Conan Doyle was photographed with Slater's defence counsel Craigie Aitchison K.C. Slater also featured in photographs which demonstrated that he had thought better of his earlier idea[400]. On July 15th, Conan Doyle's account of the appeal was published in the *Sunday Pictorial*[401].

On July 21st came the news that Slater's supporters had been waiting for. The Scottish Court of Criminal Appeal quashed Slater's conviction stating that the jury at the time had been misdirected by the judge.

The *Daily Express* of the following day announced that 'Compensation on a generous scale will be given to Slater by the government'. Figures up to twenty thousand pounds were detailed although these were clearly stated to be speculation.

Conan Doyle was delighted. When told the news by the newspaper he was quoted as saying 'Splendid! For the last fifteen years I have interested myself in Slater's case, simply because I was convinced that he never committed the murder'.

Three days later Conan Doyle was back in England and was present at Westminster Police Court, along with Sir Oliver Lodge, to give evidence in connection with charges of fortune telling which had been made against a medium by the name of Clare Frances Cantlon and Mary Phillimore the secretary of the London Spiritualist Alliance[402].

---

400 *The Daily Mirror* of July 11th.

401 Advertised in *The Daily Mirror* of July 14th.

402 The *Daily Express* of July 24th.

The following day, July 25th, it was reported, by the *Daily Express*, that the charges had been dismissed but that the defendants had been ordered to pay costs. *The Daily Mirror* of the same day reported that the costs involved amounted to thirty pounds of which the medium was to pay ten and Miss Phillimore twenty. Conan Doyle was clearly upset at the outcome. He did not approve of fortune-telling but said the situation was unjust. 'We must employ mediums,' he said, 'and those mediums must be paid. If a medium, contrary to our explicit instructions, pretends to foretell the future, we as a society are liable for aiding and abetting.... The question we now have to consider is whether it will be possible to have some sort of independent supervision'[403].

The Alliance decided not to appeal against the verdict but, according to *The Daily Mirror* of the 27th, it issued a warning to the Home Secretary that its supporters numbered 'some hundreds of thousands of voters'. The newspaper summed up by saying 'It is clear (according to Sir Arthur Conan Doyle) that the other world and its messengers are rapidly acquiring an electoral importance. Ghosts will soon be influencing votes'.

Before the end of the month ghosts took Conan Doyle to Hampshire. The *Daily Express* of July 31st reported that he had taken part in a séance at Beaulieu Abbey. A spirit of a 'wandering monk' had allegedly appeared to a woman staying at a hotel local to the Abbey. Upon following its instructions a box containing bones had been found by the estate's owner Lord Montagu.

Conan Doyle and one of Lord Montagu's friends, Sir Thomas Troubridge, were amongst those at the séance but it was reported that Conan Doyle's only contact with the spirit came when he asked it to raise the table around which they all sat if they should continue to excavate the site. The newspaper reported that 'the table swayed perceptibly'. Following this the newspaper reported that Conan Doyle was going to investigate further.

---

[403] The *Daily Express* of July 25th.

John Douglas-Scott-Montagu (1866-1929), 2nd Baron Montagu.
(Vanity Fair)

TAKING THE MESSAGE TO AFRICA

The recent court appearances surrounding fortune-telling continued to prompt reactions in the press as August commenced. The *Daily Express* of the 1st carried a letter from Conan Doyle in which, amongst other things, he expressed the hope that the extreme reaction of the law 'will lead to a reaction against it'.

Immediately below Conan Doyle's letter was another, signed simply 'A.I.' in which the writer expressed the opinion that 'People have as much right to pay the fortune-tellers to predict their future in this life as they have to pay the parson to predict it in the next'.

Three days later, on the 4th, an article was published in the same newspaper. Entitled *I Pledge My Honour that Spiritualism is True!*, it was a response by Conan Doyle to an earlier assertion by the novelist J.D. Beresford that the phenomena associated with Spiritualism had a connection to the subconscious mind. Conan Doyle welcomed the original article but disagreed with it. He went through and addressed Beresford's points before concluding by stating, with regards to Spiritualism as a whole, 'Do not examine its weakness, which is largely human weakness, but examine its strength as a living vital revelation and it will be borne in upon you that quietly and gradually something has happened in this world for which there is no parallel since the first pure days of Christianity'.

On September 9th Conan Doyle spoke at the International Spiritualist Conference held in the Queen's Hall, London. The

Daily Express of the following day singled out his claim to have received a message from Earl Haig, the senior British Army Officer during the First World War, three days after his death.

Earl Haig (1861-1928)

He explained that he had asked the relatives if they wished to hear the message as it was something only of interest to family. They had not given him a reply. He also displayed a photograph of Haig's coffin passing through the streets of London. The Field-Marshal's face could be seen over the coffin. *The Daily Mirror* of the same day chose to overlook the Haig story and focused on the fairy photographs which were also displayed and the story of a big dog which had acted as the medium for the spirit of a smaller dog. This too had been captured in a photograph that was displayed.

On the 14th the *Daily Express* published a story that was potentially embarrassing for Conan Doyle. According to the newspaper he had finally hung the painting he had purchased from William Longstaff on the wall of his Psychic Museum where it apparently covered the whole of one wall.

At the time of the purchase Conan Doyle had claimed it had been painted under psychic influence but the artist now went on record to deny this. Longstaff was quoted as saying ‘There is nothing remarkable about the picture. Unless you can call the inspiration, under which an artist always works psychic; there was nothing unusual in the way I painted it’.

It took a little over a week for Conan Doyle’s response to appear. He wrote to the paper from Bignell Wood and his response was published on the 22nd. Denying there was any discrepancy between their views, Conan Doyle stated ‘I have never thought that he was under obsession when he painted this picture…But he was certainly under strong psychic mental influence’. Conan Doyle went on to point out that Longstaff had just been to a séance and had been put in touch with a ‘vanished friend’ who was an artist. Conan Doyle asserted that Longstaff ‘was full of that spiritual elation which comes with conviction…he painted, working at great speed, a picture which depicts the whole fate of man as Spiritualists conceive it. Surely you cannot disconnect these events’.

On the last day of September Conan Doyle gave an interview on how clairvoyants could assist in the solving of crime. It was not a new subject for him but one he was clearly happy to repeatedly cover – especially when it helped to publicise his Spiritualist itinerary and his tour of Africa which was fast approaching.

Given the subject matter the press predictably brought Sherlock Holmes’s name up stating ‘The detective, with his magnifying glass, picturesque dressing gown, and scintillating deductions, may before long be a thing of the past'. Conan Doyle predicted that, eventually, there would be 'a clairvoyant in attendance at every police station and every offence will be hunted down so that crime will become very difficult, if not impossible'.

Following this, Conan Doyle took the opportunity to remind readers that Spiritualists in Britain now numbered at least two hundred thousand and stated 'We want an assurance from a party leader that we shall be free from police persecution'. This, of course, was a clear reference to the fortune-telling prosecution from earlier in the year and did rather suggest that Spiritualist votes could be had by any party that adopted a more pro-Spiritualist stance. The newspaper article went on to state that the highest concentration of Spiritualism was in the North and that Conan Doyle thought that there were around sixty thousand in Manchester alone.

Conan Doyle also attempted to quantify the level of fraud amongst mediums. 'I think I should be putting it high if I said that five per cent of mediums were frauds'[404].

This high opinion of Spiritualism and its ability to aid the cause of justice was not shared by Ingleby Oddie, the Westminster coroner. On October 12th he condemned what he called 'unwholesome dabbling in spiritualism' for the death of one David Onslow Smith. Smith, from Derbyshire, had committed suicide in the Thames and his father had given evidence that Smith had turned to Spiritualism following the death of his mother. Oddie clearly saw Spiritualism as being to blame and dismissed it as 'humbug and trickery'. The *Daily Express* decided to link this to Conan Doyle's claims of Spiritualists as an electoral force[405]. What was their purpose in doing so? One interpretation was that if political parties adopted a more favourable attitude to Spiritualists and their activities, which is what Conan Doyle wanted, in order to gain their votes,

---

[404] *The Daily Mirror* of October 1st 1928.

[405] The *Daily Express* of October 13th 1928.

tragedies like the death of David Smith would be rendered more rather than less likely.

At the end of October, Conan Doyle and his family set sail from Southampton for South Africa. In his later memoir of the trip Conan Doyle admitted that he had two motives other than spreading the Spiritualist message. The first of these was his health. He admitted to feeling run down and expressed the desire to avoid the English Winter. The second motive was nostalgia. He had a strong desire to visit parts of South Africa that he last seen at the time of the Boer War and share those places and his experiences with his family[406].

Part of the journey featured rough weather and both his sons suffered falls on board ship which left them bruised. Conan Doyle occupied a fair amount of the journey delivering Spiritualist lectures to all passenger classes.

The family arrived in mid-November[407]. They were met by local Spiritualists and press and Conan Doyle was invited to make a radio broadcast. He gave this on November 13th and used it to sketch out his position and the dates for his lectures in Cape Town. At this point he probably expected to conduct another lecture tour covering the same subjects and receiving the same kind of press coverage. However, his time in South Africa, at least as far as the media was concerned, would be well known for something far removed from Spiritualism.

On December 1st Conan Doyle arrived in Bloemfontein and took rooms at Polley's Hotel. The next day he visited the Rambler's ground where the Langman Hospital had been located during the Boer War[408]. He entered the buildings and noted that, aside from the absence of the men and suffering,

---

[406] Doyle, Arthur Conan. *Our African Winter*. Duckworth Publishing. 2001.

[407] Pugh, Brian. *A Chronology of the Life of Sir Arthur Conan Doyle*. 3rd Edition. MX Publishing 2014.

[408] Covered in the book *An Entirely New Country* by your present author.

little had changed[409]. Among the many other sites he visited was a memorial to the women and children who had died in the British Concentration Camp which had been located there. The inscription upon it was not in English and Conan Doyle misread it. He was greatly offended at the level of blame he perceived it as laying at the feet of the British and he expressed his unhappiness to a Dutch journalist who was accompanying him. The journalist lost no time in quoting him as saying that the description, according to the *Mirror*, was 'A lie and a blot on this place'[410]. He was also photographed turning his back on the memorial in protest.

His comments and actions triggered outrage. The *Daily Express* and *The Daily Mirror* editions of December 6th both covered the story. The *Mirror* reported that a crowd of three hundred people had marched on Conan Doyle's hotel to demand an explanation. The *Express* put the number a little lower at two hundred and also pointed out that this was not some unruly mob but actually an organised march that consisted of professors, lawyers, journalists and other professionals.

Rumours circulated to the effect that there was an intention to actually tar and feather Conan Doyle. Whether this was true or not is hard to determine but when the crowd reached the hotel they learned that Conan Doyle had gone out. After a period of waiting the crowd dispersed peacefully.

In the interim Conan Doyle had learned the true wording on the monument and realised that it did not paint the British in the manner he had first supposed. He later claimed that the journalist who had reported on his words could have corrected his translation at the time and that he was upset that the man had instead chosen to go for the good story. To Conan Doyle's

---

409 Doyle, Arthur Conan. *Our African Winter*. Duckworth Publishing. 2001.

410 The *Daily Express* carried a slightly different quote saying that Conan Doyle's words had been that the monument 'was a lie, an insult to this place, and to Great Britain'.

credit he immediately took steps to remedy the situation. According to the *Express* he communicated with the South African newspaper *Die Burger*. 'It has been shown,' he said, 'that I misinterpreted the real meaning of the phrase. I cannot do less than express regret and withdraw the remark'. In his book *Our African Winter* he went to great pains to point out that his decision to set the record straight was in no way motivated by news of the protestors at his hotel.

The year concluded with visits to Durban and Johannesburg with Conan Doyle noting that the former, in the opinion of his family, had been the 'jolliest town' they had been to[411].

[411] Doyle, Arthur Conan. *Our African Winter*. Duckworth Publishing. 2001.

1929

'I AM THAT GHOST'

Conan Doyle's African tour continued apace in 1929. Above and beyond the lectures Conan Doyle also found time for tourism, visiting a gold mine, the Khami Ruins and Victoria Falls. By the beginning of February he was in Kenya where he arrived in Mombasa. He did not linger but headed by train to the capital Nairobi where he stayed at the Norfolk Hotel. He was in the area for most of the next month combining tourism with Spiritualism.

On March 12th, the day before he was due to leave Nairobi to take a ship from Mombasa, he gave his last lecture at the Theatre Royal. Here he suffered an embarrassment that the press simply could not overlook.

According to the *Daily Express* of March 14th, Conan Doyle was, as usual, running through a series of lantern slides. These were of spirits, ghosts and fairies but Conan Doyle chose to focus on one slide in particular. The slide featured a ghost and the clarity of the image was something of which Conan Doyle was very proud. Before revealing the slide to his audience he described it and drew the attention of his audience to the ghost's 'hard, wicked face - not the sort of person one would want to meet alone in a dark corridor'. He went on to explain that the photograph had been taken in a haunted house in Nottingham and that he had no reason to doubt its authenticity. As the slide came up on the screen a man rose from the audience and, according to the reports, said 'I am that ghost'.

The man in question was Spencer Palmer, a Nairobi based dentist. Palmer went on to explain that he had been a member of a party of ghost hunters who had visited the Nottingham house in 1909. When the resident spirits had failed to show themselves he and his brother had arranged the fake photograph with Palmer dressing up in an old nightgown and pulling faces at the camera.

Conan Doyle apparently gave up on the photograph quite easily and, accepting Palmer's explanation, declared that he would not use it again. Nevertheless, having a photograph dismissed in which he had expressed such pride must have pained him.

However, this was not the end of the matter. Conan Doyle later recorded that he had made contact with one Mr Melton, from whom he had obtained the photograph. Melton had assured him that he had personally taken the photograph and declared the dentist's story to be a complete fabrication. Conan Doyle was frustrated that he learned this too late to prevent the dentist's version of events making it into newspapers in England and the United States[412].

The Daily Mirror of March 16th reported that Conan Doyle had left Africa the previous day primarily to be back in England in time for the General Election. The newspaper reported that it was Conan Doyle's intention to approach party leaders in order to determine which party would offer Spiritualists the most freedom from persecution.

Conan Doyle and his family found themselves in Cairo towards the end of March where they took the opportunity to visit the Pyramids and the Sphinx[413]. By the beginning of April they had reached Paris and, a little while later, they were back in England.

---

[412] Doyle, Arthur Conan. *Our African Winter*. Duckworth Publishing. 2001.

[413] Pugh, Brian. *A Chronology of the Life of Sir Arthur Conan Doyle*. 3rd Edition. MX Publishing 2014.

May was a busy month. It began with a meeting of Our Society and ended with the celebration of his seventieth birthday. June and July were relatively quiet by comparison which probably provided the opportunity for some well-earned rest. It also seems highly likely that Conan Doyle spent some of the time knocking into shape the notes of his Africa tour ready for publication.

In August the house in Bignell Wood was damaged by fire. Jean and the three children were home at the time. Conan Doyle was out for a stroll. He would later praise those who assisted in not only ensuring the safety of his family but also that of many possessions.

September saw the publication of *Our African Winter* - the account of Conan Doyle's tour of Africa. The same publisher, John Murray, put out an edition of all the Sherlock Holmes long stories that same month.

Perhaps as part of the publicity for his African memoir, Conan Doyle made a public statement on the subject of religion in which he made it clear that, in his opinion, it was the clergy that were largely responsible for the decline in Christianity. They had emptied their own churches with their doctrines and sermons.

One Rev. Bryn Thomas in Aberavon was decidedly un-amused and wrote to the *Daily Express* which published his letter on the 11th. 'Conan Doyle was once a materialist. Now as a spiritualist, he has no right to judge us'. Making it clear what he thought of Spiritualism, the Rev Thomas went on to say that Conan Doyle would better spend his time by paying 'a visit to Maskelyne and Devant's theatre at St. George's Hall, London'. There, thought Thomas, Conan Doyle should 'try and fathom the tricks there similar to those which, he says, are going to save the world'.

Conan Doyle had other plans. It was time to take the Spiritualist message to mainland Europe. Before doing so, however, he had two legal matters to attend to. The first of these was to instruct his legal representative in connection with an accusation of plagiarism. Earlier in the year an article had appeared entitled *A. Conan Doyle Sensation. Famous Author 'Lifts' Young Novelist's Plot. A Plea for Belated Justice*. This article alleged that Conan Doyle's 1925 story *The Land of Mist* had plagiarised a book entitled *The Splendid Angel* written by one J. H. Symons. It was further alleged that Conan Doyle's story *The Disintegration Machine*, which had been published in *The Strand* in January, had also stolen from a work of Symons entitled *The End of the Marriage Vow*. Given the timing, it was presumably the latter story that had triggered the article.

Conan Doyle launched a libel action against the publisher and printer of the article and this was settled on October 15th by which time Conan Doyle was in Europe. In court it was demonstrated that both of Conan Doyle's stories were in the hands of his literary agent before the respective works of Symons came out. The publisher withdrew the allegations and apologised and the printers expressed similar sentiments. Damages and costs were awarded to Conan Doyle[414]. Strangely, the author Symons appears to have had no involvement in proceedings.

The second legal matter that Conan Doyle set in motion, according to *The Daily Mirror* of October 16th, was to sue Oscar Slater. Slater had made no attempt to reimburse anyone who had contributed financially to the efforts to free him. According to the report, Conan Doyle was seeking 'some hundreds of pounds'. The report went on to say that it was likely to be some time before the action was taken forward.

By this time Conan Doyle was not in the best health. On October 19th he had begun to feel unwell and by the 21st he was in a hotel in Copenhagen – still feeling unwell. The decision was clearly made to return to England without delay and he was back in his flat at Buckingham Palace Mansions by early November[415].

---

[414] The *Daily Express* of October 16th 1929.

[415] Pugh, Brian. *A Chronology of the Life of Sir Arthur Conan Doyle*. 3rd Edition. MX Publishing 2014.

Despite his ill-health he still got involved in high-profile events. It was reported in the *Daily Express* of November 4th that Conan Doyle and H.G. Wells had both written to a man named Corbett in France who was on trial for the murder of his mother. Corbett had claimed that he had drugged his mother before shooting her to stop her suffering further from terminal cancer. Conan Doyle's letter of support, in which he had offered to act as a witness, is hardly surprising given his previously published pro-euthanasia views.

After a couple of ill-advised speaking engagements Conan Doyle returned to Windlesham where he appears to have rested without further excitement.

1930

BREAKING THE LINK

On January 22nd 1930 Conan Doyle resigned from the Society for Psychical Research[416]. He had been a member for thirty-six years, having joined at the beginning of 1893 at the suggestion of his friend and solicitor A.C.R. Williams. At that time Conan Doyle had been far more sceptical than he was now and the more he had embraced Spiritualism the less tolerant he had grown towards the sceptical stance of the SPR.

Matters came to a head when he read the January 1930 edition of the SPR's journal. It contained an article by one Theodore Besterman which strongly suggested that a series of séances, which Conan Doyle referred to as the 'Millésime sittings', were fraudulent. Conan Doyle was always sensitive to accusations of fraud but he was especially incensed as Besterman had not been present at the séances in question, whereas one Professor Ernesto Bozzano had been present and had declared the séances to be free of fraud.

In his resignation letter Conan Doyle declared that he felt the SPR was biased in favour of sceptics stating that the '...assertions of the opponents of Spiritualism are at once accepted on their face value without the slightest attempt at discriminate examination'. His letter concluded thus:

> '...my only resource is, after thirty-six years of patience, to resign my own membership and to make some sort of public protest against

[416] *Journal of the Society for Psychical Research* Volume 26 1930.

the essentially unscientific and biased work of a Society which has for a whole generation produced no constructive work of any kind, but has confined its energies to the misrepresentation and hindrance of those who have really worked at the most important problem ever presented to mankind.'

Professor Ernesto Bozzano (1862 – 1943)

Some little time later he followed this up with a circular in which he reproduced his letter to the SPR's chairman, restated many of his points and concluded with a recommendation that SPR members who felt as he did should follow his example and resign. He stated that such people would find a home with the British College of Psychic Science which, according to him, boasted '…mediums at hand to be tested, a good library, an excellent quarterly magazine, and an atmosphere which is progressive and not stagnant.'

The SPR leadership, despite the severity of Conan Doyle's attack, might have elected to accept the resignation and say no more. However, Conan Doyle's call on members to leave was not something that they could leave unchallenged. In their March journal, they published a series of responses to his accusations (which were also reproduced in full). They drew attention to Conan Doyle's many writings, his long membership of the SPR and, finally, his health which they knew to be poor. All three were cited as reasons why they did not wish to respond, but their collective hand had been forced. The first response came from the chairman, Lawrence Jones, to whom Conan Doyle's original resignation had been sent. Jones tackled many of Conan Doyle's points and clearly was not sympathetic to his position. He concluded thus:

> 'If the Society's investigations into physical phenomena have throughout its history been infrequent, this is due to the high standard of control conditions on which the Society has always, and properly, insisted, and to the preference shown by physical [sic] mediums for the much lower standard maintained elsewhere.'

He went on to say:

> 'It is, however, to be noted that sittings held in complete darkness, for the most part without control and without any searching of those present, sittings at which phenomena were produced which cannot be paralleled in the records of any sittings held under good control conditions, are described by Sir Arthur as "on the very highest possible level of psychical research." Further comment is superfluous.
>
> 'The theory that since Myers's death the Society, or the Officers or Council, have developed an Anti-Spiritualistic bias is as lacking in foundation as the contrary theory (which we have also heard expressed) that in recent years it and they have become uncritically Spiritualistic.'

The chairman's response was followed by another from Besterman in which he challenged Conan Doyle's argument and his accuracy. Both were clearly impaired by poor health in his opinion.

The *Daily Express* covered both Conan Doyle's resignation and the Society response in its issue of March 19th. It noted that there had been six resignations from the Society since Conan Doyle's resignation and only two of those had cited the circumstances that had triggered Conan Doyle's exit.

Conan Doyle was asked to comment on the response from the SPR. 'I am not at all bitter about the matter,' he said. 'I want more attention given to spiritualists, and more courtesy shown to them'.

He went on to say, 'The Society do not appear to appreciate the efforts of people who are attempting to gain more knowledge of the subject of spiritualism. You do not get anywhere by sneering. We want more experiments and knowledge and to secure that I think it is necessary for the society to have more sympathetic people in the seats of the governors'.

DOYLE'S WORK IS DONE

At the beginning of May Conan Doyle drew up a new will. It must have felt, to some extent, as if the world was already moving on without him. His sons Denis and Adrian were developing their love of fast cars by entering numerous competitions. This hobby was occasionally getting them into trouble and Adrian had already been fined for speeding back in March. It would have been difficult for Conan Doyle to criticise his son on this matter given his own motoring history.

The Daily Mirror of May 23rd carried an opinion on Sherlock Holmes which was not presented as a direct quote from Conan Doyle but, nevertheless, sounded very much as though it was. 'One can have too much even of one's own good things. An author likes to be known for *all* that he has written and he generally prefers work less applauded than his popular triumphs. But writers can do nothing about it. The public give this life to their work. And it is useless to argue with the public'.

It is possible that this resigned attitude towards Sherlock Holmes's enduring popularity had been in response to the sixteenth annual report of the Carnegie United Kingdom Trust which had revealed that detective stories were fast becoming the most popular library books[417].

Jean's brother Patrick Stewart Leckie died at the beginning of June following a fall down some stairs at the Royal Pavilion

---

[417] The *Daily Express* of May 10th 1930.

Hotel in Folkestone. According to *The Daily Mirror* of June 11th the inquest took place on the 10th and Conan Doyle was a witness. He testified to the effect that his brother-in-law suffered from Bright's Disease and had often complained of giddiness. Conan Doyle laid emphasis on the fact that his brother-in-law had been of 'very temperate habits'. The funeral took place on the 12th.

On July 1st Conan Doyle led a deputation of Spiritualists to the Home Office. It was his latest attempt to get the government to look at the various laws which he felt were being used to persecute mediums. He had not been expected to lead the deputation on the day even though that had been the original intention. Due to his poor health he was to have been replaced by one Frederick Charles Hannen Swaffer – a journalist who had worked for the *Daily Mail* and *The Daily Mirror* and now worked for the *Daily Express*. Swaffer later reported that he was replaced by Conan Doyle 'at the last moment' when it was deemed that Conan Doyle was well enough to go. The identity of the person who made the determination that Conan Doyle was up to the task was not made clear but it seems likely that it was Conan Doyle himself rather than an independent doctor.

Upon his arrival at the Home Office Conan Doyle tried to deliver his speech standing but gladly sank into a chair when the Home Secretary asked him to do so. According to Swaffer's later reports, Conan Doyle spoke brokenly and tapped his heart with the fingers of his right hand throughout the meeting. Jean was at his side with smelling salts. His speech was listened to sympathetically but with no commitment from the government.

Swaffer said farewell to Conan Doyle as they left the Home Office and later reported that he knew they would not see each other again. 'He had willed himself to live long enough to head the protest - and then he went away to die'.

At around this time, presumably realising that he was close to death or at least no longer fit enough to take an active part in the movement, Conan Doyle resigned as President of the London Spiritualist Alliance. These events done, he returned home to Windlesham. Five days after his visit to the Home Office he suffered a heart attack and he died on the morning of July 7th with his wife at his side. His famous, and often reported, last words to Jean were 'You are wonderful'[418].

The news of Conan Doyle's death reached Herbert Greenhough Smith at *The Strand*'s offices before the end of the day. The issue of the magazine being worked on at the time was that for September and it was due to go to the press the next day. While it might have looked to the magazine's readers that it was slow to comment on the passing of its famous contributor, Greenhough Smith had, in fact, written his thoughts down less than twenty-four hours after news of Conan Doyle's death had reached him.

227

The Passing of Conan Doyle

By THE EDITOR OF "THE STRAND MAGAZINE."

The header from The Strand obituary of Conan Doyle

Over four pages Greenhough Smith attempted to give a sketch of the man who he viewed very much as a friend as well as a great writer. He admitted that his writing was hurried but

418 The *Daily Express* of July 8th 1930.

he did a good job of fitting Conan Doyle's seventy-one years into so small a number of pages.

'We think of him first as a great story writer, and next, in his later years, as the burning crusader in the cause of Spiritualism. But he lived life, and enjoyed life, to the full'. Greenhough Smith went on to recall the arrival on his desk of the first Sherlock Holmes story from the, then largely unknown, writer.

> 'The STRAND MAGAZINE was in its infancy in those days; good story-writers were scarce, and here to an editor, jaded with wading through reams of impossible stuff, comes a gift from Heaven, a godsend in the shape of a story that brought a gleam of happiness into the despairing life of this weary editor. Here was a new and gifted story-writer; there was no mistaking the ingenuity of plot, the limpid clearness of style, the perfect art of telling a story.'

Greenhough-Smith went on to discuss Joseph Bell and the "death" of Sherlock Holmes in *The Final Problem*. He concluded his piece thus:

> 'As everybody knows, the adventure in Lauterbrunnen Pass was *not* the end of Sherlock Holmes. The end, alas, has come now, with the death of his creator. Doyle's work is done - and, in whatever sphere, it was well done.'

The press naturally produced a lot of column inches following Conan Doyle's death. The *Daily Express* reported that, like the Houdini's before them, Conan Doyle and Jean had agreed a code word before his death so that she would know when communications from the other side were genuine. This fact was revealed to the newspaper by eldest son Denis. His brother Adrian spoke of tests which his mother knew that would also aid her in identifying when her late husband was truly in contact.

The Daily Mirror of July 8th was blunt when speaking of Conan Doyle's legacy. It spoke of Sherlock Holmes, the books on the Boer War and the Great War, and the campaigns for Edalji and Slater. When it came to Spiritualism it undoubtedly spoke for the majority when it said 'His "spiritualism" is a matter of controversy. We neglect it. It is as the creator of

Sherlock and Watson, the immortal pair, that he will be remembered. As their father he is adored by a reading world now almost entirely devoted to detective novels'.

The newspaper was taken to task for its attitude towards Spiritualism and, a few days later, printed a response in which it took the opportunity to 'remind ardent believers that thousands of people do not agree with them'[419].

The *Daily Express* of the following day reported that Conan Doyle was to be buried in the gardens of Windlesham beside his small writing hut. It also added that a memorial service was being organised to take place at the Albert Hall on the following Sunday. *The Daily Mirror* of the same day gave the name of the minister destined to officiate at the funeral as Rev. Brayton Thomas.

On Friday July 11th Conan Doyle's funeral was held at Windlesham. *The Daily Mirror* of the 12th reported that some four hundred people had stood upon the front lawn and that their number had included authors, spiritualists and many local villagers. Of the family there were Jean, Adrian and daughter Jean[420]. Eldest son Denis was in his room suffering from laryngitis. The newspaper reported that his bedroom window was kept open in order that he could hear the service.

Rev. Thomas read out what the newspaper described as 'an expression...of the whole family's attitude towards death'. At the conclusion of this the coffin was taken to the writing hut and lowered into the grave.

In the aftermath of Conan Doyle's funeral, Spiritualism was arguably a hotter topic than it had been during his final days. Jean made token attempts to speak on the subject and she was

---

419 *The Daily Mirror* of July 11th 1930.

420 According to Georgina Doyle, Mary was also present at the funeral although she cannot be made out in photographs.

just as successful in stirring up opponents. When she stated that there were mediums in the early church she was criticised by the Rev. Desmond Morse-Boycott. Morse-Boycott was in turn challenged by one John Lamond who took it upon himself to fight Jean's, and Spiritualism's, corner[421]. This act undoubtedly went in his favour when he later sought to become Conan Doyle's first British biographer.

July 13th saw the memorial service at the Albert Hall. *The Daily Mirror* of the following day carried a photograph of Jean sitting next to the empty chair intended for her late husband's spirit to occupy. On the 16th the same newspaper reported that mediums across the world were reporting that they had either established contact with Conan Doyle or had received messages concerning him. In the same article it was stated that Jean had received a message from her late husband during the Albert Hall event but no details were provided.

The article also carried news that would have pained Conan Doyle. An official Home Office spokesman reported that no changes were proposed following Conan Doyle's earlier visit - '..the laws under which prosecutions are made against Spiritualists still stand, and the responsible authorities are there to see that these laws are enforced'.

On August 5th, in New York, Conan Doyle and what he believed in were effectively mocked by the American mentalist Joseph Dunninger. Dunninger had very much stepped into Houdini's shoes by heading up the investigating committee for the *Science and Invention* magazine. This offered over four thousand pounds to any medium able to produce 'spiritualistic phenomena which Mr Dunninger cannot duplicate by stage tricks'[422].

That evening Dunninger proceeded to produce the spirit of Conan Doyle before an audience containing members of the press and mediums. During the course of the demonstration Conan Doyle's spirit appeared and asked to shake hands with

421 The *Daily Express* of July 22nd 1930.
422 The *Daily Express* of August 7th 1930.

the reporter from the *Daily Express*. The reporter complied and later wrote that the hand he had shaken was 'indisputably human'. Tambourines were thrown across the room, Conan Doyle's head materialised and a paraffin gloved hand made by Conan Doyle's spirit was left behind along with a message on a slate which read 'The great bond of all is love. – Doyle'.

Of course it was all magic and this was Dunninger's point. The whole exercise was designed to rubbish mediums who had claimed to have been in contact with Conan Doyle. Despite this, one medium named Madame Tavarozzi insisted, as Conan Doyle had himself done to Houdini, that Dunninger had mediumistic skills and had genuinely summoned the spirit of Conan Doyle.

The Daily Mirror was not impressed by events of this sort and, in its issue of August 8th, it stated, with reference to the families of believers such as Conan Doyle, that 'it must be perplexing and humiliating for them to receive reputed messages, of the usual anodyne description, with mediumistic references, from all parts of the world – particularly from the magicians of America, whence come revelations too frequent and fantastic to be convincing'.

It concluded by stating 'The sort of posthumous publicity thus attached to honoured names must be far from pleasant to those who cared for the once "earth-bound" possessors of them'.

Someone else who had claimed to be in contact with the spirit of Conan Doyle was his widow. The *Daily Express* of August 11th reported that Jean had confirmed to an audience of nearly three thousand spiritualists that she had received a personal message, the authenticity of which she was certain.

The revelation was made in the Queen's Hall and the medium responsible for conveying the message was one Estelle Roberts. Roberts had been the medium present at the Albert Hall event back in July but it was not made clear whether this was the occasion to which Jean was referring.

The coffin of Arthur Conan Doyle is brought into the garden of Windlesham (The Collection of Brian Pugh)

Arthur Conan Doyle's coffin is conveyed to its grave next to his writing hut
(The Collection of Brian Pugh)

The Daily Mirror of September 22nd reported that the unsettled value of Conan Doyle's estate was estimated at thirty-thousand pounds. Jean stated that it would have been far more if he had not been so devoted to Spiritualism. Further to claiming to have had additional messages from her husband, Jean stated that he was presently enjoying a holiday and that as he learned about the workings of the next life he would let the family know.

For the time being, as Herbert Greenhough-Smith had stated, 'Doyle's work is done - and, in whatever sphere, it was well done'.

BIBLIOGRAPHY

Cooper, Joe. *The Case of the Cottingley Fairies*. Hale 1990. ISBN 0-7090-3935-2.

Doyle, Arthur Conan. *Memories and Adventures*. Wordsworth Editions Ltd. 2007. ISBN 978-1840225709.

Doyle, Arthur Conan. *Our African Winter*. Duckworth Publishing. 2001. ISBN 9780715630846.

Doyle, Arthur Conan. *The Coming of the Fairies*. University of Nebraska Press 2006. ISBN 978-0-8032-6655-1.

Doyle, Arthur Conan. *The Wanderings of a Spiritualist*. Hodder and Stoughton. 1921.

Doyle, Georgina. *Out of the Shadows*. Calabash Press. 2004. ISBN 9781553100645.

Duncan, Alistair. *An Entirely New Country*. MX Publishing 2011. ISBN 978-1908218193.

Gibson, John Michael and Green, Richard Lancelyn. *A Bibliography of A. Conan Doyle*. Hudson House, New York. 2000. ISBN 9780967750002.

Gibson, John Michael and Green, Richard Lancelyn. *Letters to the Press*. Martin Secker & Warburg Ltd. 1975. ISBN 9780664213114.

Hall, Trevor H. *Sherlock Holmes and his creator*. Duckworth Publishing 1978. ISBN 0 7156 0873 8.

Lamond, John. *Arthur Conan Doyle: A Memoir*. John Murray 1931.

Lellenberg Jon, Stashower, Daniel, Foley, Charles. *Arthur Conan Doyle: A Life in Letters*. Harper Press. 2007. ISBN 9780007247592.

Lycett, Andrew. *Conan Doyle: The Man who Created Sherlock Holmes*. Orion. 2007. ISBN 9780297848523.

Murchison, Carl. Ed. *The Case For and Against Psychical Belief*. Clark University 1927.

Nollen, Scott Allen. *Sir Arthur Conan Doyle at the Cinema*. McFarland & Co Inc. 2004. ISBN 9780786421244.

Pugh, Brian. *A Chronology of the Life of Sir Arthur Conan Doyle*. 3rd Edition. MX Publishing 2014. ISBN 9781780926384.

Sandford, Christopher. *Houdini and Conan Doyle*. Duckworth Overlook 2011. ISBN 978-0-7156-4146-0.

Spencer, Frank. *The Piltdown Papers*. Oxford University Press 1990. ISBN 019 858 5233.

Whitt, J.F. *The Strand Magazine 1891-1950 A Selective Checklist*. 1979. ISBN 0950670006.

Zecher, Henry. *William Gillette: America's Sherlock Holmes*. Xlibris 2011. ISBN 9781453555811.

INDEX

6th Royal Sussex Volunteer Regiment, 155

A Duet, 37, 92

A Scandal in Bohemia, 33

A Study in Scarlet, 55, 84

A Word of Warning, 373

Adelaide Town Hall, 238

Adelphi Hotel (Liverpool), 58, 60

Adelphi Theatre (London), 64, 80

Adventure of Copper Beeches, 138

Adventures with Authors, 43

Aeolian Hall, 297

Albert Hall (London), 70, 214, 405, 406, 407

Aldwych Club, 219

All Saints Church, 56

Amateur Billiard Championship, 131, 132

An Entirely New Country, xxi, 28, 45

Argus, 243, 265

Artillery Hall (Hull), 71

Ashwell, Lena, 39

Associated Sunday Magazine, 122

Auckland Star, 256

Australian and New Zealand Luncheon Club, 205

Authors' Club, 48, 55

auto-wheel, 131

Auto-wheel, 72

Ball, Alec, 114

Barnardo's, 48

Barrie, J.M., 80, 84, 120, 125

Bates College, 288

Beach Hotel, 90

Belfast News-letter, 334

Belfast Telegraph, 332, 333, 334

Bell, Dr. Joseph, 110, 111

Bennett, James O'Donnell, 162

Beresford, J.D., 380

Bernhardi, General Friedrich von, 133

Bernhardt, Sarah, 93, 119, 127

Besant, Walter, 48

Besterman, Theodore, 397

Bexhill-On-Sea, 138

Bignell Wood, 339, 342, 382, 391

Blair, Captain Gordon Campbell, 128

Bloemfontein, 384

Blow, Mark (photographer), 250

Blue Mountains, 260, 268

BMA Congress, 136

Boirac, Professor Emile, 196

Bond, Frederick Bligh, 350

Bozzano, Professor Ernesto, 397

Brigadier Gerard, 58, 64, 92

Bright, Addison, 80

Brighton, 71, 72, 131, 171, 342

Bristol Hippodrome, 274

British College of Psychic Science, 398

British Empire League, 244

British Industries Fair, 361

British Museum, 57, 311, 337

Brock, Henry Matthew, 103, 104

Brookfield, Charles, 121

Brown Palace Hotel, 312

Buckingham Palace, 195

Buckingham Palace Mansions, 341, 392

Burns Detective Agency, 145

Burns, William, 145, 155, 164

Burroughes Hall, 226

Caillard, Adrien, 138

Cambridge, 47, 48, 105, 277

Canada, 107, 149, 150, 152, 313, 314

Cardiff Evening Express, 206, 208

Carmer, Count, 106

Carnarvon, Lord, 311

Carnegie Hall, 284, 288, 289

Carroll Theatre, 295

Carter the Great, 255

Carter, Howard, 311

Casement, Roger (Sir), 60, 62, 90, 107, 174

Caxton Hall, 195, 335, 338

Challenger, Professor, xxii, 93, 113, 123, 325

Channel Tunnel, 132, 133

Charter, Marguerite Remington, 150

Chesterton, G.K., 113

Christian Evidence Propaganda, 249

Chronicles of Cleophas, 350

Churchill, Winston, 148

Cleave, 28

Collier's Weekly, 34, 35

Coney Island, 151

Congo Free State, 60, 68

Congo Reform Association, 60, 61, 62

Constantinople, 27

Cook, Sir Joseph, 244

Copenhagen, 392

Corelli, Marie, 311

Cottingley Fairies, 228, 231, 251, 257, 259, 356

Crawford, Francis R., 39

Crawford, Professor W.J., 196

Crippen, Hawley Harvey, 94

Criterion (restaurant), 114

Crowborough, xxii, 56, 57, 61, 72, 90, 103, 128, 154, 155, 163, 214, 329

Crowborough Beacon Golf Club, 95

Crowborough Gymnasium Club, 95

Crowborough Volunteer Training Corps, 163

Crystal Palace, 45, 105, 109

Cumberland, Stuart, 208, 213, 276

Cummins, Geraldine, 350

Curtis, Catherine, 291, 292

D'Oyly Carte Opera Company, 103

Daily Chronicle, 199

Daily Express, 27, 29, 34, 39, 43, 45, 47, 48, 55, 56, 59, 63, 68, 69, 70, 71, 77, 81, 85, 86, 88, 89, 90, 91, 93, 104, 105, 110, 119, 124, 125, 126, 127, 128, 132, 133, 135, 136, 138, 140, 147, 148, 149, 152, 154, 155, 156, 158, 166, 167, 185, 186, 187, 195, 208, 211,214, 215, 216, 217, 218, 226, 231, 232, 234, 251, 252, 274, 275, 277, 281, 283, 296, 304, 307, 312, 314, 316, 317, 322, 323, 329, 330, 332, 335, 337, 338, 339, 340, 341, 342, 345, 350, 356, 362, 363, 365, 367, 368, 369, 373, 374, 375, 376, 377, 378, 380, 381, 382, 383, 385, 389, 391, 393, 399, 402, 404, 405, 407

Daily Herald, 238, 240

Daily Mail, 41, 42, 82, 157, 161, 208, 234, 313, 402

Daily Observer, 249

Danger! And Other Stories, 200

Davos, 63

Dawley, Herbert, 291

Dawson, Charles, 57, 113, 123

de Heredia, Charles M., 302

Dear Old Charlie, 122

Death and the Hereafter, 206, 214, 245

Delphic Club, 218

Detective of the Surgery, 110

Die Burger, 386

Divorce Commission, 127

Divorce Law Reform Union, 92

Dominion (newspaper), 256, 257

Doyle, Connie, 59, 166, 183, 272

Doyle, Denis Percy Stewart Conan, 56

Doyle, Innes, 43, 49, 59, 72, 80, 85, 86, 97, 99, 107, 135, 171, 172, 195, 200, 207

Doyle, Kingsley Conan, 45, 46, 49, 53, 55, 61, 70, 71, 72, 85, 93, 107, 127, 172, 176, 181, 185, 195, 199, 217, 220, 235, 238, 263, 274

Doyle, Mary, 35

Doyle, Mary Conan, 69, 91, 331

Dresden, 45, 49, 53, 69, 71

Dunninger, Joseph, 406

Dupin, Auguste, 55

Easter Uprising, 174

Eclair Film Company, 138

Edalji, George, 27, 28, 125, 215

Edinburgh University, 113, 177, 292

Edinburgh, Orkney and Shetland Literary and Scientific Association, 112

Edward VII (King), 82

Edwin Drood, 368

Elcock, Howard, 310, 321, 325, 353, 356

Elektra, 93

Elvey, Maurice, 273

entitled *Our Reply to the Cleric*, 218

Erskine, Professor Alexander, 218

Evelyn-White, H.G., 322

Evening News, 245

Evening Post, 257

Exploits of the Anzacs, 205

Fairbanks, Douglas, 313

Farnham Herald, 274

Father Brown, 113

Fenning Company, 138

Ferrier, Sir David, 207, 208

Festival of Empire, 105, 109

Fires of Fate, 58, 59, 63, 68, 308

Free Lance, 258

Freeman's Journal, 245

French, Field Marshal Sir John, 167

Frohman, Charles, 29, 38, 64, 91, 95, 311

Gardner, Edward, 230, 246

Garrick Theatre (New York), 95

Gazette, 277, 356

George, David Lloyd, 181

Germany and the Next War, 133

Ghost of the Moat, 367

Gilchrist, Marion, 124

Giles, Dr. William, 237

Gillette, William, 29, 38, 58, 64, 83, 96, 311, 374

Gilmer, Albert Hatton, 29

Globe Theatre, 91, 94

Goligher Circle', 196

Goligher, Kathleen, 196

Gorefield, 308

Gow, David, 213

Grace, W.G., 48

Grand Central Hotel, 236

Gray, Clifton D., 288

Grayshott, 199, 263

Griffiths, Frances, 229, 230, 246

Grotrian Hall, 341, 362, 364, 367, 374, 376

Haggard, H. Rider, 48, 126

Haig, General Sir Douglas, 168

Hale, Arthur, 134

Hall, Trevor H., xxi, 112

Hapgood, Norman, 34, 35

Harbinger of Light, 269

Harding, Lyn, 83, 85

Hardy, A. F., 80

Hawkins, Anthony Hope, 48

Hayes, John, 42

Hippodrome, 123

His Last Bow, 33, 181, 185, 186, 275

Hodder and Stoughton, 126, 296, 323

Holborn restaurant, 119

Holborn Restaurant, 93, 231

Holiday, Gilbert, 96, 98

Holmes, Sherlock, xxii, 27, 28, 33, 34, 38, 40, 45, 58, 64, 68, 82, 83, 84, 88, 90, 92, 93, 96, 97, 103, 110, 112, 113, 115, 121, 126, 127, 134, 136, 138, 145, 149, 155, 173, 181, 183, 185, 186, 214, 220, 228, 245, 249, 272, 273, 275, 276, 281, 282, 287, 289, 293, 295, 308, 310, 311, 312, 314, 317, 322, 324, 325, 329, 332, 333, 340, 349, 353, 355, 361, 363, 364, 374, 375, 382, 391, 401, 404

Hope, Anthony, 48, 120, 125

Hope, William, 289, 300

Hornung, E.W., 80, 166, 272

Hotel Ambassador, 286

Hotel Metropole, 27, 55, 58, 85, 93, 131

Hotel Shelburne, 151

Houdini, Harry, xxiii, 223, 224, 225, 226, 227, 230, 284, 289, 290, 291, 293, 294, 295, 298, 299, 300, 301, 302, 312, 313, 353, 354, 355

Hughes, William Morris, 236

Humbert, General Georges, 173

Hylan, John Francis, 287

Imperial Copyright Act, 114

International Church Congress, 218

International Psychic Gazette, 263

International Spiritualist Conference, 380

International Spiritualist Congress, 339

Irish Home Rule, 107, 150, 174

Irish News, 333, 334, 335

Irving, Henry, 64, 81

Jastrow, Joseph, 356

Jeffries, James, 65, 67

Jerome, Jerome K., 120

Johnson, Jack, 65, 67

Jones, Lawrence, 399

Joseph Bell, M.D., F.R.C.S., J.P., D.L., etc. An Appreciation by an Old Friend, 112

Joseph Henri Honoré Boex aka J.H. Rosny, 148

Kenya, 389

King, Claude, 84, 86, 87

Kingsway, 39, 122

La Force Mystérieuse, 148

Lamond, John, 92, 406

Langman Hospital, 384

Le Maison Temperley, 127

Le Temps, 149

Lee, Arthur, 85

Lewis, Irving Jefferson, 64

Liberty, 353, 355, 361

Life After Death, 199

Light, 171, 172, 176, 213, 228, 317, 337, 344

Littlehampton, 90, 91

Liverpool, 58, 59, 60

Lloyd's Sunday News, 297

Lockard, Edmund, 364

Lodge, Sir Oliver, 185, 186, 210, 226, 231, 232, 324, 345, 367, 377

London Spiritualist Alliance, 290, 307, 377, 402

Longstaff, Will, 375, 382

Lyceum Club, 196

Lyric Theatre (London), 59

Magee, Reverend J.A., 218

Maison Temperley, 119

Manchester, 71, 88, 185, 215, 383

Manly Pacific Hotel, 250

Mark Cross Police Court, 134

Marylebone Spiritualist Association, 297

Maskelyne, Nevil, 208, 219

McAlpin Hotel, 290

McQuilland, L.J., 186, 187

medium in the mask, 213, 344

Melbourne Cricket Ground, 243

Melodrama of the Ring, 77

Memories and Adventures, 172, 323

Micah Clarke, 54

Middlesex Hospital, 48

Midland Station Hotel, 333

Midlothian, 110

Millard, Victor R., 254

Millward, Charles, 96

Molly Maguires, 145, 164

Mombasa, 389

Moody-Manners Company, 63

Morel, Edmund Dene, 59, 61

Moriarty, Professor, 35, 84

Murchison, Carl, 356

Mystery of Boscombe Vale, 138

National League for Opposing Woman Suffrage, 135

Neilson-Terry, Dennis, 274

Nelson and Sons, 45

New Gallery Kinema, 337

New York Morning Telegraph, 64, 66

New Zealand Herald, 254, 255, 256, 258

Newcastle, 70, 106

Newcastle Town Hall, 70

Newnes, George, 88, 89, 141

Newton, Lord, 172

Norfolk Hotel (Kenya), 389

Northern Star, 265

Northern Whig, 333, 334

Northern Whig and Belfast Post, 333

Norwood, Eille, 273, 311, 312

Oddie, Ingleby, 383

Old Bailey, 174, 344

Oldham, Leslie, 166

Olympic Games, 41, 125

Order of Nichan-i-Chefakat, 27

Order of the Medjidieh, 27

Ossining, W.M., 164

Otago Daily Times, 254, 258, 259

Our African Winter, 386, 391

Our American Adventure, 310

Our Second American Adventure, 321

Our Society (or Crimes Club), 196, 391

Paget, Sidney, 33, 36, 141, 310

Paget, Walter, 140, 141, 142

Palmer, Spencer, 390

Park, William, 365, 369

Pearson, Arthur, 90

Pearson's Magazine, 310

Pemberton, Max, 33, 124

Perrin, William Willcox, 299

Petit Bleu, 68

Petty's Hotel, 247

Pheneas, 303, 342

Pheneas Speaks, 362

Phillpotts, Eden, 119, 120

Piccadilly Hotel (London), 72

Pickford, Mary, 313

Pictures of Psychic Phenomena, 240

Pietri, Dorando, 41, 43

Pilgrims Club, 125

Plymouth, 70

Poe, Edgar Allen, 55

Polley's Hotel, 384

Portsmouth, 196, 215, 217

Press, 257

Price, Harry, 289, 290, 310

Prince Henry of Prussia Cup, 105, 106

Prince of Wales's Theatre, 122

Princess Theatre, 29

Psychic Bookshop, 330, 337, 356, 362

Queensbury, Marquess of, 121

Ragtime, 123

Ranjitsinhji, Kumar Shri (Ranji), 47

Raphael Tuck & Sons Ltd, 41, 152

Reginald Brett (Viscount Esher), 79

Richards, Wesley, 256

Richet, Charles, 350

Rickard, Tex, 66, 67

Roberts, Estelle, 407

Roberts, Sydney, 43

Robinson, Bertram Fletcher, 33

Rodney Stone, 63, 65

Roosevelt, Theodore, 85

Rotary Club of Belfast, 333

Rothaker, Watterson, 292

Royal Bath Hotel, 104

Royal Opera House, 93

Royal Pavilion Hotel, 402

Saintsbury, H.A., 83, 86

Salle Wagram, 339

Samson, 38

Sandow, Eugen, 81

Savoy, 125

Saxby, Jessie, 112

Schwensen, Clara, 97, 100

Science and Invention (magazine), 406

Scientific American, 301, 302, 316

Seaman, Owen, 85

Selfridge, Harry Gordon, 140

Shackleton, Sir Ernest, 324

Shakespeare Theatre (Liverpool), 58

Shaw, George Bernard, 120, 124, 128, 148

Silver, Christine, 84

Simpson, Joseph, 103, 104

Slater, Oscar, 124, 126, 148, 150, 152, 332, 365, 366, 369, 376, 392

Smith, Cecil de, 45

Smith, Herbert Greenhough, 34, 403

Society for Psychical Research, 171, 289, 300, 307, 309, 350, 397

Society of Authors, 114

South Africa, 54, 107, 384

Southampton, 311

Southsea, 215, 225

Spiritual Society of St. John, 236

Spiritualism, xxi, xxiii, 171, 172, 186, 190, 196, 197, 205, 208, 215, 217, 218, 219, 220, 223, 226, 228, 231, 234, 238, 240, 241, 243, 244, 245, 247, 249, 251, 257, 259, 263, 265, 267, 268, 283, 284, 286, 287, 290, 293, 294, 297, 307, 313, 322, 326, 333, 334, 338, 339, 341, 345, 355, 362, 363, 374, 383, 384, 389, 391, 397, 404, 405, 410

Spiritualists' National Union, 214

St Mary's Hospital, 93, 107, 195

Stern, Major Albert, 181

Sterndale, Dr. Leon, 92

Stevens, Edwin, 96

Stewart, Rev. Josie, 316

Stoll Film Company Limited, The, 273

Stonyhurst, 292

Strand Theatre, 103

Styles, Kenneth, 231

Sun Hall (Liverpool), 71

Sunday Express, 210, 212, 283, 374

Sunday Pictorial, 377

Sunday Times, 245

Sussex Petty Sessions, 361

Swaffer, Frederick Charles Hannen, 402

Symons, J. H., 392

Table Talk, 244

The Adventure of Shoscombe Old Place, 361

The Adventure of the Blanched Soldier, 353

The Adventure of the Creeping Man, 310

The Adventure of the Dying Detective, 136, 140

The Adventure of the Illustrious Client, 325, 330

The Adventure of the Lion's Mane, 355

The Adventure of the Red Circle, 103

The Adventure of the Red-Headed League, 308

The Adventure of the Retired Colourman, 355

The Adventure of the Second Stain, 353

The Adventure of the Sussex Vampire, 321, 329

The Adventure of the Three Gables, 353

The Adventure of the Three Garridebs, 325, 329

The Adventure of the Veiled Lodger, 361

The Adventure of Wisteria Lodge, 35, 36

The Adventures of Sherlock Holmes (film series), 272

The Astounding Crime on Torrington Road, 374

The Australasian, 245

The Beryl Coronet, 138

The Book I Most Enjoyed Writing, 283

The Brisbane Courier, 266

The British Campaign in France and Flanders 1917, 214

The Bruce-Partington Plans, 41, 49

The Case for Spirit Photography, 304

The Case of Oscar Slater, 125

The Casebook of Sherlock Holmes, 363

The Catholic Press, 266

The Coming of the Fairies, 228, 296, 299, 376

The Crime of the Congo, 60

The Crown Diamond, 127, 273, 275, 317

The Daily Chronicle, 162, 167

The Daily Mirror, 45, 48, 54, 71, 80, 86, 88, 93, 95, 105, 111, 123, 124, 126, 134, 139, 148, 161, 163, 172, 174, 181, 185, 199, 205, 214, 223, 224, 234, 272, 275, 283, 299, 308, 309, 311, 313, 315, 322, 325, 339, 340, 344, 345, 350, 356, 362, 369, 373, 375, 378, 381, 385, 390, 392, 401, 402, 404, 405, 406, 407, 410

The Daily News, 244, 269, 338, 375

The Detective in Fiction, 314

The Devil's Foot, 82, 90, 92, 96, 97, 98

The Disappearance of Lady Frances Carfax, 114

The Disintegration Machine, 392

The Edge of the Unknown, 355

The Empty House, 35

The End of the Marriage Vow, 392

The Evening Standard, 223, 290

The Flag, 37

The Graphic, 96

The Great Boer War, 45

The Grey Dress, 37

The Hicks Theatre, 91

The History of Spiritualism, 350

The Horsham Times, 265

The Hound of the Baskervilles, 34

The House of Temperley, 77, 78, 82, 87, 89, 90, 139, 140

The Human Argument, 238, 248

The Illustrated London News, 96

The Land of Mist, 325, 332, 337, 392

The Last Galley, 104, 105, 113

The Lost World, 91, 105, 113, 119, 122, 125, 126, 136, 291, 292, 331, 337, 368

The Mail, 242

The Man with the Twisted Lip, 45

The Marlborough Express, 253

The Mazarin Stone, 127, 275

The Musgrave Ritual, 138

The New Revelation, 210, 245, 308, 334

The New York Times, 55, 59, 82, 95, 106, 126, 133, 134, 149, 150, 151, 162, 164, 166, 176, 187, 196, 218, 272, 283, 284, 286, 287, 288, 289, 291, 292, 293, 299, 301, 302, 303, 311

The North Western Courier, 237

The Northern Miner, 265

The Order of Light, 236

The Play Pictorial, 77, 78

The Poison Belt, 126, 127, 136, 148

The Pot of Caviare, 34

The Problem of Thor Bridge, 282

The Queenslander, 267

The Register, 236, 240, 241

The Reigate Squires, 138

The Religious Argument, 238, 249

The Return of Sherlock Holmes, 34

The Richmond River Express and Casino Kyogle Advertiser, 248

The Romance of Medicine, 93

The Royal Magazine, 310

The Second Stain, 34, 353

The Secret Woman, 119

The Sign of Four, 138, 312

The Silver Blaze, 138

The Singular Experience of Mr J. Scott Eccles, 35

The Society of American Magicians, 290

The Speckled Band, 83, 84, 85, 87, 90, 91, 95, 103, 138, 275

The Spectator, 152

The Splendid Angel, 392

The Stolen Papers, 138

The Stonor Case, 83

The Strand, 34, 35, 36, 88, 92, 96, 103, 114, 115, 122, 123, 125, 140, 141, 142, 145, 155, 183, 185, 195, 200, 230, 231, 251, 252, 272, 275, 282, 296, 310, 321, 325, 330, 337, 353, 355, 356, 361, 362, 368, 392, 403

The Studio, 145

The Sunday Mirror, 271

The Sydney Morning Herald, 237, 247, 251

The Sydney Stock and Station Journal, 251

The Tiger of San Pedro, 35

The Times, 72, 107, 122, 148, 166, 223, 274

The Tragedy of the Korosko, 34, 58

The Truth About Oscar Slater, 365

The Unmasking of Robert-Houdin, 224

The Valley of Fear, 148, 155, 164, 165, 183, 356

The Vital Message, 215, 218

The Wanderings of a Spiritualist, 207, 233, 242, 249, 253, 260, 274, 283

The War Illustrated, 161, 163

The Weekly Dispatch, 274

The Westminster Gazette, 251

The White Company, 364

Théâtre des Nations, 119

Theatre Royal (Nairobi), 389

Theosophical Society, 230

Thomas, Rev. Brayton, 405

Thomas, Tom, 205, 210

Those Others (Poem), 215

Three of Them, 195, 200

Titanic, RMS, 123

Tréville, Georges, 138, 139

Troughton, Walter, 145

tuberculosis, xxii, 28, 368

Tunbridge Wells, 48, 134, 135, 157

Turkey, Sultan of, 27

Tutankhamen, 311, 322

Twidle, Arthur, 36, 49

Under the Clock, 121

Undershaw, xxi, 28, 30, 34, 274, 322

Viscountess Rhondda (Viscountess Rhondda), 335

Voltaire, 314

Wall & Co, 73

Wall, Walter, 206

Wallace, Alfred Russel, 241

Waller, Lewis, 58, 64

Waterloo, 63, 64, 311

Watson, Dr. Archibald, 237

West End Cinema, 139

Wheels of Anarchy, 33

Whitefield's Tabernacle, 70

Whitehall Rooms, 55, 93

Whitington, Ernest, 241

Wild, Sir Ernest, 344

Wilde, Oscar, 121

Wiles, Frank, 145, 183, 310, 356, 361

Williams, A.C.R., 397

Windlesham, 1, 28, 29, 30, 38, 41, 43, 44, 45, 49, 53, 55, 61, 62, 68, 71, 72, 91, 95, 106, 113, 125, 135, 136, 145, 199, 200, 207, 211, 212, 215, 220, 225, 303, 315, 363, 393, 403, 405

Windsor and Richmond Gazette, 234

Winslow, Dr. Forbes, 248

Wood, Alfred (Woody), 53

Woodward, Arthur Smith, 57, 123

Worker, 245, 267, 268

Wright, Arthur, 229, 230, 231

Wright, Elsie, 229, 230, 246

Also from MX Publishing

Sherlock Holmes Short Story Collections

Sherlock Holmes and the Murder at the Savoy

Sherlock Holmes and the Skull of Kohada Koheiji

Look out for the new novel from Mike Hogan
– *The Scottish Question.*

www.mxpublishing.com

Also from MX Publishing

Our bestselling books are our short story collections; 'Lost Stories of Sherlock Holmes' , 'The Outstanding Mysteries of Sherlock Holmes', The Papers of Sherlock Holmes Volume 1 and 2, 'Untold Adventures of Sherlock Holmes' (and the sequel 'Studies in Legacy) and 'Sherlock Holmes in Pursuit', 'The Cotswold Werewolf and Other Stories of Sherlock Holmes' – and many more……

www.mxpublishing.com

Also from MX Publishing

"Phil Growick's, 'The Secret Journal of Dr Watson', is an adventure which takes place in the latter part of Holmes and Watson's lives. They are entrusted by HM Government (although not officially) and the King no less to undertake a rescue mission to save the Romanovs, Russia's Royal family from a grisly end at the hand of the Bolsheviks. There is a wealth of detail in the story but not so much as would detract us from the enjoyment of the story. Espionage, counter-espionage, the ace of spies himself, double-agents, double-crossers...all these flit across the pages in a realistic and exciting way. All the characters are extremely well-drawn and Mr Growick, most importantly, does not falter with a very good ear for Holmesian dialogue indeed. Highly recommended. A five-star effort."
The Baker Street Society

Links

MX Publishing are proud to support the Save Undershaw campaign – the campaign to save and restore Sir Arthur Conan Doyle's former home. Undershaw is where he brought Sherlock Holmes back to life, and should be preserved for future generations of Holmes fans.

SaveUndershaw
www.saveundershaw.com

Sherlockology
www.sherlockology.com

MX Publishing
www.mxpublishing.com

You can read more about Sir Arthur Conan Doyle and Undershaw in Alistair Duncan's book (share of royalties to the Undershaw Preservation Trust) – An Entirely New Country and in the amazing compilations Sherlock's Home – The Empty House and the new book Two, To One, Be (all royalties to the Trust).

www.ingramcontent.com/pod-product-compliance
Ingram Content Group UK Ltd.
Pitfield, Milton Keynes, MK11 3LW, UK
UKHW020926170726
473358UK00001B/36